Giving with a Thousand Hands

Advance Praise for the Book

Giving with a Thousand Hands

The Changing Face of Indian Philanthropy

Pushpa Sundar

OXFORD

UNIVERSITY PRESS

OXFORD
UNIVERSITY PRESS

Oxford University Press is a department of the University of Oxford.
It furthers the University's objective of excellence in research, scholarship,
and education by publishing worldwide. Oxford is a registered trademark of
Oxford University Press in the UK and in certain other countries.

Published in India by
Oxford University Press
YMCA Library Building, 1 Jai Singh Road, New Delhi 110 001, India

First Edition published in 2017

ISBN-13: 978-0-19-947068-6
ISBN-10: 0-19-947068-5

Printed in Adobe Garamond Pro 11/13
by Tranistics Data Technologies, New Delhi 110 044
Printed in India by Replika Press Pvt. Ltd

To
The Legacy of Sampradaan
Pioneer in Promoting Philanthropy

Shat-hast Samahar Sahasra-hast San Kir
(Collect with a hundred hands and give it away with a thousand)
                                    —Vedic Sukti, Atharva Veda, 3.4.5A

Contents

Foreword

Pushpa Sundar's book, *Giving with a Thousand Hands: The Changing Face of Indian Philanthropy*, documents the progress of philanthropy in India, and the distance that remains to be covered for large numbers of deprived people to benefit from developmental efforts.

Even after nearly seven decades of independent life, India continues to face persistent social challenges on multiple fronts—health, nutrition, sanitation, education and skill development, safety and welfare of women and children, state of migrant workers, and so on. Add to these the issues related to water scarcity and urban poverty. Development projects aimed at modernizing India leave other casualties in their wake—irreparable environmental damage, community dislocations, and denial of rights to resettlement and livelihoods. These challenges need to be addressed with the backing of the state and society. In civil society, it is not enough that there are people with the means; they also need the heart to be of help.

The philanthropic work that Pushpa's book highlights is part of the welcome response from concerned individuals in the business world. They realize that business cannot succeed in a society that fails. It is morally and practically untenable for islands of prosperity to survive in an ocean of poverty and deficiency. Companies can no longer wash their hands off social responsibility by saying 'we pay taxes and we generate employment'. In a society like ours, which has an ever-widening gap between the rich and the poor, business, with its managerial and financial resources, has to contribute actively towards community welfare. As beneficiaries of capitalism, philanthropists can contribute in a big way by partnering with civil society and government to make development happen, equitably and humanely.

From the beginning, Thermax was conscious of our social responsibility. In the late 1960s, in his welcoming note, A.S. Bhathena, my father, urged the young recruits to 'fight against poverty, disease, communalism, despondency and indolence...' The decision to focus on the areas of energy and environment, so relevant to public life, also was a conscious choice. Rohinton, my husband, advocated the positive social role that business has to play in a country of disparities and deprivations, like India. His belief that 'profit is not just a set of figures, but of values', has always guided Thermax.

My son met with a fatal road accident when he was 25 years old. Having studied abroad, poverty in our country bothered him and he wanted our personal funds to be deployed for social causes. A few years after his demise, the family started helping many social causes. Besides CSR, I do hope people with high net worth reach out to the needy to bridge the gap between the rich and the poor.

This is Pushpa Sundar's second book. I am glad the book, while acknowledging the good work done so far, also points to what remains to be done. I do hope this book inspires many more to invest their money and more importantly, their sense of care and concern.

Anu Aga
Chairperson of the Thermax Foundation
Member of Parliament, Rajya Sabha

Preface

I am not a philanthropist, nor likely to be one, lacking the wherewithal, as well as the broad vision which enables one to bet on risky but potentially winning ideas in the interest of society. To be sure, I have contributed my mite, both as alms, and in response to appeals for good causes. But, as I am at pains to explain in this book, charity is not philanthropy.

But if I have not engaged *in* philanthropy I have certainly engaged *with* it for thirty plus years. The engagement began in 1984, when as Programme Officer with the India Office of the Ford Foundation, I was asked by a grantee which Indian sources could be tapped to help their social organization.

Unable to answer the question, I began an exploration into indigenous philanthropy. I realized that social development in a society needed more than government intervention to make it happen. At the same time, there was much desire on the part of many individuals to contribute either their time or money for the purpose. Starting with a workshop in 1985, the journey led me to research and to write on Indian philanthropy; to found an organization for promoting it; and to advocate the need for it at different fora.

I naively believed that it was possible to promote philanthropy, to motivate people by making them aware of the need to give, and to channelize the donated resources to where they were most needed. But exactly how naïve this vision was, became apparent when I and a small core group of public minded people set up the Sampradaan Indian Centre for Philanthropy in 1996 for the purpose. It was a hard and uphill—albeit worthwhile—task.

Back then, donors were not interested in finding out how to be more proactive, how to get more bang for the buck from their money. The general attitude was one of indifference. On the other hand, non-profit organizations, always long on purpose and short on funds, were keen to know which donors would be interested in their particular work. One group held the purse strings; the other needed not only their compassion, but even more, their money. The question was how to bring them together. It led me personally, and Sampradaan as an organization, to explore the contours of Indian philanthropy, and to learn how it was similar to and different from that elsewhere in the world; to seek the basic information on who gives, for what purpose, why, and how. And then to try and make sense of the learning in order to apply it to the Indian situation.

I am happy to say that, in the ways the book describes, the situation has changed for the better since my journey began.

This book is the result of my explorations, past and present, and my hope for the future.

Acknowledgements

There are many people without whom this book would have remained an idea in my head.

As the Founder Director of Sampradaan, I had the opportunity to interact with a number of people and organizations who deepened my understanding of Indian philanthropy. They are too numerous to name, but mention must be made of Dr M.B. Athreya, former Professor at IIM Calcutta, and co-founder of Sampradaan; the late Mr Rusi M. Lala, then at the head of the Sir Dorab Tata Trust, and his team, but especially Tara Sabawala; the team at the Sir Ratan Tata Trust; and the team at the Ford Foundation while I was there, but especially Lincoln Chen and David Arnold. Our interactions opened the first windows to me in my study of Indian philanthropy.

I also owe a debt of gratitude to Lester Salamon, Director of the Center for Civil Society Studies at the Johns Hopkins Institute for Health and Social Policy Studies, USA, who ran the programme of International Fellowships in philanthropy. My stint there as a Senior International Fellow in Philanthropy gave me an exposure not only to American Philanthropy but also the European and Asian traditions, and vetted my desire to learn more about Indian philanthropy.

My thanks to the Governing Council of Sampradaan, who made it possible for me to write this book by sanctioning me a grant before the demise of Sampradaan.

Thanks are also due to India's leading philanthropists of the Old Economy—Ratan Tata, Jamshyd Godrej, Arvind Mafatlal, the late Suresh Neotia, Bharat Ram, Venu Srinivasan, M.V. Subbiah, C.K. Birla, and many others—who many years ago made time to meet me and give me insights into traditional business philanthropy, especially of their own families or business groups.

The philanthropists of the New Economy, among them Shibulal, co-founder of the Infosys Group, Sudha Murthy of the Infosys Foundation, Rohini Nilekani of Arghyam, and Kiran Mazumdar-Shaw, Chairman of Biocon Technologies and the Biocon Foundation, gave me insights into the changes that have occurred in the tradition of philanthropy. Among them, I would especially like to acknowledge Kiran Mazumdar-Shaw, a remarkable woman entrepreneur, and a warm human being, who, in spite of a very busy schedule, made time to meet me at short notice. Thank you all.

Fellow travellers in the philanthropy space—Dileep Ranjekar, Director of the Azim Premji Foundation, Anmol Vellani of the India Foundation for the Arts, Noshir Dadrawala of the Centre for Advancement of Philanthropy, Deval Sanghavi of Dasra, Pushpa Aman Singh and N. Venkatakrishnan of the GiveIndia Foundation, Don Mohanlal, fomer CEO of the Nand and Jeet Khemka Foundation—stimulated my own thinking, and I acknowledge my debt to them.

I also acknowledge with gratitude Anu Aga for very kindy writing the Foreword for this book, and Lester Salamon, David Arnold, and Rohini Nilekani for their kind messages, which they sent promptly inspite of much pressure on their time.

Sanjay Aggarwal of AccountAid, Amitabh Behar, CEO of the National Foundation for India, Pradeepta Naik, former Director of Sampradaan, Dr M.B. Athreya, Nandini Sundar, and Aparna Sundar all very kindly read different chapters of the book. Their comments were invaluable. Thank you all.

Vishnu Saksena helped me to find research assistance. Utkarsh Mishra and Meghali Roy helped me fill some gaps at different times. The Library of the India Habitat Centre offered a quiet and conducive space to reflect and write, and the staff were quietly helpful. My thanks to them too. I would also like to thank the editorial team at Oxford University Press.

My final debt is to my family—Sundar, Aparna, and Nandini—for being there for me always, offering criticism and encouragement equally, in large doses.

Abbreviations

ADB	Asian Development Bank
AIIMS	All India Institute of Medical Sciences
ARY	Arogya Raksha Yojana
AVARD	Association of Voluntary Agencies in Rural Development
BAIF	Bharatiya Agro Industries Foundation
BHU	Benaras Hindu University
BPAC	Bangalore Political Action Committee
CAF	Charities Aid Foundation
CAP	Centre for Advancement of Philanthropy
CEMS	Centre for Emerging Market Solutions
CF	Community Foundation
CRY	Child Rights and You
CSO	Civil Society Organizations
CSR	Corporate Social Responsibility
DICCI	Dalit Indian Chamber of Commerce & Industry
ESOP	Employee Stock Ownership Plan
FATF	Financial Action Task Force
FCG	First Givers Club
FCRA	Foreign Contributions Regulation Act
FICCI	Federation of Indian Chambers of Commerce and Industry
FICCI-SEDF	FICCI Social and Economic Development Foundation
FY	Financial Year
GDP	Gross Domestic Product
GER	gross enrolment ratio
HDI	Human Development Index
HEFA	Higher Education Financing Agency
HNWIs	High Net Worth Individuals

HR	human resource
HRD	Human Resources Development
HUF	Hindu Undivided Family
IIM	Indian Institute of Management
IIT	Indian Institute of Technology
InsaF	Indian Social Action Forum
IT	Information Technology
ITC	India Tobacco Company
MIS	management information systems
MNC	multi-national company
MoU	Memorandum of Understanding
NABARD	National Bank for Agriculture and Rural Development
NARF	Native American Rights Fund
NGO	Non-governmental Organization
NRIs	Non-resident Indians
NWBs	New Wealth Builders
PRIA	Society for Participatory Research in Asia
RGVN	Rashtriya Gramin Vikas Nidhi
TERI	The Energy Research Institute
TPI	The Philanthropy Initiative
SEZ	Special Economic Zone
SF	Sainik Foundation
SICP	Sampradaan Indian Centre for Philanthropy
SIT	Special Investigative Team
SNDT	Srimati Nathibai Damodar Thakersay
SRCC	Sri Ram College of Commerce
TIFR	Tata Institute of Fundamental Research
TISS	Tata Institute of Social Sciences
TSIS	Thermax Social Initiative Foundation
UHNWI	Ultra High Net Worth individuals
UWC	United World College
VANI	Voluntary Action Network India
VDCF	Valley Dew Community Foundation
VHAI	Voluntary Health Association of India
WBCF	West Bengal Community Foundation

Introduction

Aadanam hi visargaya, satavarimuchamiva samudrajalam utsrashtam, aadate hi jalam ravi.

(Noble men like clouds, acquire goods [wealth] only to redistribute them, just as the sun draws water from the sea, only to return it in the form of rain.)[1]

When there is no compulsion to do so, gifting away a portion of one's wealth to improve society or benefit the less fortunate may seem inexplicable. But deep in every human being is a yearning which goes beyond material wealth and a comfortable life for oneself; a yearning for a meaning and purpose to life; a desire to belong to a cause bigger than them, and to make a difference to someone's life or to society at large. That is why altruistic giving for the love of humanity is considered one of mankind's noblest instincts.

Altruistic giving, or giving out of compassion and without expectation of a material return, has been variously described as charity, philanthropy, or social investment. The terms 'charity' and 'philanthropy', in particular, are frequently used interchangeably, but in fact each has a different nuance since each evolved at different times and in different contexts. This book is about Indian *philanthropy* and not charity. The distinction is important to the narrative.

---

[1] Quotation from Kalidas, *Raghuvamsham*, fifth century AD.

A Question of Definition

Charity, defined as the voluntary giving of money to those in need, is the term used since the earliest times, and continues to be the most popularly used. It applies equally to giving by an individual as well as to giving by companies or other organizations. The motive behind charity is compassion and a desire to alleviate distress and need of all kinds. It is palliative, not curative in nature, and aims to provide immediate relief, not to root out the cause of the distress. It takes a short-term, not a long-term view of a problem. It is purely impulsive. When people give alms or even a donation to a cause, they are not concerned with the long-term impact of their action. Charity makes no claim that it is given in order to reduce inequality or to promote social justice.

Examples of charity are giving alms to a beggar, or fish or food to a hungry man, or giving money to a cancer patient for treatment. Modern charity includes random and ad hoc donations given on request for particular causes, which could be relief for earthquake or war victims, or for a school, or a charity show. Normally, these would be one-time donations and comparatively small, with no commitment to continue giving.[2]

Philanthropy, on the other hand, is the *planned* use of wealth for transforming society for the good of all. It implies the use of a scientific spirit and method in giving, for the purpose of social advancement. It is not limited to alleviation of poverty but includes giving to bring beauty and refinement to society. Further, it assumes that social ills such as poverty, educational failure, or criminal behaviour can be identified, attacked, and cured.

Underlying philanthropy is the idea that with great wealth comes great responsibility, embodied in the concept of *noblesse oblige*. Money, if utilized appropriately, has the power to do many great things. Hence, wealth creators have an unsaid responsibility of

---

[2] In the West, charity mainly referred to almsgiving for relief of poverty or allied ills, but in traditional Indian usage the scope of charity was not so limited. It included giving for temples and religious needs, but also for secular long-term purposes such as establishing schools, planting trees along roadsides to give shade to travellers, building wells, bathing ghats, *dharamshalas* (rest houses), and so on.

utilizing a portion of their wealth for the betterment of society. This act of promoting the welfare of society through altruistic giving is called philanthropy. In fact, philanthropy covers a broad range of giving—of time or service, non-monetary resources, as well as money. But inevitably, the greater focus is on the giving of wealth.

Philanthropy springs from the same impulse as charity, namely compassion, but is not synonymous with charity. While giving alms to beggars is in the nature of charity, providing vocational training so that those unemployed need not resort to begging would be philanthropy. Supporting cancer research instead of donations to individual cancer patients illustrates the same difference. It has been aptly said that charity puts ambulances at the bottom of a cliff whereas philanthropy would fence the top of the cliff so that people do not fall off.

Philanthropy can be individual, that is, by an individual for individual benefit or for the good of many; or it can be collective, referring to a pooling of individual donations and collectively applying them to address a social problem on some scale, as is done by social action organizations. It also refers to giving by a corporate body or organization because with the development of joint stock companies, the corporation came to be seen as a distinct social and legal entity, and altruistic giving by a company for a social rather than a commercial purpose came to be referred to as corporate philanthropy. Corporate philanthropy is essentially a charge on a company's profit, and therefore a Board or collective decision.

One criterion for judging whether giving is charity or philanthropy is how it is applied. If the contributions are made collectively through an organization for the purpose of bringing transformative change, then those contributions, though small, ad hoc donations by individuals, can still be considered philanthropy; but if they are used for purely ameliorative purposes, such as earthquake relief, even if collectively used, then one must still consider them charity. A second, especially modern, distinction between the two is that of scale. Philanthropy implies giving on a large scale or undertaking social projects with large-scale impact, either geographically or qualitatively.

While charity has existed from time immemorial, philanthropy, in the way defined, developed in the late nineteenth and early twentieth century, when the new generation of wealthy elite in the West, like Andrew Carnegie and John Rockefeller, referred to as the 'robber barons' for the way they made their money, began using the wealth so amassed to explore new modes of charitable action which would go beyond amelioration to the root causes of social dysfunction. In India, the pioneering industrialist Jamsetji Tata independently began to use his wealth for what he called 'constructive philanthropy', to distinguish it from the traditional charity then prevailing.

A society needs charity as well as philanthropy, since different kinds of situations need different kinds of responses. Charity is necessary to meet emergency situations, especially in a society like India, which has no health insurance or social security for individuals. Philanthropy of visionary individuals, on the other hand, either using their own money or that of a company which they head, is catalytic in nature, and necessary to back innovation, experimentation, and risk-taking on unproved but potentially worthwhile projects/causes.

Each approach has its place, but when talking about development, philanthropy is the more appropriate concept. This book is therefore not about charity but contemporary Indian philanthropy and its role in the development of India.

Purpose and Scope

A lamentable lack of knowledge about the contours of Indian philanthropy and how it has contributed to Indian society has led many non-Indians and Indians alike to believe that India lacks in philanthropy, and to make misleading statements such as that by Dean Nelson, the Telegraph Media Group's South Asia editor, based in New Delhi for four years. In 2009 he sarcastically commented, 'What does it say about India that its most active philanthropists right now are Bill Gates and Prince Charles?' According to him, though some Indian wealthy have given money to charity, nothing is on any great scale or with any real ambition in India itself. He goes on to say, 'Instead of developing original ideas to unleash the potential of its hundreds of millions of untouchables and backward castes, many of its wealthiest figures are more often seen feathering their own spiritual nests by donating large sums to Hindu temples.'[3]

[3]   Dean Nelson, 'Where Are India's Great Philanthropists?' *The Telegraph*, 28 July 2009.

This is simply not true, neither in the past nor at present. Though Indian philanthropists as a whole could undoubtedly do much more, my study of the historical evolution of philanthropy in India, namely *Beyond Business: From Merchant Charity to Corporate Citizenship* (Sundar 2000), shows the richness of Indian philanthropy before and immediately after Independence, though later on, philanthropy was, on the whole, in decline.

Contemporary philanthropy too has numerous inspiring examples, with many philanthropists like Azim Premji, Ratan Tata, Kiran Shaw Mazumdar, Shiv Nadar, and Kris Gopalkrishnan contributing to India's social, economic, and cultural development with key philanthropic contributions.

It is this gap in knowledge and perspective which this book seeks to fill. The book's main objective is to improve knowledge of contemporary Indian philanthropy by documenting and analysing its nature, sources, scope, practice, and changes in it over the last quarter century. The goal is to provide a sound base for an enlightened discourse to enlarge and improve the practice of philanthropy. A second objective is to critically examine Indian philanthropy so as to highlight not only its achievements but also its shortcomings.

My earlier book had stopped at the nineties of the last century. Since then, much has changed, both in the Indian economy and society, and in how Indian philanthropy sees its role. This book documents those changes.

As mentioned before, this is a book on *contemporary* Indian philanthropy. It covers a span of roughly a quarter century, from 1991, a landmark year for India's economy, to the present. In 1991, the economy faced an unprecedented foreign exchange crisis which forced the government to liberate India's economy from the walls of protection that government controls had erected round it after Independence. The budget introduced by Manmohan Singh as Finance Minister in 1994 set the economy on an upward path and led to the second wave of wealth creation, which has had a transformative impact on Indian philanthropy.

Given the way we have defined philanthropy, the attention perforce is mainly on the rich and the ultra-rich, though cognizance is also taken of the collective philanthropy of smaller individual donors aggregated by social organizations.

In the spirit of an Indian tradition of philosophical enquiry which explores the Ultimate Reality by saying *Neti Neti*, 'it is not this, not this', I would like to spell out right at the outset what this book is not.

It is not meant to be an academic book, but is written largely for the interested public and the informed lay reader, though academics may also, I believe, benefit from the analysis and the extensive referencing and bibliography provided.

It does not include volunteering and donation of non-monetary resources in the analysis, though philanthropy, in its broadest sense, includes these.

Though religious philanthropy continues to be a strong presence in India, an analysis of this is not attempted here, because an earlier book (Sundar 2001) had dealt with it separately.[4] The focus is only on secular philanthropy, and therefore only on modern secular trusts and foundations and not on religious charitable organizations such as *mutt*s and *waqf*s.

Some of the issues discussed in the book include:

- The role that philanthropy can play in society, and why India needs philanthropy
- Is charity the same as philanthropy? Are Indians more charitable than philanthropic?
- The emergence of corporate social responsibility as a new paradigm for giving, and whether it can be equated to philanthropy
- The role the state plays in encouraging or restraining philanthropy
- The implications of the infrastructure deficit for the size and quality of Indian philanthropy
- The changing face of Indian philanthropy, including the profile of new donors, with women as an emerging sub-set
- How the management of philanthropy has changed
- The effectiveness of Indian foundations as vehicles for the expression of philanthropy

---

[4] Pushpa Sundar, *For God's Sake* (New Delhi: Sampradaan Indian Centre for Philanthropy, 2001).

- What philanthropy has meant for higher education in India, and what needs to be done to encourage more and better giving for education
- Why Indian philanthropists are donating huge amounts to educational institutions abroad and not enough to their own country's institutions
- And finally, what ails Indian philanthropy, and how the deficit can be removed

The approach of the book is to combine history and contemporary interdisciplinary material. For each of the topics I first give a brief history before going on to describe the contemporary position, so as to indicate the nature and direction of change.

I have used some primary material comprising interviews done by me over a period of time; archived material; published and unpublished material of the Sampradaan Indian Centre for Philanthropy (SICP); and reports including those of the government. In addition, I have used secondary material from published sources on religion, urban history, business history, history of social work, biographies, newspaper reports, and journal articles, supplemented by my own experience of the past thirty years in studying or promoting Indian philanthropy.

Since it deals with contemporary times, which is history in the making, there is more dependence on media reporting and personal conversations than on archival material or published books, which are few for this period. It is also the reason why it is not possible to talk of the impact of contemporary philanthropic work with any degree of confidence.

I conclude that philanthropy has a vital role to play in India, and it is important to encourage it through a variety of measures, as spelled out in the last chapter.

The Changing Face of Indian Philanthropy: An Overview

How Indian Philanthropy is Unique

While there undoubtedly are similarities in philanthropic motives and practices all over the world, and in a globally interlinked world change in one part of the globe immediately impacts the others, it is also true that the form philanthropy takes in any society depends uniquely on a society's history, ethical, cultural, and social traditions, and on economic and political organization. As these change, so do theory and practice. This is as true of India as anywhere else.

Indian philanthropy has several distinctive features. For one, it is a very old tradition going back several thousands of years, which has its origins in religiously ordained or faith-based giving. Religion continues to play an influential role in Indian philanthropy, while in the West it has accounted for less and less with modernization. In India, many would-be philanthropists, even today, are motivated to give by the tenets of their religion, by saint-like figures such as Mahatma Gandhi and Mother Teresa, or by modern gurus such as Mata Amritanandamayee and Sri Sri Ravi Shankar, among others.

Two, it is rooted in a social structure in which extended families, especially business families consisting of several generations, live together and hold property in common, and kin and family ties are very strong. As will be noticed later, this has a somewhat restraining effect on the giving of wealth to society.

Three, India's business sector, which produces the bulk of its wealth, is made up mostly of family enterprises belonging to several traditional business communities following different religions and commercial traditions. This makes it difficult to distinguish family philanthropy from company philanthropy, since there are many overlaps between family and company interests.

Some business communities, such as the Parsis, the Marwaris, the Gujaratis, and the Chettiars, have established not only business dynasties but also dynastic philanthropic traditions.

The development of philanthropy also varies between regions because of very different social, economic, and political backgrounds.

Four, while the trust or foundation is as popular a mechanism for philanthropic giving in India as it is in the West, there is a strong preference for hands-on philanthropy or keeping operational control of philanthropic activities in the donor's hands. Consequently, there are very few grant-making foundations in India compared to the West, and most foundations are what would be called 'operating foundations'.

Five, in Western capitalist societies, private initiative and abhorrence of government are ingrained values which have encouraged private philanthropy. In India, on the other hand, there is a strong dependence on government, first because of colonial rule and then due to the adoption of a socialistic pattern of society and planned development to make up the development deficit. Modern Indian industry and business were born in colonial India and matured in a post-independence, controlled economy. The state has, therefore, played a more critical role in shaping philanthropy in terms of the space it has allowed or not allowed for creating, retaining, and disbursing wealth. Sometimes it has been positive, at others, very negative.

History

Ameliorative charity for distress relief is evident throughout Indian history. By and large it was personalized and ordained by religion. However, the traditional Hindu term for charity, *daanam*, is broader than the Western definition of charity and somewhat akin to the modern concept of philanthropy. It goes beyond distress-relieving alms directed only to the poor, to gifts for promoting education and scholarship, planting of trees, and for improvement of the physical and social environment of the community as a whole through provision of civic amenities. The concept of charity in the other religions of India was similarly broader (more in Chapter 3).

However, in no case was charity envisaged as social intervention which engages with the social situation to effect changes in the very base of social problems, such as institutionalized inequality, which is what modern philanthropy is about. Philanthropy in this sense has a somewhat shorter history in India, beginning in the mid-nineteenth century.

Till then, the Indian economy was primarily rural, with agriculture as the main occupation, though there were several urban centres with high levels of affluence and refinement. In villages particularly, there was a strong sense of interdependence and community, manifested in concentric circles of obligation radiating outwards from the family, to the caste and the village. The welfare of the indigent and victims of fate or natural calamities was the responsibility first of the joint family, and then of the caste or the occupational organizations such as caste associations and guilds, and finally of the village as a whole, through the village *panchayat* (council), which not only arbited in disputes but also mobilized community resources in times of famine or floods or for celebration of festivals. Temples and other places of worship served several functions other than religious, offering food and shelter to the needy, and serving as foci for community events, cultural and others. In towns, the family, caste, and community associations played the same role.

These institutions of civil society, such as guilds, caste associations, *gram panchayat*s (village councils), and *nagar panchayat*s (town councils), were supported by individual and organizational charity.

Charity was an ingrained practice in most families, and among the wealthy it was aided by the fact that there was little outlet for wealth. Some was invested in real estate or in good living in ornate houses. A little was spent on secular display, but not too much, because an obviously wealthy man was a target for extortion. But the larger portion went to religious or religiously sanctioned charity. People gave both directly and through their businesses and social organizations.

The wealthy endowed temples or other religious buildings and paid for preserving and repairing them; or contributed to the upkeep of monasteries, for conduct of religious festivals and rituals, and for free pilgrimages for members of their religion. Many merchant communities had the practice of setting aside a fraction of their income or profits for charitable works and causes. Some merchant organizations levied cesses on their members, the proceeds of which went to charitable causes.

By the third decade of the nineteenth century, this traditional charity began to change from being largely religious, ameliorative in nature, and confined to members of their own community, caste, or religion, towards being more secular, more inclusive in terms of caste, creed, and community, and more oriented towards bringing progress to society through Western-style modern institutions. Though the more enlightened wealthy began to diversify their charitable giving in content and intent, they continued the older forms of gifting as well; and many did not change at all, and thus a mix of 'charity' and 'philanthropy' has continued to this day.

The changes began well before the development of indigenous industry in the mid-nineteenth century, the most important reasons being the spread of Western education, the influence of missionaries, and encouragement by officials. But industrialization, which led to the first wave of major wealth creation, accelerated and strengthened the trend.

The first fifty years of the twentieth century were golden years for Indian philanthropy. Whereas in the earlier period only two or three large and modern trusts had been set up, this period witnessed a proliferation of trusts and foundations. What is significant is that though the wealth of these foundations, in many cases, came from the business of the founder, they were not 'corporate' foundations as understood today, but were the outcome of the personal decision and charity of the founder; many were bequests out of personal fortunes.

The trusts either established prestigious institutions or gave money to others to create and maintain them. Many of the leading trusts began to view giving as an instrument of social change, but mostly, the trusts preferred to initiate and operate their own philanthropic projects and the bulk of the funds were utilized by them on projects which also served to memorialize family members, only smaller amounts being given to outside projects.

Since its beginning, Indian philanthropy has played a significant role, whether in terms of ideas, institutions, or innovations. One has only to look at the physical and institutional facilities of most cities—parks, drinking-water stands, auditoria and halls, planetariums, hospitals, museums and art galleries, as well as universities and research institutions—to appreciate this contribution.

Private philanthropy also led the way in supporting new fields of endeavour—girls' education, art, engineering, commercial and technical education, textile technology, management education, and scientific and medical research. The state later used the experience and expertise generated to widen the field and disseminate the gains more widely.

To give just a few instances: many of today's well-known public institutions like the Sir J.J. School of Arts, the Sir J.J. Hospital, the

Bombay University, the Indian Institute of Science, the Tata Memorial Centre for Cancer Treatment and Research, the Tata Institute of Social Sciences, the Tata Institute of Fundamental Research (TIFR), Banaras Hindu University, the Annamalai University, the Birla Institute of Technology in Pilani, the Birla Planetarium in Calcutta, and the Shri Ram College of Commerce and the Lady Shri Ram College for Girls in Delhi, were all endowed by Indian philanthropists such as Sir Jamsetji Tata, Jamsetji Jeejeebhoy, Raja Sir Annamalai, Lala Sri Ram, and G.D. Birla.

Many of the wealthy, like Jamnalal Bajaj and G.D. Birla, also contributed financially to Gandhi's freedom struggle, as well as his nationalist reconstruction work. After Independence too, philanthropists like Kasturbhai Lalbhai and the Sarabhai family of Ahmedabad supported the establishment of the Physical Research Laboratory, the Indian Institute of Management, and the like.

However, philanthropy was largely by and for urban areas, in one's own backyard, in terms of geography, and in some cases towards members of one's own caste or religion.

Between 1960 and 1990, Indian interest in philanthropy began to decline as the state began to assume welfare functions and taxed the rich heavily. People looked to the state to perform the welfare functions previously performed by temples, guilds, or village councils and such other voluntary civic agencies.

The Government's licensing and taxation policies stifled entrepreneurship and wealth creation, encouraged black money, and left less legitimate wealth in the hands of individuals and companies. Such measures sapped the philanthropic spirit of the wealthy as well as of the ordinary individual, and both voluntary action and institutional growth came to depend almost entirely on government funds. The large inflow of official and private international aid for both relief and development, which began around 1960s, also replaced domestic philanthropy as a source of funds for social action and let the wealthy off the hook, though charitable trusts and foundations continued to be established, partly as tax saving devices.

It is only at the end of the twentieth century, with a partial roll back of the state and legitimization of private enterprise, that Indian philanthropy is once again coming into its own. The story of

Indian philanthropy up to the nineties has been covered by me in the book *Beyond Business* and elsewhere, and is therefore not being repeated here.[5]

Indian Philanthropy Today

Revival of Interest

Though many of the wealthy have engaged in philanthropy to a greater or lesser extent since time immemorial, Indian interest in philanthropy has been sporadic, spurred only by periods of large scale wealth creation, or large scale needs such as wars, drought, and famine, or some exogenous stimulus such as social reform, the freedom struggle, and Independence, or a resurgent civil society.

In the history of modern Indian philanthropy there are only two key periods when there was much interest in philanthropy—the early twentieth century before Independence, and the present. In between, there has been a major hiatus.

In the early twentieth century there were important public debates regarding the need to reform existing practices of charity and philanthropy in India. The debates were particularly directed at religious giving and religious organizations. There was a general sense that traditional Hindu forms of giving were wasteful and inefficient and had to be changed. The issue was also discussed by Muslims and Sikhs. The measures canvassed for reform included legislative action to regulate charity. Later, Mahatma Gandhi's national reconstruction campaigns served the same purpose of stimulating an interest in philanthropy. The result was a democratization and secularization of charity. It became more substantial, more institutionalized, and more inclusive, and was re-channelled into constructive areas of concern such as modern education, social

---

[5] See Pushpa Sundar, *Beyond Business: From Merchant Charity to Corporate Citizenship* (New Delhi: Tata McGraw-Hill, 1999); Pushpa Sundar, 'Philanthropy in the Building of Modern India', in Mathieu Cantegreil, Deep Chanana, and Ruth Kattumuri, eds, *Revealing Indian Philanthropy* (London: Alliance Publishing Trust, 2013), pp. 31–9; and, 'Business, Society and Philanthropy', in *Footprints of Enterprise: Indian Business through the Ages* (New Delhi: FICCI/Oxford University Press, 1999).

service, and social action.[6] But subsequently, there has been little debate on substantive issues or serious scholarship.

The present interest in philanthropy, at both a practical and intellectual level, is essentially one of the unforeseen and unexpected fallouts of the Indian growth story. The two main reasons for this interest are increased wealth and the increased inequality throughout the world, including in India.

Increased Wealth

The Indian economy grew at a steady 6–7 per cent on an average every year in the last few decades. According to the 19th Annual World Wealth Report 2015, India has seen a whopping 211 per cent increase in its wealth over the last fifteen years, much higher than the US, UK, Japan, France, and Germany. The per capita wealth has risen from about $900 in 2000 to $2,800 in 2015. India is now the tenth richest country in the world, ranked according to total individual wealth, though when ranked according to per capita income, it comes last among the top twenty countries.[7]

Estimates of the number of Indian billionaires vary depending on the agencies doing the ranking, but most rankings of the world's richest individuals invariably have numbers of Indians among them.

According to the Knight Frank Wealth Report for 2016, there has been a rise of 340 per cent in Ultra High Net Worth Individuals (UHNWIs) in India in the last ten years, whereas globally the growth has only been 61 per cent. India presently has 6,020 UHNWIs (those with more than $30 million in net assets) and the number is expected to grow 5 per cent by 2025.[8]

---

[6] Carey Watt, *Serving the Nation: Cultures of Service, Association and Citizenship in Colonial India* (New York and New Delhi: Oxford University Press, 2005), p. 73.

[7] Capgemini and RBC Wealth Management, The 19th Annual World Wealth Report 2015, www.worldwealthreport.com. Total individual wealth has been defined in the report as private wealth held by all the individuals in each country.

[8] Knight Frank Wealth Report 2016, http://www.knightfrank.com/wealthreport for Report 2016.

The October 2015 issue of Forbes Magazine lists Asia's fifty richest families. Of these, fourteen are Indian business families, with two of them, the Ambani and Azim Premji families, in the top ten. In the number of global billionaires, India ranks sixth among the top ten countries.

This new wave of wealth creation and increased wealth in the hands of High Net Worth Individuals (HNWIs); the awesome contribution of Rs 8,846 crores by business tycoon Azim Premji to his foundation for education, the largest ever donation by an Indian; and the big ticket donations by other Indian philanthropists to institutions abroad have all put the spotlight on Indian philanthropy. The high profile pledging of 50 per cent of their wealth to philanthropy during their lifetimes by American billionaires Bill Gates and Warren Buffet, and their visits to India in recent years to encourage Indian billionaires to do the same, have stimulated an interest in philanthropy. There is interest in India and abroad in knowing how Indian billionaires spend their money, and how much, if at all, they give to philanthropy.[9]

It has also led Indians and non-Indians alike to wonder why a country with so much wealth, technical know-how, and management talent gives so little back to its own people, and leans instead on foreign donors. Considering that India has been a recipient of international charity since Independence, there is a feeling in India and abroad that rich Indians must now shoulder some of the responsibility for the development of their own country. International donors in particular are interested in finding out whether and when they can divert their wealth to other needy countries.

Possibly, there is also an undercurrent of self interest in the global desire to know about Indian philanthropy. The fact that several wealthy Indians, among them Ratan Tata, Anand Mahindra, and N.R. Narayana Murthy, have made large philanthropic contributions

---

[9] Buffet and Gates started the Giving Pledge in 2007 to encourage other billionaires to give away at least 50 per cent of their wealth during their lifetime. By 2015 the number of individuals and families signing the Pledge had risen to 137. Azim Premji and G.M. Rao are two of the Indian billionaires who have signed the Pledge; there are also several Indian Americans like Vinod Khosla and Manoj Bhargava among them.

to Harvard, Yale, and other leading Western universities has aroused an understandable hope on the part of other foreign institutions that Indian philanthropists can be enticed to give to them as well.

Finally, civil society has grown by leaps and bounds, and its need for funds has increased. While foreign agencies have provided valuable aid so far, they can, and have been accused, of bringing foreign agendas, and introducing foreign values not accepted by Indian society as a whole. Besides, foreign aid is on the decline, not only because of slowing global growth but also because of India's success on the economic front, which is why foreign donors do not see the need to give aid to India. Increased difficulty in accessing foreign aid by non-government organizations (NGOs) due to the government's restrictive policies has made the necessity for indigenous funds to fill the gap left by foreign aid even more urgent, and has further added to the interest in Indian philanthropy.

Growing Inequality and Social Need

The growth in wealth in India and elsewhere has only increased the gap between the wealthy and the poor. If there is a recurring theme in most conversations about development today, it is that of inequality, which has become one of the prime global concerns now. According to a recent Oxfam Report, sixty-two people, fifty-three of them men, own as much wealth as the poorest half of the entire world population and the richest 1 per cent own more than the other 99 per cent put together. The wealth gap is widening faster than anticipated. The wealth of the richest sixty-two people has risen by 44 per cent in the five years since 2010, from $542 billion to $1.76 trillion. The average annual income of the poorest 10 per cent of people has risen by less than $3 each year in almost a quarter century.[10]

In India, inequality of income, wealth, and opportunity is further compounded by inequalities due to gender, caste, and religion.

Inequality on all fronts is manifested in social malaise of all kinds. Indian statistics on health, infant mortality, malnutrition, and access

---

[10] Oxfam Report January 2016, reported in *The Economic Times*, 19 January 2016, '62 People Own Same Wealth as Half the World: Oxfam'.

to basic needs such as housing, water, and toilets are among the worst in the world. India ranks a lowly 130 out of a total of 180 nations in the latest UN Human Development Index (HDI). There is endemic corruption. Farmers are committing suicide due to mounting debts caused by failure of rains. In many places, people are locked in battles with companies over land acquisition and wages; besides, conflicts between castes or between communities are causing enormous loss of life and property.

At the same time, the aspirations of ordinary people are high. They want India to be a land of opportunity, and are restless to share in the prosperity they see around them. The government is unable, on its own, to meet these growing social needs or aspirations.

It is in this context of reducing inequality, social and economic, that philanthropy becomes significant. People are looking to philanthropy to power alternative solutions and one of the debates is around whether inequality is best reduced through taxation or philanthropy. Clearly, taxation has its limits, whereas experimentation and innovation has in the past helped solve humankind's intractable problems. Frequently, governments do not have the spare resources for experimental and creative work which may or may not yield results, and which, moreover, needs freedom from red tape and procedural strait jackets. In the past, philanthropic monies have provided the support for creative ideas and innovations, which in turn have led to exponential progress. This is why the possibilities of philanthropy are being more seriously explored.

Role of the Media

The interest in Indian philanthropy has been fed by greater media coverage, both national and international. The national media has demonstrated an undreamt of power to motivate people and to mobilize resources for charity. The news channel NDTV, for instance, ran a very successful Save the Tiger campaign. *The Times of India*, similarly, ran a Teach India campaign for educated Indians to teach the underprivileged. This media power has been used not only to motivate, but also to ensure accountability in recipients.[11]

[11] Pushpa Sundar, 'Whither Indian Philanthropy'. Mimeo, 2006.

Abroad, *The Harvard Business Review*, *Forbes Magazine*, *The New York Times*, *Wall Street Journal*, and *The Economist* have all covered Indian philanthropy at some time or the other recently. In 2011, The Philanthropy Initiative's (TPI) Center for Global Philanthropy hosted 'Philanthropy and Social Change in India', an event co-sponsored by New England International Donors.

Companies Act 2013

Finally, the Companies Act of 2013 has added a new term and a new paradigm to altruistic giving in India—that of corporate social responsibility (CSR). In a replay, the old custom of setting aside a certain amount for charity/philanthropy by rich families or merchant firms has been replaced by a compulsory contribution of 2 per cent of profits by government diktat. Clause 135 of the Act makes it mandatory for companies of a certain size and profitability to devote 2 per cent of the average net profits of the past three years to what are called CSR activities. This, once again, has increased the interest on the part of companies in how philanthropy has been done in the past and how it can be done now.

Increased Potential for Philanthropy

If there is an increased interest in philanthropy, both at the practical and intellectual level, there is also an increased potential for it.

Indian philanthropy comes from five main sources, namely individual charitable giving; corporate giving; donations and grants by foundations and trusts; donations by religious organizations; and diaspora philanthropy, that is, giving by non-resident Indians (NRIs). The potential of each of these has increased due to the expansion of the economy.

Apart from the greatly increased numbers of HNWIs, India's greatly expanded middle class is also more charitably inclined due to the feel good factor induced by an expanding economy. With 23.6 million people, it accounts for 3 per cent of the global middle class, and is estimated to have almost one fourth of the country's wealth, at $780 billion.[12] Many of the pioneering entrepreneurs who

---

[12] Credit Suisse, *Global Wealth Report*, October 2015.

created the new wealth have come from this educated and globally connected middle class. In contrast to inherited wealth, most of which is expected to be passed on to the children, the new wealthy hold middle class values of thrift and self-help and appreciate that opportunities for advancement are perhaps more important than inherited wealth. They are therefore keen to offer others the same opportunities they have received, and are ready to give away large amounts of their wealth in their own lifetimes.

Moreover, in common with other countries of the globe, India's increased life expectancy means that the number of elderly persons has gone up. Among these, the numbers of the affluent elderly are increasing, and they are interested in and able to engage in philanthropy for another reason. Families today are smaller than they used to be, many have children settled abroad who, moreover, are disinterested in, or unable to inherit, property in India. For them, giving away their wealth makes sense. As a result, many are exploring the hitherto unusual option of making bequests to social action organizations.

The Indian diaspora too, estimated to number 20 million, including a number of affluent NRIs, has become majorly interested in philanthropy. The Indian diaspora in America, now numbering more than 1.9 million Indian-born immigrants and another 1.6 million Americans with Indian ancestry, is perhaps the most influential. They have amassed significant wealth and 27 per cent of them earn more than $140,000, putting them in the top ten of earners nationally. The combined annual discretionary income of Americans of Indian origin is approximately $67.4 billion.[13]

This successful diaspora is now seeking opportunities for repaying a debt to their home country, to their alma maters, and to their home villages, towns, and regions. The brain drain witnessed in the early years of Independence is now beginning to show a reverse flow, at least in money terms. It is estimated that if the American Indian diaspora directed 40 per cent of their philanthropic giving to India, $1.2 billion would flow from the diaspora to Indian causes. Not only would it dwarf official US aid to India ($116.4 million in financial

[13] Migration Policy Institute, RAD Diaspora Profile, 'The Indian Diaspora in the United States', Appendix 1, July 2014.

year 2014), but it would also represent more than half the entire amount of official development aid received by India from all countries from 2005 to 2013, at $2.2 billion on an average.[14]

Importantly, whereas earlier money flowed from this diaspora to their families and local communities, it is now looking to support social organizations working on national causes. Consequently, more and more ways and mechanisms to make this reverse flow possible are being explored, ranging from promotion of online giving by organizations such as GiveIndia, to the establishment of counterpart foundations by several Indian NGOs like CRY, ASHA, and others, to the offering of tax benefits to the NRI donors in their own country. Diaspora philanthropy is thus growing, and in recent years has become a significant source of funds for non-profit organizations engaged in development and welfare. At the same time, the potential is far greater than is being tapped, principally because of lack of information and proper mechanism through which this money can be channelled to social action organizations, regulatory constraints like Foreign Contributions Regulation Act (FCRA) rules, lack of trust in Indian NGOs, and a disconnect with India by second generation diaspora.

Because of globalization many Indian companies with a global presence are aware of corporate philanthropy in other countries and feel that they too would be judged by their contributions to the community. They are therefore willing to give more for social development. At the same time, there are many more multi-national companies (MNCs) in India, willing and interested in contributing to India's social development.

The uncertainties of our times have also stimulated an interest in religious and spiritual matters so that giving to religious organizations is at an all-time high. There is both a potential and an opportunity to bring some of this money into organized secular philanthropy.

Finally, technological developments in information and communication technology have provided powerful tools for donors and would-be donors to learn about and contribute to new developments and opportunities worldwide.

---

[14] Rohit Menezes, Sonali Madia Patel, and Daniel Pike, 'Giving Back to India', Impact India, *Stanford Social Innovation Review*, Stanford, USA: 17–23, Fall 2015.

Increased Giving

In response to the new stimuli, India's pool of philanthropic capital is growing. According to the Bain and Company's *India Philanthropy Report* for 2011, giving is said to have increased from 0.2 per cent of gross domestic product (GDP) in 2006 to 0.3–0.4 per cent in 2010, though the present reality is that Indians still give just 1.5–3 per cent of their annual household incomes, as against 9 per cent by Americans.[15] The Country's Wealthy have reportedly increased their contributions to philanthropy from 2.3 per cent of household income in 2010 to 3.1 per cent in 2011.[16] The Bain and Company's *Annual Philanthropy Re*port for 2015 indicates that the country has added more than 100 million donors since 2009, and the amounts donated have increased. Moreover, a third of the current donors expect their donations to increase in the next five years and under the right conditions, giving in India can reach significant and impactful proportions.

However, the philanthropy space is skewed. There are sophisticated donors working with organized non-profit organizations to create impactful change. At the other end are donors who are ad hoc givers who give to ever-changing new causes and organizations, as well as non-profit organizations seeking new donors all the time.[17]

Changes in Modes of Giving

Profound long-term changes in the world economy have led to a rethinking of the way philanthropy is practised. India is no exception. Three major trends are visible in India. One, there is a major change in the profile of the new donors. The new rich and therefore the new donors come from non-traditional backgrounds, engage in philanthropy at a younger age, and include more women and individuals from previously disadvantaged backgrounds such as the Dalits. Two, the concept of philanthropy has broadened to include CSR contributions and funding of social entrepreneurship. In India,

---

[15] Arpan Sheth, *India Philanthropy Report*, Bain and Company, June 2011.

[16] *India Philanthropy Report*, Bain and Company, 2012.

[17] *India Philanthropy Report*, Bain and Company, June 2015.

because it has been made mandatory for companies of a certain size, CSR has become a major player compared to family foundations and individual philanthropy by HNWIs. New terms such as 'venture philanthropy' and 'social investment' have emerged, signifying a new approach to giving. Social impact, also known as Social Return on Investment, is being emphasized.

Three, the practice of philanthropy is changing partly because many governments in the world, including India's, are unable to address growing social needs without private sector contribution, and partly because many Western foundations have seen reductions in assets and income. This has forced philanthropists and philanthropic organizations to rethink their roles and ways of working.[18]

The changes in global economies have led to a debate on three themes: the need for philanthropy to address growing inequality and problems such as migration, international as well as rural–urban; the tendency to see philanthropy in terms of investment in the form of free loans, soft loans, and equity investments rather than donations and grants; and the need for cooperation and partnership, especially with government and other philanthropic organizations. The key challenges before philanthropy are considered to be maximizing impact, achieving scale, focusing on inequality and social change, lack of data to guide policy, and achieving a more conducive legal and fiscal environment.[19]

There are changes in philanthropic preferences too, to reflect new emerging needs. The focus is shifting from the traditional favourites—education and health—to children, nutrition, women's issues, water, sanitation, and environmental concerns; and from establishing prestigious institutions towards supporting grassroots initiatives.

The way philanthropy is managed is changing too in various degrees, with measurement of impact becoming important.

Further, organized philanthropy is more diverse than ever before. There are many new foundations and companies engaging in

---

[18] Anthony Tomei, 'Changing Roles in a Changing World', *Alliance magazine*, 1 June 2013.

[19] Andrew Milner and Caroline Hartnell, 'Philanthropy in a Changing World Economy: How is Philanthropy Changing?', *Alliance magazine*, 1 June 2013.

philanthropy; more intermediary organizations to service new donors; a new class of professionals engaged in the business of giving for welfare and development; and a new group of professionals raising funds for charitable causes, who make good use of modern technology.

New types of philanthropic organizations have emerged, such as Giving Circles—rather like women's kitty parties but with the objective of engaging in philanthropy together; community foundations; Donor Advised Funds; online portals (e.g., Give India, Give to Asia, etc.); and foundation like intermediaries engaged in both collecting and disbursing funds (CRY, HelpAge, Concern India). Also new means of giving are visible like payroll giving, and internet giving.

In spite of several positive changes, there are still several negative features in the ecosystem which constrain giving, the most important of which is the donor's lack of trust in intended beneficiaries, and lack of an infrastructure to promote giving. Nor has the government played a particularly facilitating role.

Finally, old-style charity, characterized by ad hoc, small, unplanned, and informal giving for immediate relief of distress, and largely for religious and local community projects, continues alongside, and is far larger than modern philanthropy, giving rise to a deep divide in the charitable sector which parallels the rural/urban, poor/rich divide—or what is commonly called the Bharat–India dichotomy. Organized philanthropy or social investment for long-term change is urban and centred on NGOs, social entrepreneurs, and foreign donors. Both donors and recipients talk a common language of strategic philanthropy, programme planning and design, grant making, evaluation, monitoring, governance, transparency and accountability, FCRA, and so on.

Charity, on the other hand, is largely centred on rural and *mofussil* (semi-urban) India, and the middle and lower class individual giver, the small retailer, trader, and businessman, and impact is a word not heard at all.

The Study of Indian Philanthropy

While Indian philanthropy is increasing and changing, its study lags behind, unlike in the USA and other Western countries, where philanthropy is a subject of serious study. There are numerous centres and university departments for the study of philanthropy in the USA, such as the Centre on Philanthropy at Indiana University and the Centre for the Study of Philanthropy at New York City University. In India there are none. Indians are yet to think of philanthropy as a serious discipline-worthy of research.

Extant Scholarship and Gaps

Consequently, the corpus of knowledge on modern Indian philanthropy is meagre, though material is more plentiful about the historical tradition of charity. Studies in business history, such as those of D. Tripathi (1984), Makarand Mehta (1981, 1991), and Margaret Herdeck and Gita Piramal (1985), touch on charity tangentially. Biographies and autobiographies of great industrialists such as Jamshetji Tata, G.D. Birla, K.K. Birla, and Lala Shri Ram, who were also great philanthropists, mostly deal with their subjects as businessmen, though they contain some sections on their philanthropic activities.[20]

The only studies which deal with the history of philanthropy are Mr R.M. Lala's excellent studies of the Tata Trusts, namely *The Creation of Wealth*, and the *Heartbeat of a Trust*, and R.P. Masani's two books, *N.M. Wadia and His Foundation* (1961) and *The Role of Wealth in Society* (1956). But in each, the attention, with the exception of the last, is only on one business family.

Dadrawala's book (2003) is a series of case studies of modern business philanthropists, while Mathew Cherian (2014) deals with religious philanthropy as a part of his interest in the history and working of India's civil society. There are also some books on diaspora philanthropy.

But beyond these, there is an overall dearth of work taking a comprehensive look at Indian philanthropy and exploring the interrelationships between philanthropy and its wider context on the lines of David Owen's seminal book *English Philanthropy*

---

[20] Some of the recent biographies and autobiographies are those of Vinay Bharat Ram (2011), G.D. Birla (2003), and K.K. Birla (2012).

1660–1960 (1965). My own work over the years has tried to fill in some of the gaps.[21]

Contemporary empirical research is almost non-existent, limited to reports of some leading consultancies such as McKinsey and Company and Bain and Company, and civil society organizations such as the now extinct Sampradaan Indian Centre for Philanthropy, Centre for Advancement of Philanthropy, and Charities Aid Foundation. Recently, there have been some articles in newspapers and journals on different facets of business philanthropy such as sponsorship, CSR programmes, and the contributions of individual donors; but these hardly constitute a corpus of systematic analysis about levels and mechanisms of giving, philanthropic preferences, and so on. Mostly, they are descriptive and not critical analyses.

There is, in particular, a lamentable lack of quantitative data on the size of philanthropic giving in India, either in the total or disaggregated according to sources. Some estimates are available about the volume of individual donations from some surveys conducted by the organizations mentioned above, as well as Sampradaan Indian Centre for Philanthropy (SICP) and Society for Participatory Research in Asia (PRIA) in 2001 and 2002 respectively, and more recently by the Charities Aid Foundation India. But there are no quantitative estimates about the volume of giving by foundations and trusts to other social organizations, or giving by the other sources, though some tentative and partial estimates are available.

There is no central enactment governing the establishment of public trusts and therefore no single source of data on numbers; nor have there been any independent surveys of giving by individuals, corporations, foundations, or foreign donor organizations; hence there is no way of knowing the total philanthropic contributions, or what percentage of net profits go for philanthropy, and so on.

[21] Sundar, *Beyond Business*; 'The World of Indian Foundations', *Directory of Indian Donor Organisations,* 1998. Paper first written for the seminar on 'Trusts, Philanthropy and Development' organized by the Indian Centre for Philanthropy at IIC, New Delhi on 28 January 1998. 'Charity for Social Change and Development: Essay on Indian Philanthropy', 1997.

For other publications and works by the author, please refer to the bibliography.

Tax and other government policies have a direct bearing on whether profits are channelled into philanthropy or not, and for which causes. But there is hardly any research on whether tax incentives have in fact stimulated charity, and whether these resources would have come forth irrespective of incentives; whether the present subsidy regime is regressive, giving more advantage to the richer donor; whether an amnesty scheme for black money abroad, if it is invested into large philanthropic projects is feasible or not; and so on. If a larger impact on social progress is the desired goal, we need to devise policies which will link up philanthropic resources with large and important national goals and programmes.

More importantly, there is little theoretical analysis of philanthropy in the context of wealth creation and distribution.

Critiquing Philanthropy

The recent economic crisis in the West, the growing gap between the rich and the poor everywhere, and the various financial scams which have surfaced not only in India but the rest of the world as well, have raised larger questions about the creation and distribution of wealth, and especially about the ethics of philanthropy.

The excesses of capitalism have led to a search for alternatives to capitalistic production. Whether philanthropy can be an alternative has been questioned by many, including Rev. Dr Martin Luther King Jr. who said, 'Philanthropy is commendable, but it must not cause the philanthropist to overlook the circumstances of economic injustice which make philanthropy necessary'.[22]

So one of the questions being raised is how should the system be changed so that the incentive to create wealth and use it for the common good is retained, but not its excesses, and what is the role that philanthropy itself can play in this? A related question is, what impact will an alternative system have on the nature of philanthropy? The experience of the Soviet Union makes for a good case study.

---

[22] Quoted by Darren Walker in 'Why Giving Back Isn't Enough' *New York Times*, New York edition, 17 December 2015.

A second related question is whether philanthropy is only a way of ensuring the status quo of social structure and power equations.

Gandhi's doctrine of trusteeship of wealth was criticized on the grounds that he encouraged voluntary giving by the rich in order to prevent a more drastic restructuring of society and redistribution of wealth, which would have led to a more egalitarian society.

Today again, critics of big money are accusing the big Western foundations of perpetuating the status quo of power and privilege. The Ford Foundation, which has long had removal of social inequities as a programme goal, is accused of having failed to deliver on the promises to change entrenched systems of power. Instead of funding structural changes to deal with racial discrimination and labour exploitation, such as radical Black Power movements or labour unions, which would have struck directly at the root of the existing wealth and power distribution, it is said to have supported only peripheral measures such as education programmes for poor neighbourhoods, or black leadership.

Other big foundations, including new ones like the Gates Foundation, are accused of having avoided confrontation with systems of power and privilege, and in some instances of producing new relationships of inequality. The Gates Foundation, for instance, while claiming to address inequality in educational achievement, is said to simultaneously promote competitive approaches which build market opportunities for private educational service providers, without improving outcomes for poor students.[23]

Because of the many financial scams which have surfaced lately, the latest being the Panama Papers scandal about stashing away of fortunes by the rich and powerful in secret tax havens, even legitimate wealth is coming to be looked upon with suspicion. The origins of the great fortunes, whether legitimate or illegitimate, on which their philanthropy rests, has become a matter of great interest. Gustavus Myers, in his 'History of the Great American Fortunes', argued that after years of enjoying their wealth the robber barons became great philanthropists to give themselves a new character. Myers pointed

---

[23] See Kohl Arenas, 'Can Philanthropy Ever Reduce Inequality?' *Transformation*, 8 July, https://www.opendemocracy.net/transformation/ erica-kohlarenas/can-philanthropy-ever-reduce-inequality.

out that the libraries endowed by Andrew Carnegie owed their origin to wealth produced by underpaid and overworked employees.[24]

Using philanthropy to whitewash fortunes was not a new phenomena at the time, nor limited only to America. Nor will it be the last. Philanthropy has ever been used to gain status and acceptance in societies across the globe and across time. Many of the fortunes made by India's great philanthropists of the late nineteenth and early twentieth century were derived from the opium trade with China, or other unethical business practices.

Some of the great fortunes today, in India and elsewhere, also rest on questionable means. Phil Knight, the founder and chairman of the athletic gear company Nike, is today the fifteenth richest man in the world and a philanthropist. In February 2016 he made a gift of $400 million towards a $750 million endowment meant to pay for young leaders from around the world to attend graduate school at Stanford. But his fortune rests on profits made by Nike from sweated labour in South East Asia, though the company has since adjusted worker's salaries and started community development and micro credit programmes in order to regain its reputation.[25]

This issue raises the question whether good ends justify questionable means, a question which is yet to be answered satisfactorily.

Philanthropists themselves, either individuals or companies, seem unable to see the contradictions in their behaviours, as far as ethics is concerned. Companies will pollute the community's source of water with their operations on the one hand, and fund health programmes on the other; or they make their money through employing women or children in sweatshops on the one hand, and fund women's empowerment or children's nutrition programmes on the other.

Individuals like Ramalinga Raju, the promoter of the Indian company Satyam will, for instance, spend crores of personal and company money on philanthropy on the one hand, and defraud shareholders and other stakeholders on the other. The Indian Tobacco Company (ITC) makes its profits from harmful-to-health tobacco, and yet is one of the most generous among companies as far as spending for

---

[24] See Christopher Caldwell, 'Donor Beware', *Wall Street Journal Review*, Saturday–Sunday, 12–13 March 2016.
[25] Caldwell, 'Donor Beware'.

development of communities is concerned. In India, philanthropy has also been used to mask tax evasion and to launder black money, especially in the education sector.

It seems unlikely that foundations, even in America, will undermine their own power and privilege to back radical social change which will put people back in the driving seat.[26] And it looks more unlikely to happen in India, given that Indian foundations have always avoided confrontation with either the government or civil society.

Beneficiaries of philanthropic money, whether NGOs or other organizations, almost certainly will not, or cannot, afford to challenge how the philanthropists generate their wealth, how they want to spend their grant money, or to question their breaching of ethical behaviour. Therefore, it is up to independent thinkers and activists to raise these questions about philanthropy and social justice through research and public debates, so that philanthropy may play a truly useful role in society.

In the West there is also much preoccupation with the power of philanthropists over government policies, so much so that a Commission (the Filer Commission) had to be appointed to investigate abuse of philanthropic money and power. In India the question has not arisen so far because till now philanthropy has been very low key and philanthropists have avoided conflict by taking non-partisan positions on policy issues, either directly or indirectly. But it is possible that as Indian foundations expand and become influential, the question may arise.

Because a demand for incentives is always made by philanthropists and others as a way of promoting philanthropy, another question which arises is, are not tax incentives for philanthropy a contradiction in terms? Is it true charity or philanthropy to expect something in return for giving out of generosity of heart?

A final question which needs to be confronted, especially in the context of widespread inequality, is who benefits from philanthropy? As Francie Ostrower (1997), Caldwell (2016), and others have argued, big philanthropy tends not to be egalitarian. In fact, it is explicitly elitist in its choice of individuals and institutions and regions to benefit. Western philanthropists have endowed museums, art galleries, elite universities and the like, which are largely used

[26] See Arenas, Arenas, 'Can Philanthropy Ever Reduce Inequality?'.

by the elite, and as noticed above, critics have pointed out that not enough attention has been paid to what is called 'social justice philanthropy'. But whether philanthropy, if it is to be voluntary, can indeed be made egalitarian is debatable.

Giving for elite causes or institutions has been justified by many of the leading philanthropists themselves on the ground that it is the government's role to equalize spending to take care of poorer sections and regions. The role of private money is to encourage excellence wherever found, so that society as a whole may progress. Carnegie believed, 'wealth passing through the hands of the few, can be made a much more potent force for the elevation of our race than if it had been distributed in small sums to the people themselves'.[27]

Jamsetji Tata voiced a similar opinion in his oft quoted idea of constructive philanthropy. He said, 'What advances a nation or community is not to prop up its weakest and most helpless members as to lift up the best and most gifted so as to make them of the greatest service to the country. I prefer this constructive philanthropy which seeks to educate and develop the faculties of the young men.'

Indian philanthropy of the earlier era tended to be like the Western variation in its elite orientation. Judging from the evidence in the following pages, it does not appear to be so today.

It has become necessary to revisit the many questions mentioned above, so that new philanthropy may grow on the right track. This book does not claim to have answered these questions. To answer them is outside the scope of this book. Its limited purpose is to provide some material for debate and further exploration. As has been wisely said, sometimes raising the right question is more important than giving an answer that is wrong.

To conclude, Indian society is undergoing multiple transformations and is faced with daunting challenges. Philanthropy should be a part of the solution. Though both the volume of philanthropy and dialogues about it have increased, Indian philanthropy is still a mere footnote in the main text of development discourse, rather than a mainstream concern. The stories have not yet merged to form a single strong narrative or public discourse on philanthropy and its role in India today. It is my hope that a discourse will be stimulated by this book and that it will take Indian philanthropy to a new high.

---

[27] Carnegie, quoted in Caldwell, 'Donor Beware'.

PART I

AN ETHIC OF GIVING

Giving and caring are not only public values that need to be cultivated, but they should also give rise to an ethic of giving in which how you give matters as much as what you give.
        —James A. Joseph, Former US Ambassador to South Africa and Professor Emeritus of Public Policy, Duke University

1

Why India Needs Philanthropy

Wealth is most commendable, provided the entire population is wealthy. If however, a few have inordinate riches while the rest are impoverished, and no fruit or benefit accrues from that wealth, then it is only a liability to its possessor. If on the other hand, it is expended for the promotion of knowledge, the founding of elementary and other schools, the encouragement of art and industry, the training of orphans and the poor—in brief, if it is dedicated to the welfare of society—its possessor will stand out before God and man as the most excellent of all who live on earth and will be accounted as one of the people of paradise.[1]

Giving on a large scale for the benefit of society is praiseworthy, but by all accounts, not easy. As the Greek philosopher Aristotle and many leading philanthropists in the world, including Warren Buffet and Azim Premji have pointed out, giving away money for social change and transformation requires even more prescience, more imagination, and more executive skill, than making it. Then why do people engage in philanthropy? And what good does philanthropy do to society? Social and political theorists have debated these questions for

[1] Abdu'l-Baha, *The Secret of Divine Civilization* (Wilmette, Illinois, Baha'i Publishing Trust, 1956, reprinted 1971).

centuries, and the answer is that philanthropy meets multiple needs in a human being as well as in society.

For an individual, philanthropy, like the quality of mercy, is twice blest—it blesseth not only him that takes but also him that gives. For the recipient the benefit is obvious. For the giver, it fulfils a spiritual and moral need. But does it have any larger role or purpose in society as a whole? The short answer is yes.

Philanthropy's Role in Society

The distribution and proper utilization of wealth has engaged the human mind almost as much as its creation. How to ensure an equitable social order in which there is no exploitation and in which wealth is used not only to take care of the poor and needy, but also to bring beauty, art, and knowledge to all, has been, and continues to be, a vexed question. Philanthropy has long been considered as one solution for creating a good life and an equitable society.

Philanthropy plays several roles in society but in the main, there are four. One, philanthropy supplements government provision for social needs, and assists in its efforts to bring development to society.

Two, it plays a role in reducing inequalities of wealth and opportunity in society.

Three, it plays the role of a catalyst, triggering positive transformative change in society. By providing independent private resources as seed funds, philanthropy acts as an incubator for great ideas and drives innovation. Strategic philanthropy invests in long term solutions to the larger problems facing society.[2]

Finally, it acts as a countervailing force, helping to build a strong civil society to rein in an all too powerful government or an exploitative market to safeguard the rights of citizens.

Each role and its relative importance is described in some detail in the following in order to show why India needs philanthropy.

---

[2] Council on Foundations, 'Defining Philanthropy's Role in Society', Council on Foundations, Philanthropy Roundtable, Forum of Regional Association of Grantmakers, Undated. http://www.foundationsonthehill.org/docs/Defining-Philanthropys-Role-in-Society.pdf on 6 November 2012.

Supplementing Government Provisions

While philanthropy can certainly supplement government provisions for education, health, the arts, or sports, it can only be a small, and not its best role, since the resources of philanthropy are generally limited and on a much smaller scale than government budgets for the same. Though the budget of the Bill Gates Foundation, currently the biggest philanthropic organization in the world, is bigger than the GDP of some countries, it is still miniscule as a portion of international wealth, and cannot compensate for internal government spending even for a small country, because it is focused on only one or two issues, such as healthcare. Besides, the government can get supplementary contributions for its social spending by levying further taxes, though there is a political limit to how much taxes can be increased; alternatively, it can make contributions to social programmes compulsory, as has been done by the Indian government in the case of education cess or mandatory CSR contributions. Private philanthropy cannot do either.

Besides, the total wealth of the rich is not wholly available for meeting social needs, and, being dependent on market valuation, is notional and subject to fluctuations. According to a calculation by the Business Standard Research Bureau, if the total wealth of India's ten richest business people as of December 2010 were added up, the figure would come to Rupees 5.6 trillion, the amount spent by the central and state government in 2010–11, on what the Economic Survey calls 'social services', meaning health, education, and sundry other schemes (according to the Budget Estimates for 2010–11). Even if all these rich people were to give the entire or a bulk of their holdings to social causes, it is only the dividend income from these shares (which is a percentage of their face value, not market value) that would be available for investment—and that, in turn, is a function of how the company concerned performs.

There is another reason why philanthropy cannot function as a substitute for the government. Philanthropic agendas are rarely truly objective and depend on the interests and other motives of the donors. They would, in all likelihood, focus on only the one or two needs that are judged most important by them, and other causes or organizations would be at a disadvantage. Philanthropy by the rich is unlikely to address social needs and issues in a balanced way.

Again, philanthropic activities tend to be confined by the limitations of a corporation's location and capabilities. An individual donor or a company generally gives to causes near where they are located or in which they have a special interest. For instance, a company will give preference to building schools in its backyard rather than in a place far away, with no connection to its business. Individuals generally concentrate their giving in places or causes with an emotional connect, as was the case with the industrialist G.D. Birla and his home town, Pilani. So, the geographic impact of their giving is very limited compared to government spending.[3]

But while philanthropic resources can never match state budgets for development in size, they can certainly supplement government provisions, often being more efficiently spent, and better at reaching the beneficiaries than government agencies. But more importantly, as an alternative to government funding, they offer choice and independence in action to the users.

Reducing Inequality

Philanthropy's role in reducing inequality is indirect. Direct transfer of resources from the rich to the poor on any large scale is simply not a practical proposition for reducing inequality, as the experiment with communism has shown. Besides, even the most generous philanthropic society in the world such as the USA, with its philanthropic giving amounting to around 2 per cent of its GDP, has not been successful in reducing inequality. As Thomas Piketty has shown in his seminal book, *Capitalism in the Twenty-First Century* (2014), inequality in America today is greater than ever before.

Many people, especially with leftist ideology, do not believe that philanthropy has any role to play in reducing inequality, and that for redistribution of income there is no substitute for taxes and

---

[3] See Kanika Datta, 'Charity Begins in Governance', *Business Standard*, 31 March 2011.

government spending on social needs. These ensure that the money goes to those who need it the most, does not make them dependent on the whims of donors, and has wider geographic impact.

Few will deny that good governance, rather than philanthropy, even on a large scale, will ensure faster growth and remove poverty,. But good governance is a scarce commodity, especially in developing countries. Besides, heavy taxation can be counterproductive. According to *The Economist* (20 January 2011), the right way to combat inequality and increase mobility is by governments keeping their focus on pushing up the bottom and middle rather than dragging down the top: investing in (and removing barriers to) education, abolishing rules that prevent the able from getting ahead, and refocusing government spending on those that need it the most.[4] If this can be done consistently, the government undoubtedly has an edge over philanthropy as far as reduction of inequality is concerned.

But inequality can certainly be reduced *indirectly* by philanthropy. Picketty admits that though reduction of income inequalities does not come automatically with the progress of capitalism, there are powerful forces that can mitigate inequality. These he identifies as diffusion of knowledge and skills, and these can be influenced by state policies on education and access to training and skill development. He does not mention philanthropy in this connection, but philanthropy, alongside the state, can also provide access to education, training, and skills.

When the large American foundations were established, the 'robber barons' had made unprecedented wealth while the labour received only a small share. But their philanthropic efforts helped to ameliorate labour conditions both directly and by putting pressure on the government.

Though philanthropy cannot reduce inequality by itself, it can support reforms which may lead to a more equitable distribution. Writing in September 1958 about American philanthropy, historian Irving Wylie wrote, 'If America expected her philanthropists to be sensitive to current needs, she also expected them to be aware that

---

[4] *The Economist*, 'The Rich and the Rest: What To Do (And Not Do) about Inequality', 20 January 2011.

there was a limit to what even the wisest and most liberal charity could accomplish. ... Philanthropy was no substitute for social justice. ... America preferred benefactors who did not view philanthropy as an antidote to reform *but rather than as an admission that reform was necessary. To give was to confess the need, and to confess the need was to open the door to change* (Emphasis mine).'[5]

So, the role of philanthropy is not to reduce inequalities of income directly, but to reduce *inequality of opportunity* and provide access to a high quality of life.

Picketty asserts that the equalizing process cannot work properly without inclusive educational institutions and continuous investments in skills, and this philanthropy can ensure, if not exclusively, either as a supplement to government efforts or in partnership with the government.

What differentiates American capitalism from all other forms of capitalism is its historical focus on both the creation of wealth (entrepreneurship) and the reconstitution of wealth (philanthropy). Philanthropy has been recognized as a crucial contributor to the stability of American society and culture and to the process of economic development.[6]

According to Andrew Carnegie, considered one of America's greatest philanthropists, no system can or should maintain complete equality between the drones and the bees, because differential rewards are necessary for progress. Yet, he said, it was also true that the capitalists as a class reaped far more than they had sown and therefore they owed it to society to return the surplus wealth which was not their due. This surplus, he held, should be utilized for the betterment of one's fellowmen and enlightenment and progress in society.

Those who, like Carnegie, made their fortunes in the first 'Gilded Age', created foundations that, in turn, contributed to greater and

---

[5] Irving Wylie, 'The Reputation of the American Philanthropist: A Historian's View', *The Social Service Review*, September 1958.

[6] Zoltan J. Acs and Sameeksha Desai, 'Democratic Capitalism and Philanthropy in a Global Economy', *Jena Economic Research Paper No. 2007–056*, Jena, Germany, September 2007.

more widespread economic prosperity through opportunity, knowledge creation, and entrepreneurship. By 1940, twelve of the thirteen families in control of two hundred of the nation's largest non-financial corporations had their own foundations. It is acknowledged today that no institution in the US private sector has had a greater impact on society, especially on research and development, than these foundations. For instance, before he died, John D. Rockefeller gave back 95 per cent of his wealth to society to support knowledge creation, which ultimately led to advances in the fields of agriculture and health and the creation and funding of great research centres such as the University of Chicago and the Brookings Institution. In the words of Warren Weaver, 'foundations have freed large parts of the world from the curse of diseases such as malaria and yellow fever; have brought enjoyment of the arts to millions of people; have created and helped support universities and research institutes; ... have importantly contributed to our growing knowledge of physical and living nature',[7] and so on, in a large catalogue of contributions to human welfare.

Finally, unlike in the contemporary period, the rise in inequality in the US in the first 'Gilded Age'(prior to 1930) was accompanied by a falling incidence of poverty, thanks to the advances made by the philanthropic contributions of the 'robber barons'. There was a sharp decline in income inequality between 1913 and 1948.[8]

In present times, Warren Buffett justifies his philanthropy by saying that life is about planting trees for others to sit under. He wasn't born with a silver spoon in his mouth, but he went to excellent educational institutions that were endowed by philanthropy. In other words, the system empowered him and he utilized the opportunities available. Having sat under a tree that nurtured him, he now wants to plant trees for others by giving away 99 per cent of his wealth. He believes that while a market system works best to create and sustain

[7] Warren Weaver, *US Philanthropic Foundations* (New York: Harper and Row Publishers, 1967).

[8] Zanny Minton Beddoes, 'For Richer, for Poorer: Growing Inequality is One of the Biggest Social, Economic and Political Challenges of Our Time. But it is Not Inevitable'. *The Economist*, 13 October 2012.

prosperity, philanthropy, as well as state support, must lend a helping hand when individuals cannot access the market. So, capitalism must flourish along with philanthropy. But philanthropy must remain a matter of individual choice—because to make it mandatory would be tantamount to socialism.[9]

However, not all agree about philanthropy's ability to ameliorate the ills of capitalism. If philanthropy depends on wealth and wealth leads to inequality, then, as Pier Mario Vello and others point out, we have the paradox that the existence of philanthropy is inextricably linked to the problems it attempts to solve.[10]

Peter Buffet, Warren Buffet's son, points to the inherent contradictions in philanthropy—giving back something even as more lives and communities are destroyed by the system that creates vast amounts of wealth for the few. Calling it 'giving back' makes it sound better, he says, but feels that it should be called 'conscience laundering'—feeling better about accumulating more than any one person could possibly need to live on, by sprinkling a little around as an act of charity.[11]

His objection, however, is not so much to philanthropy as to *charity* which just keeps the existing structure of inequality in place through handouts, and ensures a perpetual poverty machine. Philanthropy, on the other hand, can help. Used as risk capital which leads to systemic change through innovation, it can trigger more employment and incomes. According to him, money should be spent trying out concepts that shatter current structures and systems that have turned much of the world into one vast market. He pleads for new ways of thinking, or use of philanthropy as a catalyst.

On balance, while philanthropy by itself cannot reduce inequality, it can *aid* in reducing it.

[9] *Business Standard*, 'One can create jobs and still be a Santa Claus: Buffet', 25 March 2011. From http://articles.timesofindia.indiatimes.com/2011-03-25/edit-page/29187698_1_philanthropy-capitalism-plant-trees.

[10] Anthony Tomei, 'Changing roles in a changing world', *Alliance Magazine*, 1 June 2013.

[11] Peter Buffet, 'The Charitable-Industrial Complex', *The New York Times*, 26 July 2013.

Philanthropy as Catalyst

This is the third role of philanthropy—acting as leaven in bread. Properly used philanthropy can stimulate creativity and innovation. Philanthropy, free of the short-term pressures from voters and shareholders that constrain governments and for-profit companies, can solve many problems that the other two might find difficult. In the words of Waldemar Nielson, the role of philanthropy is 'to help generate some fresh ideas and to test some new methods that might provide for equity and efficiency, humaneness and effectiveness, in social programs'.[12] Ideas and experiments seeded by private wealth can, upon success, find their way into public policy and implementation, though not necessarily with the same success.

According to Brian O'Connell (1986), a former President of the Independent Sector, a coalition of voluntary organizations, foundations, and corporations promoting giving in the USA, the rationale for philanthropy is not that it provides succour to the needy more efficiently and in a more humane manner than government agency, but the quality of what the philanthropic funds can do. He calls it the 'extra dimension' in the pursuit of progress and happiness. Philanthropy provides for seeing and doing things differently. It does not replace government or other basic institutions but provides additional means of addressing our problems and aspirations and helps to keep the basic institutions responsive and effective. Both the commercial and political market-places are subject to levelling forces which may threaten the pursuit of excellence. But philanthropy allows pluralism—many sources of initiative, many conflicting beliefs, many competing economic units, many kinds of institutions—to flourish and allows pursuit of excellence.[13] He gives the example of ten great ideas which created transformative change in the world, and which were backed by philanthropy.[14] Nelson Mandela was supported by wealthy well-wishers while he cast the first stone at Apartheid, just

---

[12] Waldemar A. Nielson, *Golden Donors: A New Anatomy of the Great Foundations* (New Jersey: Transaction Publishers, 1985, reprinted in 2001).

[13] Brian O'Connell, *Philanthropy in Action* (Washington: Foundation Center, 1987).

[14] O'Connell, *Philanthropy in Action*.

as G.D. Birla, Jamnalal Bajaj, and other wealthy magnates put their wealth at the disposal of Mahatma Gandhi while he experimented with non-violent struggle to free India from the British.

Governments, in general, are hopeless at spotting great ideas. They work through committees and too many heads ensure that the genuine creative idea—the one dissenting voice that can make a difference—gets stifled.

According to O'Connell, philanthropic resources can help to:

- discover new frontiers of knowledge
- support and encourage excellence
- enable people to exercise their potential
- relieve human misery
- preserve and enhance democratic government and institutions
- make communities better places to live
- nourish the spirit
- create tolerance, understanding, and peace among people
- remember the dead[15]

O'Connell illustrates each of these from the history of American philanthropy. To mention only a few, Daniel Guggenheim, in whose name the Guggenheim Foundation was later established, gave early financial support to Robert H. Goddard to test rockets when many were sceptical of the feasibility of rockets. That early support led, in time, to man's first steps on the moon.

To provide equal opportunity and empowerment, the Ford Foundation provided funding for a pilot project that developed into the Native American Rights Fund (NARF) which provided discriminated Indians access to lawyers and legal processes. This gave a big fillip to the native American Rights Movement.[16]

The government may have larger resources, but there is scepticism about its ability to deliver social services effectively and in a 'humane', non-bureaucratic manner. Philanthropy can do what the government will not or cannot, or, because of its size and nature, should not. Experiments are best made by private institutions on a

---

[15] O'Connell, *Philanthropy in Action*, p. 9.
[16] O'Connell, *Philanthropy in Action*, pp. 56–7.

smaller scale before public funds are committed in large amounts on schemes which are not as yet proven.

The leading philanthropist of our time, Bill Gates, offers this rationale for philanthropy which is worth quoting at some length:

> While private markets foster many stunning innovations in medicine, science and technology, the private sector still under-invests in innovation—dramatically. There are huge opportunities for innovation that the market ignores because those taking the risk capture only a small subset of the returns. Innovations for the poor suffer from both of those market limitations. The market is not going to place huge bets on research when there are no buyers for a breakthrough.
>
> This explains why we have no vaccine for malaria today, even though a million people die from it every year. In this gap, government plays an important role. It can offer services where the market does not and thus provide a safety net. To some extent, it also fills in where the market leaves off in funding innovation. But government faces its own obstacles to funding innovation. It generally does not take the long view, because election cycles are short. Government is averse to risk, given the eagerness of political opponents to exploit failures. Unlike the private market, government is good not at seeding numerous innovators but at backing only the ones that make progress.
>
> So when you come to the end of the innovations that business and government are willing to invest in, you still find a vast, unexplored space of innovation where the returns can be fantastic. This space is a fertile area for what I call catalytic philanthropy. And once you've found a solution that works, catalytic philanthropy can harness political and market forces to get those innovations to the people who need them most.[17]

Gates encapsulates the catalytic role of philanthropy thus: 'Risk takers need backers. Good ideas need evangelists. Forgotten communities need advocates.'[18]

[17] Bill Gates, 'The Power of Catalytic Philanthropy', http://forbesindia. com/article/philanthropy-awards-2012/the-power-of-catalytic-philanthrop y/34209/1?utm=slidebox#ixzz2dSEtDrMx.

[18] Gates, 'The Power of Catalytic Philanthropy'.

To sum up in the words of John Gardner, 'The best philanthropy is money wedded to talent and imagination'.[19]

Strengthening Civil Society

The fourth main role of philanthropy is to build a strong civil society to act as a countervailing force. A well-functioning democracy needs a strong civil society, one that is supported by active citizens' groups as well as by philanthropic institutions. The importance of non-state actors stems from the limitations of the state. As independent entities, they are free to innovate and experiment with new technologies, methods, and concepts. They have a capacity to function as social critics and policy advocates, and provide the much needed balance between the role of government institutions and market organizations.

Plural sources of support for such organizations are necessary because, as the popular saying goes, he who pays the piper calls the tune. Whoever provides the money can dictate what is to be done with his/her money. He/she can thus influence the nature and direction of action by an individual or organization. Many private organizations working for social change may be in opposition to the state, market, or extra-national forces, which makes it possible that any of the latter may withhold support in conflicting situations. Business is unlikely to support actions which are directed against the power of the state because it will affect them adversely as well. Therefore, if a plurality of actors is necessary to act as a counterforce to state power and market excesses, a plurality of funding sources is necessary for independence of action. Traditionally, such support for reformative action has come from private philanthropic funds. It is necessary to have independent philanthropic organizations which are endowed by business—but free from their daily compulsions of profit making—or by wealthy families.

In the USA, public policy reform, especially to secure rights for the disadvantaged, has been supported by US Foundations. Every public policy reform movement in the history of the United

---

[19] John W. Gardner, Quoted in O'Connell, *Philanthropy in Action*, p. 44.

States—whether against slavery, or for women's suffrage, civil rights, education reform, peace movements, judicial reform, public housing, healthcare, or environmental conservation—has had its roots in philanthropic instinct, and each was brought to birth by an institutional means: voluntary non-profit associations (NGOs or civil society organizations).

The very first foundation in the US to address major national policy issues was the Peabody Education Fund in 1867. Later foundations made more systematic attempts to shape public policymaking, using the influence of their elite boards, moulding public opinion by campaigns of public information and education, creating demonstration projects, using their own funds to leverage public funds, direct lobbying, and exploiting legal mechanisms as necessary or useful.[20]

Why India Needs Philanthropy

India needs philanthropy to play all the four roles mentioned above, but most of all the last two, because of its own specific context.

After almost sixty years of planned development and a massive commitment of public funds, the spectre of poverty refuses to go away. India's ranking in the Human Development Index (HDI) is still very low, and even as India has seen massive wealth creation in the last few decades, social disparities have widened.[21] The net worth of the billionaire community has increased several folds, and is enough to eliminate absolute poverty in this country. The wealth of these billionaires is around 22 per cent of the country's GDP, comparable to that in the UK and USA, while many live on a pittance.[22]

One is daily witness to the extremes of inequality. Plush high-rises such as Mukesh Ambani's twenty-seven storey home, Attila, overlooks hovels of the extreme poor; air-conditioned schools for

[20] See James Allen Smith, *Foundations and Public Policy Making: A Historical Perspective*, Working paper, California, USA, 2002.

[21] Buffet, 'Charitable-Industrial Complex'.

[22] The exact numbers in the statistics may differ because they are from different sources which often do not use the same methodology. But the differences should not matter here because they are used here for indicative purposes.

rich kids coexist with government schools with few basic facilities, and big plush shopping malls with disorganized markets; five-star hospitals for the rich coexist with government facilities where poor patients line the corridors.

Though, in education, there is near-universal enrolment of children in schools at the primary level, and infant mortality rates have declined from 64.9 for every 1,000 births in 2000 to 46.1 in 2012, serious challenges remain. Despite higher enrolments, India's young continue to be poorly educated and lacking in skills. For example, less than a third of school-going children in Class III can read a Class I text, according to the provisional 2013 report from Pratham, one of India's largest education NGOs. On the public health front, India still ranks 130th among 180 nations on the United Nation's HDI, which includes scores for maternal and child mortality. Medical resources remain sparse, and a World Health Statistics report counted India among the most likely countries to face a shortage of health workers.[23] India needs philanthropy because government provisions for such things remain inadequate and do not reach the needy.

As for inequality, the gap is not only in real wealth, but also in opportunity. Aspirations are high, and there is a desire for equal opportunity and a sense that social mobility is possible.

Inequality in India is troublesome because in addition to 'patrimonial' capitalism there is also 'rentier capitalism' in India. Indian capital earns unfairly high returns on capital not due to entrepreneurship and innovation alone. Influence and connections, especially in lucrative land deals and government contracts, lead to a cornering of wealth, which is again passed on through generations, with little returns to society in terms of growth. Moreover, there is little evidence of such *rentier* wealth, accumulated by politicians and businessmen alike, going into philanthropy; most of it seems to go to acquiring power and patronage. Though several politicians have established charitable trusts and NGOs, very often these are not truly non-profit and are used to evade taxes or for dispensing patronage. Finally, there is also the inequality created by high returns to the very

[23] Arpan Sheth, *India Philanthropy Report 2013*, Bains and Company, Mumbai, 5 March 2013.

unequally distributed human capital, which represents lost economic opportunities for India's poor.[24]

Forces such as globalization, technological advance, and geopolitical conflicts have introduced new challenges as well as opportunities. Though India is ranked to become one of the superpowers, the benefits of such progress, as has been made, have not reached the poorest and the marginalized. The government has been unable to meet the social deficit or bridge the rural–urban, caste–class, and educational divides by itself.

The respective spheres of the three main protagonists in society—the state, the market, and civil society—are being revalued, and the boundaries realigned. The civil society is being called upon to play a greater role in national life because of the dissatisfactions with the state and the market operating on their own.

There is a general sense that unless something is done to avoid it, there will be social unrest, and since wealth-creation is both allowed and facilitated by the government, the rich must use at least some of it to help society in at least as efficient a manner as the government would use it, had it been taxed. It is in this context that philanthropy's role in India has to be understood.

Need for Plural Sources of Funds

Philanthropy, as a part of civil society, must either itself undertake projects of betterment, or provide resources to other civil society actors for the creative non-governmental response needed to meet the situation. Its role is to make each sector more effective, either by itself or in partnership with the other two sectors.

The potential social and political conflict created by inequalities was managed in the West by creating a welfare state, but that option is not open to India, partly because the government lacks the capacity both to raise the necessary revenues and to deliver the social services. Non-state action, therefore, becomes important.

[24] See Mihir Shah, 'Fairy Tale Capitalism', *The Indian Express*, 24 April 2014; and Ashoka Mody and Michael Walton, 'Story of a Fraying Capitalism', *The Indian Express*, 14 May 2014.

As it is, in the last two decades India has seen a tremendous growth in not-for-profit organizations, also called NGOs, who supplement government efforts to address the problems of poverty and social and economic inequity.

However, private, non-government support for social development has not grown commensurately with the need. The bulk of the funds needed by NGOs come from either the government or foreign multilateral, bilateral, and private donor agencies like the Aga Khan Foundation and the Ford Foundation.

While both government and foreign aid are invaluable sources, there is an urgent need to build up an alternative third source for three major reasons: one, government funding is beset with a lot of red tape and inflexibility; moreover, the government is often itself the problem against which NGOs are fighting. Two, foreign funding is often governed by geopolitical considerations so that funding can be unstable, and unless the agendas are set locally, can be divorced from local needs and perceptions. Moreover, to receive foreign funds, permission under FCRA (Foreign Contributions Regulation Act) is necessary, and this is becoming ever more difficult and cumbersome. Three, India's developmental problems are so vast that no one agency can, by itself, meet all the needs. Partnerships between different funding sources are necessary to complement and supplement each other. To ensure independence of action and sustainability of the NGO sector, therefore, it is important to tap the private philanthropic sector consisting of individual donors, public charitable trusts, and foundations and corporate donors. The potential for leveraging funds for welfare and development from these private indigenous sources is far greater than has been tapped so far.

On the plus side is the fact that there is a great deal of wealth within the country; that India has a tradition of giving for worthy causes; and that there is still a great desire in most people to contribute their mite for removal of poverty and bring progress to the country. Therefore, it is philanthropy's role as a catalyst of change, and as a countervailing force, that is of the greatest consequence in India.

Regarding the catalyst role, philanthropists in India are faced with two diametrically opposed choices: either to encourage excellence and enable people to exercise their potential, or to relieve human misery. Given the scale of human economic need in India, and a socially unjust society, per force the emphasis of both government provision and such philanthropy as exists has been on the latter, with the former taking a back seat. Quantity and scale have taken precedence over quality and pursuit of excellence, though there are examples of the latter as well. Funding knowledge for the sake of knowledge, for exploration and discovery, for encouraging inventors and inventions, has received lower priority. But India needs philanthropy most of all for experimentation and innovative ideas. The formation of the Breakthrough Energy Coalition is an example of this kind of philanthropy. Formed by an international group of twenty-eight titans of industry such as Bill Gates, Ratan Tata, Mukesh Ambani, Jack Ma, and Mark Zuckerberg, it will invest in technologies that will bring affordable, reliable, and carbon-free power from the research lab to the market, give a push to clean energy and so prevent global warming, and improve the lives of the poorest by giving them clean affordable energy.[25] Philanthropists today must become more conscious of the need for quality funds such as these to trigger an explosion of innovation.

This is not to say that smaller amounts of money collectively used to bring about slow, long-term change through education and health are not needed. Collective philanthropy is also needed, but it is more readily available. Big funds to support big ideas are rarer, but can have exponential impact.

Ensuring Space for Democratic Dissent

Philanthropy has an equally important role to play in supporting civil society at this period of time because intolerance of dissent seems to be growing and freedom of belief and expression is under attack.

The phenomenal growth of the Indian civil society is undoubtedly one of the most important developments of our time. Many citizens' associations and civil society organizations are active in every district and town of the country and have supported citizens to claim their rights and to organize self-help efforts.

Surprisingly, while a dearth of resources is recognized as a major limiting factor for its further development, philanthropy's role as a

[25] Reported in *The Times of India*, 'Led by Gates, 20 biz titans launch clean tech coalition', 1 December 2015.

countervailing force against the excesses or dominance of government and in keeping dissent open—and therefore democracy vibrant—has not been stressed enough.

Efforts at social mobilization and demanding accountability from governance institutions are on the verge of being squeezed out of existence for want of flexible and durable funding. Hardly an Indian name comes readily to mind for having supported these kinds of initiatives after Independence, except for the Tatas. Philanthropy that supports a few hundred or even thousands of schools or clinics is not as important as that which makes the government, at all levels, accountable for poor governance.

After Independence, catalytic funds for experimentation and innovation as well as advocacy for policy change have largely been provided by foreign aid, both private and official. From supporting civil rights groups protesting an inequitable trading system, to helping them protest climate change negotiations which favoured the rich rather than the poor, or genetically modified crops, foreign international organizations have attempted to shape a global order which is at least minimally just for everyone. They have also helped NGOs influence policy decisions to ensure citizens' rights to minimum levels of health, safety, conditions of work, transparency in government, education, food free from contamination, and clean air and water. But now foreign donors like the Ford Foundation are coming under attack for supporting Indian civil society organizations (CSOs) to do all this.

Receipt of foreign money by CSOs has been used by the government as a weapon against them to stifle dissent. When the India Against Corruption movement was at its peak, its moving spirit, activist Anna Hazare was accused of being anti-national because of taking foreign funds for his movement. He publicly denied the allegations, pointing out that the accounts of his organization had been audited and were in the public domain. The allegations, he said, were to divert attention from the demand for a strong *Lok Pal* Bill which the Campaign was demanding to counter corruption in the government.

The magazine *Civil Society*, on 8 June 2013, reported a similar case of action against an NGO for its protest activities. On 3 May, the Union Home Ministry slapped a notice on the Indian Social Action Forum (INSAF), a coalition of NGOs and people's movements, suspending its FCRA registration and freezing its bank account on the ground that the Forum's activities are 'prejudicial and against public interest'. The immediate provocation was that InsaF had organized and staged a protest against the Asian Development Bank (ADB), accusing the Bank of causing displacement and loss of livelihoods by promoting privatization.

In their own defence CSOs alleged that the government is pursuing a double-edged policy. It is co-opting civil society organizations to create awareness and to enhance the success of its welfare schemes, and at the same time, it is using tools like the FCRA against NGOs fighting violence perpetrated by the state and corporate entities.

Since then, there have been other instances of NGOs being hauled up for violating the FCRA. In April 2015, the Ford Foundation and sixteen other foreign donors were asked to take government permission before granting any money to NGOs, on grounds of national interest and security, because the Gujarat Government had accused it of funding 'anti-India' activities of activist Teesta Setalvad's NGO Citizens for Justice and Peace and the allied Sabrang Trust. These were said to have fomented communal disharmony. Now, Teesta's Sabrang Trust is facing cancellation of their FCRA permission, which is an effective way of ensuring that the organization ceases to be active, since indigenous funds cannot replace the aid that has supported it so far.

Similarly, Greenpeace has been accused by the Ministry of Foreign Affairs of stalling power plants and depriving the nation of low-cost energy by protesting against thermal power generation at plant sites, and its foreign funding has been suspended.

Under the latest change in rules under FCRA, NGOs will have to report on the foreign funds received and used by them for 'civil rights advocacy', to include research, seminars, conferences, and publications, as well as submit details of social media accounts on Facebook or Twitter—all moves to straight jacket NGOs into compliance with government policies.[26]

These actions seem part of a closer government watch on NGOs who are critical of government policy, especially in the environment and human rights field.

---

[26] For further details see Aman Sharma, 'Tighter Norms for NGOs to Track Foreign Funds' in *The Economic Times*, 19 June 2015.

Indian money is needed not only because foreign aid is on the decline, partly due to slowing global growth and partly because of India's success on the economic front, so that foreign donors do not see the need to give aid to India; but more precisely because foreign aid is becoming harder to access for socially sensitive causes. Indigenous philanthropy is needed to fill the gap if the space for legitimate dissent is not to shrink.

In the final report of the Inquiry into the Future of Civil Society, carried out by the Carnegie UK Trust, it is recommended that philanthropy should move from specific issues such as social needs and social care to a broader focus on key areas such as democratization of media ownership and content, developing a participatory and deliberative democracy, strengthening the financial stability of the civil society sector, and building a low-carbon economy.[27] These are also the areas which Indian philanthropy needs to support if democracy is to flourish in India.

The Downside of Philanthropy's Power

There is also a downside to the power of philanthropy which has to be recognized. After centuries of successful policy advocacy by philanthropic foundations in the USA, these foundations are now being accused of being too powerful and influencing government policies in self-interest. For instance, looking at global health, there is no denying the impact the Bill and Melinda Gates Foundation has had on many Governments' policies—what should be done and what should not receive support. It is also claimed that by virtue of its scale, the Gates Foundation has driven a lot of other players off the field, though deeper research is needed to substantiate these charges.[28]

---

[27] 'Role for philanthropists in shaping the civil society of the future', 25 March 2010, downloaded from philanthropy/UK: inspiring giving, at http://www.philanthropyuk.org/news/2010-03-25/role-philanthropists-shaping-civil-society-futureon 6 November 2012.

[28] Laurie Garrett, Senior Fellow for Global Health at the Council on Foreign Relations, quoted in Shanaz Musafer, 'Power of Policy-making in the Hands of Philanthropists', BBC News, 2 September 2012.

The power to do good with a lot of money makes a philanthropist influential on public policy; say those against the power wielded by foundations. 'The rich have a great deal of power that can be exercised and can reshape the character of a country', says writer and journalist George Monbiot, who is also a social justice and environmental campaigner. He claims he is 'in favour of philanthropy as long as it does not allow too much power for the giver over the political system'. 'But that is exactly what ends up happening', he says: 'You are diverting money into areas which suit your political interests and away from those that don't.'[29]

So far this problem has not arisen in India where philanthropic funds are miniscule compared to government budgets, no one philanthropist is big enough to influence policy, and philanthropists in any case have not aspired to influence social policy. They are too busy lobbying for their own commercial interests.

It has been observed that there is a tension between the right of the wealthy to spend their money as they see fit and the desire of politicians to exercise their mandate to implement what they believe to be the will of the people. Views differ on how to achieve these goals and which goals actually matter, and concerns are raised when individuals or individual organizations are seen to be dominating the field. It is a tension which only multiple sources of funding—either private or private-cum-public—allowed to be applied freely, can solve.

But granting that India needs philanthropy, what is needed for it to flourish? From the experience of many countries of the world, including India, it is clear that the level, nature, and impact of philanthropy in any society is deeply influenced by two main factors: one, a culture of giving, which in turn depends on the intellectual and ethical traditions of a society which motivate a people to give; and two, an environment which transforms the desire to give into the positive act of philanthropy. The next chapter looks at India's culture of giving, and what philanthropy amounts to, while a later chapter discusses how to promote it.

[29] Quoted in Musafer, 'Power of Policy-making'.

2

Are Indians Charitable?

That gift is good, which is made to one from whom no return is
expected, with the feeling that it is one's duty to give and which is
given in proper place and time and to a worthy person.
— The Bhagavadgita (Ch.17, text 20)

Are Indians charitable? The simple answer is yes. Are Indians philanthropic? Unfortunately, the answer would have to be 'not very'. This
apparently contradictory statement becomes clear if the distinction
between charity and philanthropy explained in the previous chapter
is kept in mind. The traditional culture of giving in India is rooted in
the religious injunctions to give in charity. Philanthropy is a modern
add-on.

The Culture of Giving

Charity was an ingrained practice in traditional families of all faiths
throughout India, encouraged by religious teachings. The Hindu
Upanishads declared charity as the highest virtue, and enjoined a
householder to give in charity on all important occasions such as a
birth, death, marriage, visiting a holy place, raising a crop, sending
a child to school for the first time, recovery from illness, and so on.
The Hindu term for charity, namely *daanam*, included giving to meet
social needs such as care of the environment, education, needs of

travellers and of whole communities in times of famine, floods, or fire, in addition to giving to individuals in need.

In Jainism charity is a fundamental principle and amongst the six daily duties enjoined by the religion.[1]

Zoroastrianism, the religion of the Parsis, neither glorifies poverty, nor deprecates riches, but enjoins instead, industry, self-help, and deeds of beneficence and promotion of public welfare.

Christianity, too, makes giving central to its teaching. Time and again Christ exhorted people to give, saying, 'Freely ye have received, freely give'. It further includes the giving of service as part of the giving by an individual.

Islam, likewise, extolls charity, wise stewardship of wealth, and rendering help to the less fortunate. But the concept of charity is somewhat different than that in Hinduism and the other religions. According to the Quran, wealth does not belong to individuals, only to God. Charity as wealth spent for personal satisfaction is not a valid idea in Islam. It has a more engaged sense. To give in charity is not merely the duty of an individual who has wealth, but it is also the right of the poor to get their share.

Charity has two forms: voluntary and obligatory. *Zakat* falls in the obligatory category, and is the most important philanthropic act in Islam. The idea of zakat is that people purify their wealth by giving a share of it to God. Zakat purifies possessions and makes them pleasing to God. Purification of an individual's possessions takes place through helping others. Zakat, defined as a certain percentage of one's acquired property or profit for the year that is paid to the needy, is one of the five main pillars of Islam. Zakat can range from 2.5 per cent to 10 per cent of one's profit, depending on the nature of the property and the conditions under which it was acquired.[2]

Of the voluntary forms, *wakf* is the central one in India. The owner of a property voluntarily dedicates it to God, and gives up all rights to it. The ownership of God implies that it may revert to and

[1] For Jainism, see Michael Carrithers and Caroline Humphrey, eds, *The Assembly of Listeners: Jains in Society* (Cambridge: Cambridge University Press, 1991).

[2] Sachiko Murata and William C. Chittick, *The Vision Of Islam* (New York: Paragon House, 1994), p. 16.

be applied for the benefit of human beings. The society and community exercise control over the property through a *Muttawali*, or the manager appointed by the owner. In India, wakfs are religious trusts, but instead of the community, it is the state which controls them and nominates people to the boards.[3]

In sum, individuals, families, and businesses traditionally gave for both religious and secular purposes, and for individual and community needs.

The concept of pooling community resources for community betterment has also existed in some form in both rural and urban areas from ancient times. Guilds and village and town councils collected money from their members to meet common needs, especially in times of emergency such as droughts, famines, and floods. In the temple town of Tirupati, there existed an institution called the 'sthanattar', which was a temple committee of eminent men of the city to run the temple on secular lines. The committee invested the funds donated to the temple in endowments beneficial to the community and honoured the wishes of the donors as to the use of these funds.

As mentioned earlier, modern philanthropy, which came into existence in the mid-nineteenth century as a result of the first wave of wealth-creation due to the industrial revolution, built on and transformed the older practices of charity, retaining some features and adding on others. The culture of giving, today, combines indigenous practices and global influences. But the culture of giving alone will not determine whether Indians are more charitable than people in other nations, and whether charity, or philanthropy, is the dominant pattern. The economic conditions of the time, especially per capita incomes, taxation levels which would determine how much disposable income is available for giving, the legal framework, and the nature of social need are also important determinants. Nor will simply looking at the total figures of charitable giving at a point or over time indicate whether there is more of charity or philanthropy in a given society. It is only when one disaggregates the totals and analyses the *pattern of giving* to see who gives, for what, and how, that one can take a position.

---

[3] See Mathew Cherian, *A Million Missions: The Non-Profit Sector in India* (Delhi: Authors UpFront, 2014), pp. 50–68 for more details.

Nature of Giving in India

Unfortunately, in India there are few reliable and comprehensive statistics of giving comparable to those available in the USA, UK, and other Western countries. In the USA, total giving is broken down into giving by individuals, giving by bequest, giving by foundations and by corporations, and the causes to which the sums are given are separated into different categories for data-management purposes.

In India there are no official statistics, and few surveys of charitable giving. Such surveys as are there have not used the same parameters as the Western ones, so that the data cannot be compared. Some are surveys of household or individual giving; others like those of Bain and Company focus only on HNWIs or companies. Unless the methodologies are the same for every survey in every country, comparisons are not accurate or reliable and whatever comparisons are made should be taken only as broad indicators.

But one can get a fair idea of whether there is more charity or more philanthropy if one considers small informal donations by individuals to other individuals or religious organizations, for distress relief or for religious purposes, as a proxy for charity; and large donations by HNWIs or companies for social causes or social organizations; as also numerous small individual donations to social and developmental organizations as a proxy for philanthropic giving.[4]

One of the earliest surveys of charitable giving, in 2000 and reported on in 2001, was by the Sampradaan Indian Centre for Philanthropy, Delhi.[5] It covered 6,400 households from the upper three socio-economic categories in the four biggest metros and ten cities with a population of over 1 million. The findings from the sample were projected for the entire population of those cities, which was 28 per cent of the urban population. The survey found that

---

[4] The term HNWI refers to individuals who have at least $1.1 million in investible assets, excluding primary residences, consumables, and consumer durables.

[5] The findings of the survey were presented in Sampradaan Indian Centre for Philanthropy, *Investing in Ourselves: Giving and Fund Raising in India* (Delhi: Sampradaan Indian Centre for Philanthropy, 2001).

98 per cent of the households surveyed had contributed to charity in the previous year, indicating that the charitable instinct was still strong in the Indian population. The total amount donated was Rupees 16.16 billion.

The average amount donated was Rupees 1,420 per annum. The largest number (89 per cent of households) donated to individuals, who received 50 per cent of the donations. The giving to religious organizations was also high—87 per cent of households giving 29 per cent of the total amount to them. Only 51 per cent of the households donated to social organizations, who together received only 21 per cent of the total. (The numbers do not add up to 100 per cent because many households give donations to multiple entities.)

Amongst the social organizations, the most popular purpose for which donations were made was to relieve distress of victims of calamity, followed by cultural and arts activities, education, and health. Giving for arts and culture included giving subscriptions or donations for neighbourhood activities like Durga Pooja, Ganesh Utsav, and local arts and entertainment events, and not necessarily to organizations such as museums, libraries, or art galleries, or performing arts organizations to promote art, language, literature, and serious theatre or playwriting, which could be considered philanthropy.

The motive cited for charitable giving was largely compassion, and because giving made them feel good. One of the most important reasons for *not* giving was lack of trust in non-religious organizations. This reason figures time and again in all surveys.

On the whole, the more emotive causes, such as for children or disabled persons, received more donations than the more cerebral or those whose impact is visible only in the long term, such as research of all kinds, works for social justice to empower the marginalized and disadvantaged, and advocacy for policy changes.

The pattern of giving which emerges from this survey is one of charity rather than philanthropy.

The Indian survey was part of a five-country study of giving in South East Asia, deploying the same model used in Indonesia, Philippines, Bangladesh, and Thailand. The results were compared for the top two socio-economic categories using purchasing power parity criteria.

Though the overall giving rate, that is, the percentage of households that give, is lower for India than the other countries, it is not too dissimilar. What was a cause for concern is that not only did Indians in the top two classes give far smaller average amounts per capita ($34) than did the Indonesians ($123), Filipinos ($400), and Thais ($546), but they also gave lower proportions of their income. The generosity rate, that is, the average amount given by the sample as a percentage of the average household income of the sample, is abysmally low in India, at 1.7 per cent, compared to 5.9 per cent for Indonesia, 4.6 per cent for Philippines, and 5.3 per cent for Thailand. This means that those most well-off are not giving as much as they can to society.

A second cause for disquiet was that the amounts going to organized charity, as distinct from ad hoc giving to individuals and to religious organizations, was also much smaller. This means that though the non-governmental development sector or civil society in India is as widespread and vibrant as anywhere else, it received very little financial support from the community. Only 51 per cent gave to voluntary organizations in India, compared to 82 per cent in Indonesia, 88 per cent in Philippines, and 81 per cent in Thailand. The average amount given per capita per annum was also very much smaller, at $7, compared to Indonesia's $34, Philippines' $113, and Thailand's $143. Little wonder that the Indian civil society is heavily dependent on government and foreign donors.

This comparison again indicates that whereas charity is more or less similar in all countries, philanthropy is less developed in India than in the other countries of South East Asia.

The second survey came ten years later, when incomes had gone up in India. In 2012, Charities Aid Foundation (CAF) India did a survey similar to that of Sampradaan. But the sample, at 9,000 households, was larger. This survey, too, showed similar trends. Of the sample surveyed, 84 per cent had given Rupees 50 billion to a good cause in the previous year.[6] Though the amount had increased, it was still very small in comparison to countries where philanthropy is mature, namely the USA and the UK.

[6] *India Giving Report* (New Delhi: Charities Aid Foundation India, 2012).

Not only was the total giving in the CAF survey comparatively small, but as before, only a small percentage of givers (27 per cent) had given to charitable organizations. More donors had given to individuals and religious bodies. In fact, 70 per cent of the donors said that they preferred to give directly to the beneficiaries rather than to an organization. The most common way donations were made was said to be 'give to strangers for charitable reasons', followed by door-to-door collections for religious purposes, and to individuals outside places of worship. The attitudes in relation to giving also bear out a traditional 'charity' mind set. Some of the attitudes were: 'My contribution is not going to make a difference in peoples' lives'; 'Charity is the responsibility of the government'; and 'Once I donate my money, my duty is over'.

But though charity still seemed to predominate over transformative giving, there were some encouraging changes in the CAF survey:

- 86 per cent of donors agreed that 'people should come together to help marginalized sections of society'.
- A greater number of those who earned more gave to charitable organizations rather than through informal donations, (29 per cent of those earning Rupees 10,000–19,999 a month gave to charitable organizations; this figure rose to 42 per cent of those earning Rupees 20,000 and over a month).
- Over a third (38 per cent) of those who donated money to organizations claimed to do some research about the organizations before donating.
- 65 per cent of donors said they 'want to know where/how the funds are spent'.

All these indicate a move towards planned and strategic giving. But again, the main constraining factor for not giving to organized philanthropy was said to be lack of trust in these organizations. And not without reason.

To give just one example: according to a recent newspaper report, though zakat, the 2.5 per cent share of annual savings and income that Muslim families have to give to charity, is meant to help in the economic uplift of the community, unorganized collection and under-utilization have hampered the cause. Nearly 60 per cent of the total *zakat* money collected in India is reportedly cornered by *madrassas*, including fake ones. Now, there is said to be a clamour in the community to reduce the contribution to religious seminaries and use the funds to facilitate self-employment and modern education of its members instead.[7]

More recent surveys bear out the same conclusion, that of more charity than philanthropy, and also of lagging behind other countries in giving.

The Bain and Company's *Annual Report on Indian Philanthropy 2012* showed that private charity contributions in India amount to only $5–6 billion, and as a percentage of the GDP, make up only 0.4 per cent, compared with 1.3 per cent in the UK, 2.2 per cent in the US, and over 4 per cent in the Netherlands and Sweden, though they are higher than Brazil's 0.3 per cent and rival China's 0.1 per cent. In the UK, 74 per cent of people made charitable donations in 2013, compared to 28 per cent in India.

What is disturbing is the evidence that once again India is shown to lag behind other countries in charitable giving. The Charities Aid Foundation's World Giving Index 2014, released in November 2015, shows that India is not among the top twenty countries for generosity. It ranks a low 106th behind Brazil, and last among the countries from South Asia. The proportion of givers fell sharply in 2014 as compared to 2013. Though it has more people, in absolute numbers, who help strangers, donate money, and volunteer time for a good cause, this is largely because of India's large population. But the proportion of people donating to charity in 2014 had fallen to 20 per cent, down by eight percentage points from 2013. There were also fewer people who had helped a stranger or volunteered for a cause. The research further shows that some of the world's most generous countries are also among the most deprived.[8]

Impressionistically, this appears to be true also within a country. Poor Indians, whether rural or urban, give in charity proportionately as much as, or perhaps more than, the rich.

[7] Report in *The Times of India*, 'Use Zakat Money to Promote Modern Education', 22 June 2015.

[8] 'A Global View of Giving Trends', *The World Giving Index 2014* (UK: Charities Aid Foundation, November 2015).

While Indians can certainly give more, I believe the finding that Indians are less charitable than nationals of other countries can bear review. India comes out poorly on the generosity index because the focus is on aggregated giving and no distinction is being made between philanthropic giving and charitable giving. My contention is that charity is alive and well in India, and Indians are as charitable as any other people. But philanthropy is another story.

Charity Alive and Well

Indian *charitable* giving is underestimated because most sample surveys focus only on the urban segments, and capture the more formal giving. Most charitable giving in India is of the informal kind, given as alms, given to dependents, friends, employees, and others in need, or given through informal channels. It, therefore, goes unreported, or is grossly underestimated, especially the contributions by rural givers who are themselves at the bottom of the pyramid. But undoubtedly, they too give, especially in times of disaster, to their fellow sufferers.

Anecdotal evidence, too, backs the conclusion that, though not reflected in surveys, Indians are as charitable as any other people.

The Nepal Earthquake of April 2015 is a case in point. Within days of appeals for help being issued, many fund raising organizations and portals had received an overwhelming response, so much so that many appeal campaigns like that of the *Times of India*-cum-Fabindia had to declare a temporary halt to the drive. The bottleneck, as usual, was in getting the donated resources to the actual victims, especially in the far away interior places, due to logistical difficulties. Though aid poured in, it did not reach the victims. It was either spoilt or looted. This is a story which gets repeated again and again.

Other media reports also indicate that the charitable instinct is alive and well. A day after the *Times of India* reported on the financial constraints which prevented figure skater Rajkumar Tiwari from participating in the Asian Open Figure Skating Trophy in Bangkok, people from across the country came forward to fund his trip. It was the same for the two slum boys who came out tops in the entrance exams for the prestigious Indian Institute of Technology (IIT), but could not avail of the opportunity because of lack of funds. Funds poured in when people read their story.

Similarly, Aarti Madhusudan of Chennai decided to help those homeless who sleep hungry, either because of poverty or lack of space and facilities to cook. She decided to cook rice and curry for five people and took it to pavement dwellers. She wrote of her effort on Facebook, as a result of which, small groups of people across Chennai have started dishing up and distributing a simple meal to those whom they feel need it.[9]

The analysis of the SICP and the CAF India surveys clearly show that what passes for philanthropy is really charity. Also, that small giving does not get added up into collective philanthropy for transformative change, because it does not flow in large numbers to organizations who are involved in developmental work. The reason is, as surveys and studies have again and again pointed out, people do not trust that the donations will reach the intended beneficiaries without getting hijacked by other parties on the way, or due to lack of organization and capability in the implementing agencies. It is not the charitable instinct which is missing but integrity and efficiency in charitable organizations.

In contrast to secular giving, faith-based giving is doing well, and is both creative and complex in its structure.[10] It is estimated that if the famous Venkateswara temple at Tirupati donated its annual earnings, it would become the country's second largest philanthropist.

Philanthropy in Short Supply

Meanwhile, philanthropy is in short supply in India. Those who can afford to take risks on supporting large projects for transformative change and innovation do not give enough.

---

[9] *The Times of India*, 'Cook Two Extra Meals, Launch Thousand Smiles', Chennai, 23 June 2013.

[10] See Sanjay Agarwal, *Daan and other Giving Traditions in India* (Delhi: April 2011). According to him there are many forms, rituals, themes, ways, times, and methods through which people give.

The number of 'high net worth individuals (HNWIs)' in India has grown exponentially, by any count, at possibly the fastest pace in the world. According to the Hurun Report 2016, published by a China-based luxury and events group, the number of billionaires in the world grew by ninety-nine to 2,188 individuals, 50 per cent more than in 2013. Of this, India's tally is 111 billionaires, giving it the third place in the list.[11] Their combined wealth is estimated at US$ 308 billion.

Moreover, a recent study sponsored by Citibank shows that the new rich are poised to grow the fastest in India over the next five years. While the new rich Indians will grow by 47 per cent in 2020, the growth globally will be only 7 per cent, and in Asia, 10 per cent. The number of such new wealth builders is expected to be close to 50 million, and the total value of their wealth is expected to be $879 billion, double what it was a decade ago.[12] According to Forbes Magazine, three of India's industrialists, Reliance Industries' Mukesh Ambani, Lakshmi Mittal of Arcelor, and Dilip Shanghavi of Sun Pharma are among the five wealthiest individuals in the world.

However, the distribution of wealth is highly unequal in India. Only five to six billionaires account for nearly 30 per cent of the total net worth. At the other end of the scale are an estimated 363 million living below the poverty line of rupees 32 a day in villages, and rupees 47 in cities. This, by itself, makes a persuasive case for philanthropy to share wealth more liberally with the rest of the population.

However, according to the *World Giving Index* of Charities Aid Foundation UK, India has actually come down in its ranking from 93 in 2013 to 106 in 2014, demonstrating an overall reduction in Indian philanthropy. The *Hurun Philanthropy List* for 2015 confirms this. The list has only thirty-six individuals who donated rupees 100 million or more in 2014, down from fifty last year. The total contribution of thirty-six top philanthropists in 2014–15 (November–October) totalled only to rupees 350 billion, and Mukesh Ambani, the

---

[11] Hurun Institute, *The Hurun Global Rich List 2016*, http://www. hurun.net/en/ArticleShow.aspx?nid=15703.

[12] Reported in *The Times of India*, 'No. of New Rich to Grow Fastest in India, Says Study', New Delhi, 24 September 2015.

richest Indian, contributed only rupees 3.45 billion, or 0.4 per cent of his wealth to philanthropy in 2014.[13]

Compare these figures of giving back to society with the figures the wealthy owe to society. In a current scam of unpaid debts to Indian banks, around an estimated 5,000 are declared to be wilful defaulters, with the total amount of wilful defaults coming to rupees 500 billion. Vijay Mallya, one of India's richest and most flamboyant businessmen, is said to owe rupees 90 billion in dues to banks and the government. Several other business defaulters owe somewhat smaller amounts ranging from rupees 10 billion to 50 billion. Though some of the default is due to a stressed economy and conditions beyond the borrowers' control, this does not apply to wilful default. Many of those defaulting were enjoying their lives personally. The picture that emerges is of a self-absorbed, unethical, and socially irresponsible class, mindless of the needs of others. So much for philanthropy and social responsibility!

The first generation of India's wealthy, such as Lala Sri Ram, Jamnalal Bajaj, G.D. Birla, and others had believed in simple living and big philanthropy. But today's rich are indulging in ostentatious living and spending lavishly to flaunt their wealth (in some cases borrowed wealth), rather than in philanthropic giving. Antilla (named after the legendary island off the coast of Portugal), is the twenty-seven storey skyscraper home of Reliance Chairman Mukesh Ambani, known as the richest man in India. It is a glass palace of which six levels are dedicated to exclusive parking for 170 cars; one floor for car maintenance; one for an entertainment centre with a mini-theatre that will seat fifty; three floors of terrace gardens, three floors of health club, gymnasia, and swimming pool; two floors of guest apartments; living floors for the family; and an air space floor as control room for choppers landing on the helipad above. Staff strength required to maintain it is 600 and the global firm Leighton's reported fee for designing it is said to have been $110 million!

[13] Shoaib Daniyal, 'Azim Premji Aside, Why are India's Ultra Rich So Tight-fisted When It Comes to Philanthropy?', *Scroll.in*, 11 July 2015, http://scroll.in/article/740220/azim-premji-aside-why-are-indias-ultra-rich-so-tight-fisted-when-it-comes-to-philanthropy.

London-based steel magnate Lakshmi Narayan Mittal hired a French chateau to host his daughter Vanisha's wedding in 2004. A host of Bollywood stars performed during the six-day extravaganza, which was reputed to have cost an estimated $60 million.

Vijay Mallya, till Fate caught up with him, was the undisputed king of 'good times', and India's most flamboyant tycoon: apart from his businesses, he had two helicopters, two private jets, penthouses in London, Monaco, New York, Johannesburg, and Los Angeles, a Scottish castle, several South African game lodges, not to mention a house on the most happening beach in Goa. He owns a stud farm and a stable of 250 thoroughbreds, as well as a 165-foot yacht. He is said to wear $100,000 worth of jewellery.

But when it comes to giving away money, India's rich are not very keen on loosening their purse-strings. According to the Bain and Company's *Annual Philanthropy Report* for 2011, the wealthiest social class as a whole has the lowest level of giving, just 1.6 per cent of household income. The class below the top gives 2.1 per cent and the middle class 1.9 per cent of household income, giving a median of 2.1 per cent of household income.

Though the figure of giving as a proportion of household income of the Indian rich had increased somewhat to 3.1 per cent by the time of the 2012 *Annual Philanthropy Report* of Bain and Company, it is still well below the potential for giving. A MacArthur Foundation-Intellecap study estimates that the current philanthropic contribution in India is only $8 billion per annum, whereas the potential is $22.4 billion per annum, if we benchmarked giving to US standards.[14]

The lack of giving by the rich, bar a small strata, is borne out by anecdotal evidence. US-based oncologist Siddhartha Mukherjee, whose book on cancer, *The Emperor of All Maladies*, won the Pulitzer prize, in an interview to the *Times of India* mentioned that he was disappointed with the level of philanthropic support for cancer research in India, even as he was happy to note the amazing efforts,

---

[14] MacArthur Foundation-Intellecap Report, *Strengthening Philanthropic Giving and Impact Investing for Development in India* (Delhi: McArthur Foundation, March 2016).

individual and organizational, at the grass root level in palliative care. Both state and philanthropic support for cancer research is very poor in India, the only exception being the Tata Institute for Cancer Research, Mumbai, whereas data shows that philanthropic support can have transformative effect on cancer research, so necessary to wipe out the disease.[15]

One more instance will make this clear. Indian actor Aamir Khan's Sunday talk show *Satyameva Jayate*, aired some time ago on the TV channel Star Plus, made a big splash by presenting pressing social issues to the Indian public, but in terms of charitable donations stimulated by the show, it was not a big success. Though about 400 million viewers watched the show, it raised less than $305,000 for its recommended charities. That amounts to a tiny fraction of one cent per viewer. In fact, it is about 2 paise per viewer.

The only outstanding philanthropic contribution for Indian causes has been that of Azim Premji, of approximately $2 billion, to his foundation to promote education in India. However, even this awesome donation is estimated to be only around 10 per cent of his personal wealth.

It is not only that Indians are not very philanthropic. They also seem to lack imagination when it comes to choosing the causes to which to give. Education remains the most favoured cause, accounting for 84 per cent of donations, according to the *Hurun India Philanthropy List* of 2015. The Bain's *India Philanthropy Report* for 2015 puts the percentage of respondents in their survey giving to education as the highest, at 54 per cent. This is followed by child welfare, old age care, disaster relief, and healthcare. Environment and the arts had only 11 per cent and 10 per cent donors giving to the field, respectively. There are many other emerging causes which need philanthropic funding, among them research and innovation of all kinds in scientific, medical, and social science; good governance and democratic reforms; and human rights, to mention only a few.

[15] Malini Nair's interview with Siddhartha Mukherjee, 'We May Have To Learn To Live With Cancer Rather Than Die of It', *Sunday Times of India*, Delhi edition, 9 August 2015.

Indian and US philanthropy

Compare this to 9 per cent given by the wealthy in the USA. In spite of a severe recession, US charitable giving figures, from Giving USA, which has been tracking these over decades, showed only a 3.6 per cent decline in 2009 over that in 2008, to notch up $303.75 billion. What is worth noting is that corporate giving actually rose in 2009 to $14.1 billion, as did international aid, by 3 per cent, to $8.89 billion. Now it has almost reached pre-recession figures. Giving by American individuals, estates, corporations, and foundations grew by 4.4 per cent in 2013, to a total of $335.17 billion. Individual giving accounted for the bulk (72 per cent) of all charitable giving in 2013, followed by foundations (15 per cent) and companies (8 per cent). This is the fourth consecutive year of increase in giving, a period of growth that began in 2010. The single largest influence on this increase was the additional $9.69 billion in gifts made by individuals like Bill Gates and Warren Buffet over 2012.[16] As noted in chapter 1, as yet only very few Indian billionaires have followed the example of Gates and Buffet.

But, even while admitting that our rich could do better, it would be simplistic to compare our philanthropy, dollar for dollar, to the American way. Firstly, US philanthropy is exceptional and outstrips that of other developed countries. Secondly, philanthropic giving is not just a matter of writing multi-digit cheques; it is complex. Large-scale philanthropy, unlike individual charity, is a function of several factors—history, the socio-economic-cultural environment, the political and ideological underpinning of governance, fiscal policies, pressure from civil society, level of institutional development, and the opportunity for large-scale philanthropic investment. Our context, motivations, and philanthropic preferences are substantially different.

In the past, India had a rich history of giving. One has only to look around our cities to realize how much has been contributed by our wealthy to society, in the shape of endowed institutions and

---

[16] *Giving USA: The Annual Report on Philanthropy 2014,* http://npengage.com/nonprofit-news/key-findings-from-giving-usa-2014-report/.

social infrastructure of all kinds. Jamsetji Jejeebhoy was perhaps the only businessman in India's history, on whose death Mumbai came to a standstill, and flags were flown at half-mast in tribute to his munificence. More recently, many leading Indian business leaders have contributed generously to philanthropy, though the really substantial contributions in recent times have been to institutions abroad.

The reasons for the disparity in scale between Indian and American giving have to be sought deeper. Americans have always valued private initiative, and have jealously guarded against encroachments by the state. Social provision through private initiative was thus both a need and an obligation, encouraged by the state through tax laws. With inheritance tax rates of nearly 46 per cent for large estates of more than $2 million, it made economic sense for wealthy individuals to endow private foundations for charity before their death. There has never been an inheritance tax in India.

The colonial Indian government followed laissez faire policies and easy taxation of the rich, and expected and encouraged the wealthy to make up the social deficit. The consequence was flourishing philanthropy for social reform and progress, to which the growth of nationalistic feeling and Gandhi's influence also contributed. But independent India arrogated the obligations of bringing development and an equitable society to the state. India's planned, mixed economy, steep taxation, and control of profit-making as well as profit-distribution precluded a large role for philanthropy as an engine of social progress.

However, even with the most encouraging of state policies, the rich in India may still not give away half their wealth during their lifetime, as Buffet and Gates have done, simply because our culture and philanthropic preferences are different. Family and kin ties are stronger here than in America. Wealthy business families in particular tend to have joint families and extended kin networks. While many American philanthropists have publicly stated that they would rather that their children made their own way in life, wealthy Indians prefer to leave their wealth to their children, even at the risk of spoiling them. Add to this a feudal *maibaap* or noblesse oblige culture, and a strong religious influence, which means even distant relations, dependents, servants, or religious organizations are preferred beneficiaries rather than an impersonal organization.

A desire to control their philanthropic resources, rather than to adopt the more arms-length philanthropy characteristic of American foundations, and the lack of suitable opportunities that can absorb resources on the scale envisaged are cited as other reasons for not giving as much as half of one's wealth to independent organizations.

Moreover, large-scale philanthropy has always been used by Americans to win friends and influence people internationally. It is only now, with globalization of Indian business, that the Indian rich are making contributions abroad, which, partly at least, is a branding exercise.

Finally, as Gates and others have acknowledged, it takes at least two generations of wealth in the family to feel secure enough to give it away. Large-scale philanthropy from the new super rich will, possibly, come later. Wealth creation is still a recent phenomenon in India. Generally philanthropy comes at the end of a long wealth-creation curve, when the newly rich feel secure. Relatively recent accumulation of wealth by individuals inhibits philanthropy. The number of wealthy individuals in India started growing rapidly only after the economic reforms of the 1990s. Normally, it takes fifty to a hundred years for philanthropic markets to mature.

Sunil Mittal, Chairman of the Bharti Group and a leading wealth creator of the new wave, makes the same point in the following quote.

> As we create wealth or any business house that creates wealth they have a responsibility of, not only not to display their wealth in a fashion, which is hurting the sentiments, but more importantly start contributing in a very big way. ... Now, people ask why India Inc. [*sic*] not doing enough. I have a clear proposition for that; one, new found wealth, people are still not very comfortable under their skin that this is here to stay. When you come from poverty struck background, you tend to eat more. Similarly when you have come from difficult situation, you do not have the comfort of parting with your wealth.

Continuing, he said,

> As you get more comfortable, you will start seeing more and more companies joining this bandwagon. The other part that holds Indians back from doing what many in the Western world do is leaving all the money for the children. So people here will cut down a meal

for themselves, but ensure that their children are taken care of. Most wealth is left for the next generation... .[17] [*sic*]

Mittal said that he was inspired by the stories of Rockefeller and Carnegie, and how they left most of their wealth for public causes. He feels this has to happen here, and that one day he would like his Bharti Foundation to be as well known as the Carnegie Endowment and Ford and Rockefeller Foundations.

Constraints to Increasing Philanthropy

Granting that rich Indians are not as philanthropic as they should be, it must be conceded that there are several constraints to increasing philanthropy; among them:

- Lack of motivation and awareness on the part of donors, especially the newly rich, of the emerging needs and new developments which offer opportunities for engaging in philanthropy;
- Lack of information on the part of both donors and fund seekers about whom to approach and how, worthy causes and organizations, different ways of giving, and availability of tax incentives;
- Absence of research on giving, historical, theoretical, or empirical, which could provide a basis for informed giving and guide policy formulation as well as action by fundraisers, policy makers, and welfare and development organizations;
- Strong family and kin ties which preclude leaving one's wealth as bequests to social organizations, as in America;
- A lack of trust by Indian donors in both the integrity and competence of social organizations and institutions. The perceived lack of integrity and transparency means that donors fear their donations would be used for personal benefit, while the apparent lack of professionalization would lead to little impact on the

[17] CNBC TV 18, Money Control, 'Sunil Mittal: Empowering India Through Education'. 28 June 2010, http://www.moneycontrol.com/news/business/sunil-mittal-empowering-india-through-education_466356-1.html?utm_source=ref_article.

social problem. Temples or other religious organizations, on the other hand, rightly or wrongly, are trusted more and therefore a bulk of charitable giving goes to religious charity.

- In the West there is a proper set up which oversees accountable and efficient use of money by social organizations. In India, either there are no professional support organizations for donors, or they are not professionally managed. For many, it is this uncertainty which prevents them from giving.

- At least a part of the trust deficit between donors and beneficiaries is due to insufficient exposure of donors to and interaction with NGOs who have become the dominant actors in the social sector. This is related to the fact that there is no sense of community or common cause among donors who tend to act separately, without any interaction to exchange information, expertise, or experience.[18]

Some donors also list the difficulty of dealing with the government as one of the constraints. Those who have tried to open schools for the poor in collaboration with the government mention that it is often a 'nightmarish' experience.

Added to this is the fact that communities are also sometimes suspicious of donor motives, since among the poor, the Indian wealthy, especially businessmen and Indian corporations, have a reputation—not entirely unjustified—for being unscrupulous. Thus, when Rakesh Mittal of Bharti Enterprises reportedly tried to acquire land to start his schools, he faced opposition from villagers who suspected that he was trying to seize their land to set up cellular towers.

Moreover, while donors seek outcomes which are measurable, the Bains and Company's *Philanthropy Report* for 2013 mentions that there is a disconnect between donors' and NGOs' understanding of successful outcomes. The London Business School research defines impact as 'an outcome, less an estimate of what changes would have happened without any intervention', and though this measurement

---

[18] These facts were brought out by a workshop, 'On the Status of Indian Philanthropy', organized by Pushpa Sundar and Dr M.B. Athreya, in collaboration with Partners in Change, New Delhi, in December 1995.

may be highly desired, it is quite difficult to measure it in the field, particularly in India.

Based on Bain interviews, while donors seek quantitative metrics of the difference their giving makes in the lives of the beneficiaries, NGOs in the field believe that qualitative parameters, such as a greater interest in education in the younger generation, are preferable for creating true and lasting change. Under the pressure of donor expectations, however, they discount those factors—a disconnect that may ultimately lead to underperformance.[19]

Wealthy people in some parts of Asia are also wary of revealing the full extent of their wealth, partly because of cultural values which encourage quiet, unsung giving, but also lest they are slapped with taxes, a corruption investigation, or even the risk of imprisonment. As a result, data on charitable donations in Asia are likely to under-report actual levels of giving. This is true of India too.

Another reason is that donors fear being overwhelmed by demand once their willingness is made public (see chapter 9 on Foundations).

Further, whereas in the West, Wealth Managers and Professional Advisors are known to introduce philanthropy into conversations with their clients, the whole concept is missing in India. Only recently have some banks like Citibank and Stanchart started such services. But there is still a long road ahead to make the upper and middle classes more philanthropic.

Till now, in general, big-ticket philanthropy came out of company profits to create institutions, because stock market wealth was not so pronounced. Though in the first phase of wealth creation in the early twentieth century, it was personal wealth which created many of India's philanthropic institutions, after Independence, for reasons noted elsewhere in the book, personal wealth became less significant in endowing institutions. Now, huge gains have come from market capitalization, creating billionaires out of promoters shareholding in companies. But that has not been a sufficient incentive for many to share their personal wealth in spite of the crying need all round them.

[19] Arpan Sheth and Anant Bhagwati, *India Philanthropy Report, 2013*, (Mumbai: Bain and Company, 5 March 2013).

According to Anand Mahadevan, to make the rich give more, the argument should be turned from 'They have so much money they should give more', to 'They are good at solving problems, so they should engage in fighting social evils and poverty'. If the rich see philanthropy as an entrepreneurial opportunity to make a difference, they will be more motivated, like Richard Branson and Azim Premji. They will grow their social initiatives in the same way they did their business ventures.[20]

The Indian attitude to wealth has always been ambivalent. The Indian tradition embraces both wealth and sacrifice or austerity. Lakshmi is worshipped but non-possession is also an ideal of life. Between these two extremes, the possibility of making money but using it for the public good has not been popular. What is needed now is not the denigration of wealth-creation or acquisition, but glorifying the wise use of that wealth. And this has not happened post-Independence, unlike in British times when titles like Rai Bahadur were given to those who donated munificently to public causes. Today, charitable donations do not necessarily win social recognition. Instead, many of the newly wealthy see a display of wealth as the key to improving their social standing. We need to give status to philanthropy as a worthy social endeavour, recognize our philanthropists, and facilitate the giving of large sums to needy causes and organizations by creating an enabling environment and infrastructure.

The Good News

To conclude on a more optimistic note, philanthropy, if inadequate at present, is up and growing.

Bain and Company's *Philanthropy Report 2011* estimated that corporate giving in India now totals $1.5 billion—a greater than fivefold increase since 2006. From 2006 to 2010 private giving increased by 50 per cent; $2.5 billion was committed by the top ten donors. Of the country's estimated 300-plus grant-making and operational

---

[20] Mahadevan Anand, 'Be Super Rich and Be Premji', *The Economic Times,* 7 March 2013.

foundations, 62 per cent were registered after 1991. Large individual gifts, too, are becoming more common.

Bain and Company's *Philanthropy Report 2012* reveals that the encouraging trend continues, and that India's rich have increased their contributions from 2.3 per cent of household income in 2010 to 3.1 per cent in 2011. In both the 2012 and 2013 research, the majority of donors indicated that they would likely increase their donations in the years ahead. The Bains report of 2015 observes that giving continues to show an upward trend. Whereas in 2009 only 14 per cent of the adult population across India had donated cash and some 12 per cent their time, in 2013 the figure had jumped to 28 per cent of the adult population donating money and 21 per cent their time. The donors in 2013 said they will increase their giving in the next five years, especially if a vibrant philanthropy ecosystem and facilitating conditions emerge. The top two areas of concern for philanthropists in 2012—providing food and clothing, and supporting education—remained the same in 2013.

The Hurun Philanthropy list for 2016, a ranking of the most generous individuals from India, shows that of the thirty-six top donors, thirty-three also figure on the *Hurun India Rich List 2015*, indicating that almost all the top rich are at least engaging in philanthropy, commensurate with their wealth or not. Information Technology tycoon Azim Premji is the 'Most Generous Indian' for the third time in a row, donating rupees 275.14 billion, or 81 per cent of the total wealth given away by those on the list; Nandan Nilekani and Rohini Nilekani were second with a donation of rupees 24.04 billion; and N.R. Narayana Murthy third, with rupees 13.22 billion. There are thirty-six Indians in the list, down from fifty in 2014, but with twelve new entrants; twenty-six have dropped out. Average donations were higher at rupees 9 billion, up from rupees 3 billion in 2014.[21]

What is noteworthy is that the 2016 list, as that in 2015, has seen philanthropic donations by women entrepreneurs individually and also jointly with their family.

---

[21] See the *Hurun India Philanthropy List 2016* for the complete list of India's top philanthropists. The Hurun Report is published by the Hurun Research Institute, headquartered in Shanghai. It started the India lists in 2012. http://www.hurun.net/en/ArticleShow.aspx?nid=9583.

Encouragingly, both the Bain surveys and Hurun Research show young donors becoming more engaged. As the decision makers in 32 per cent of households, they often set their family's philanthropic vision. Many of the younger generation of wealthy families have returned from studying in the West and have been influenced by philanthropic practices there. They are bringing a more strategic perspective to their family philanthropy.

Therefore, as the Bain Report (2012) comments, 'facilitating these young donors and their preferred methods of donating—as well as novice donors of all ages—is crucial to the continued growth of philanthropy in India'.

At the other end, the generation of business leaders and entrepreneurs who have been building businesses and creating wealth since liberalization in 1991 has developed a mature outlook on philanthropy. Shiv Nadar, speaking at the London School of Economics in 2012, said that in the 1990s and early 2000s the businesses and wealth of his generation were new and philanthropy was not on their agenda. Now they feel a new confidence in their wealth and in their ability to turn their skills and experiences to social development, thus once again bearing out that wealth needs time to mature before philanthropy can take root.

A further cause for optimism is that Indian donors are also beginning to actively try and measure the impact of each rupee they spend, and beginning to venture into new fields.

There are other isolated instances of philanthropic engagement by the better off, which give one hope. Give India's First Givers Club (FGC), a platform to bring together likeminded individuals interested in philanthropy, has seen both its members and the amounts donated go up, showing a greater interest in philanthropy. Its members had given rupees 230 million since its inception in 2010, and in 2012–13 the 135 members had donated rupees 130 million.

The Second India Giving Challenge organized by Give India attracted 200 NGOs and fifteen corporate participants. The challenge raised rupees 19.4 million from more than 7,500 donors.

CAF, Give India, and United Way Mumbai have also structured simple workplace giving programmes which, over a 10–12 year period, have involved 100,000 individuals in a sustained giving programme, showing that if people have trust in the organizations they give to and are sure of their accountability, they will give.

The Companies Act of 2013, with its Clause 135 making it mandatory for companies above a certain size to set apart 2 per cent of average annual profits of the last three years for CSR activities, is also likely to change the giving scene in India.

It is also entirely possible that one form of altruistic giving morphs into another form over time as circumstances change. For instance, charity can become philanthropy and philanthropy can become social entrepreneurship. Let me conclude by quoting the following as a heart warming story of one such mutation:

A young man in his thirties used to stand on the footpath opposite the famous Tata Cancer Hospital at Mumbai. The grim faces of the patients and their relatives disturbed him greatly. Most of the patients were poor people from distant towns. They had no idea whom to meet, or what to do. They had no money for medicines, not even food. The young man, heavily depressed, would return home, haunted by the thought that something must be done for these people. At last he found a way.

He rented out his own hotel that was doing good business and raised some money. From these funds he started a charitable activity right on the pavement opposite Tata Cancer Hospital. The activity consisted of providing free meals for cancer patients and their relatives. Many people in the vicinity approved of this activity. Beginning with fifty, the number of beneficiaries soon rose several fold to 700, as did the number of helping hands.

Mr Harakhchand Sawla, for that was the name of the pioneer, did not stop here. He started supplying free medicines for the needy. In fact, he started a medicine bank, enlisting voluntary services of three doctors and three pharmacists. A toy bank was opened for kids suffering from cancer. The 'Jeevan Jyot' trust founded by Mr Sawla now runs more than sixty humanitarian projects.[22]

Ultimately, a society needs charity as well as philanthropy, since they fulfil different roles, and different kinds of situations need different kinds of responses. There is a place for all of them. Hopefully, India will become more philanthropic as well as charitable and also more socially responsible in the future.

---

[22] Downloaded from the internet: Nanda Cariappa <ncariappa34@ gmail.com>, subject: Fwd: Grand Salute to this Man, 31 January 2015.

3

Corporate Social Responsibility

Philanthropy's New Avatar?

One of my strongest beliefs is that corporations have an important
duty to contribute to society. No corporation can sustain its progress
unless it makes a difference to its context.
—Narayana Murthy, Chairman and Chief Mentor, Infosys

The enactment of the Companies Act of 2013 added a new
paradigm—that of corporate social responsibility (CSR)—to the
altruistic giving scene in India, by virtue of its Clause 135. Though
the Act itself is concerned with improving corporate governance,
the above clause deals with contributions by companies to social
development and is being construed as promoting philanthropy. It is
expected to add at least Rupees 30,000 to Rupees 40,000 annually to
the amounts given to charity/philanthropy so far.

The Companies Act 2013

A sub-clause of Clause 135 requires every company having a net
worth of rupees five hundred crore or more, or, a turnover of rupees
one thousand crore or more, or a net profit of rupees five crore or

more during any financial year, to spend, in every financial year, at least two per cent of the average net profits made during the three immediately preceding financial years, on social development or what are called CSR programmes.

Other sub-clauses define how a company must carry out its mandate: it must constitute a Corporate Social Responsibility Committee of the Board. The Board's report under sub-section (3) of Section 134 must disclose the composition of the Committee which has to formulate and recommend to the Board a CSR Policy indicating the activities selected from those mentioned in Schedule VII; recommend the amount of expenditure to be incurred on the activities selected; and monitor the Policy from time to time. The Board must approve the CSR Policy, disclose its contents in its report, place it on the company's website, and ensure that the activities mentioned in the Policy are actually undertaken. In such spending the company must give preference to the local area and areas around where it operates, and if it fails to comply with requirements under Section 35, the Board, in its report, must give reasons for non-compliance.

The sub-clause concerning financial contributions should have been considered only a part of the effort to make companies better governed and socially sensitive, but because of the financial contributions being made mandatory, it has received the most attention and widespread criticism or praise.

The Genesis of the Concept of CSR

By itself, the idea of making companies contribute to the development of their communities is not new either globally or in India, and goes back in the West to as early as 1926. With the development of joint stock companies, the corporation came to be seen as a distinct social and legal entity, as much a citizen of a society as an individual, with parallel social and legal obligations to contribute to society.

The concept of social responsibility of business became a subject of debate about whether the interests of society were better served by doing business better and passing on the benefits to the consumer, or by philanthropic activities. The question being asked was, 'Is the obligation of business to make better products available more cheaply, and create higher living standards in a productive society, or is it to give more in charity?[1]

By 1953, it came to be accepted that public responsibility, social obligations, and business morality were synonyms for social responsibility and referred to as 'the obligation of businessmen to pursue those policies, to make those decisions, or to follow those lines of action which are desirable in terms of objectives and values of our society'.[2]

Thus emerged the modern idea of managerial trusteeship, as opposed to individual trusteeship of wealth, namely that the company is to be managed for the good not only of the owners (stockholders) but also for the good of the economy and society. It was distinct from the older individual philanthropy of the wealthy, in being a charge on corporate wealth, and in going beyond monetary contributions to social obligation and responsible behaviour. Growing sensitivity to the social environment of business led managements to seek new ways of identifying their companies with efforts at social improvement.

This new paradigm differed also from the earlier welfare capitalism in going beyond the welfare of company employees to the welfare of society at large and encompassing all the stake holders in business—the consumer, labour, government, and society—without expectation of any direct quid pro quo. It was expressed in giving for philanthropic causes through company foundations, or directly through companies to charitable organizations, and was not limited to communities around company locations.

In India, the first public articulation of the concept of CSR of business was in 1965, at the International Conference on Social Responsibilities of Business, held in Delhi at the India International Centre. In many ways, it contributed to the enactment of the Companies Act.

Jayaprakash Narain (J.P.) was the moving spirit behind the Conference. Narain's opening speech and much of the discussion

---

[1] Morrell Heald, *The Social Responsibilities of Business: Company and Community, 1900–1960* (Cleveland, Ohio: Case Western Reserve University Press, 1970).

[2] Howard R. Bowen, *Social Responsibilities of the Businessman* (USA: University of Iowa Press, 1953), p. 6.

at the seminar concentrated on Gandhi's concept of trusteeship and whether it was practical; what could be done by voluntary means to enforce it; whether a voluntary code of conduct was sufficient or whether the state should step in and regulate business; and whether labour and shareholders also had a responsibility.

Some of the participants were against the concept of trusteeship, believing it to be negative and impractical. It was pointed out that social responsibility should not be taken to mean charity. They felt it was necessary to spell out the goals and the kind of institutions that should be evolved, instead of simply leaving it to individual conscience and moral persuasion. Moreover, the concept of voluntary trusteeship would not make much headway because due to poverty and illiteracy of consumers and the absence of consumer associations, there was no pressure on business. It was necessary to build in social audit as part of the concept of social responsibility.[3] This thinking was to find a reflection in the later Companies Act.

One of the results of the Conference was the Declaration of the Social Responsibility of Business, spelling out the need for it and pointing out that the concept was broader than charitable giving for community affairs. It included:

- justice and fair play in all dealings;
- making serious attempts at growth and development of all the factors or constituents of business from owners to consumers;
- utilization of surplus primarily for the above two purposes;
- utilization of surplus, if at all left over, for any other social purpose deemed fit for assistance, such as education, health, and research.[4]

Today's Concept of CSR

The concept of CSR has been further refined and clarified since that date, so that today CSR is defined as, 'the continuing commitment by business to behave ethically and contribute to economic

---

[3] Pushpa Sundar, *Business and Community: The Story of Corporate Social Responsibility in India* (New Delhi: Sage, 2013).

[4] Upadhyay, R.B., *Social Responsibility of Business and the Trusteeship Theory of Mahatma Gandhi* (New Delhi: Sterling Publishers, 1976).

development while improving the quality of life of the workforce and their families as well as of the local community and society at large'. (as per the *World Business Council for Sustainable Development*)

This concept of social responsibility is broader than just donating resources, whether of time or money, and includes such concerns as ethical business practices and responsibility towards all the stakeholders in business and towards the physical environment. It implies a considered Board decision based on enlightened self-interest. It is also about how business takes into account the economic, social, and environmental impact of the way it operates, what is today known as the triple bottom line.

The traditional model of corporate philanthropy was first to make a profit and then to give a portion to society out of the surplus. CSR is concerned not merely with distributing a portion of the profits but also with whether that profit is equitably distributed among all the stakeholders—disadvantaged communities, society at large, shareholders, and employees. It further means raising the bar about payment of more than fair wages, being concerned with effluent quality, preventing gender and caste discrimination, taking positive affirmative action in their favour, and so on. Corporate philosophy has gone from profitmaking as the goal to value creation as the goal.

In sum, CSR means not only doing good but also not doing bad, or put another way, maximizing positive impacts, and minimizing negative impacts. Hence in CSR the *process* of making profit is believed to be as important as the *end use* of surplus.

Far from costing the company more, it is believed that being socially responsible can actually increase a company's revenue by reduction of waste and recycling, and by causing non-monetary benefits as well, such as greater employee satisfaction and morale, leading to increased productivity, improved relations within and outside the company, and greater brand recall.

Why the Enactment?

The inclusion of CSR in the Companies Act was the culmination of several developments. There was dissatisfaction with the way corporate philanthropy was practised. It was as ad hoc as individual charity, with no policy, no designated resources or long term commitment to a cause or project; it was also dependent on the whims of a few people at the top. It ceased if profits were not made. There were no metrics to measure impact. Moreover, philanthropy existed side by side with poor governance and short changing of consumers and government. What was needed was a 360 degree concept which took account of all aspects of corporate operations, and how they impacted on society. Merely giving away of surplus resources was not enough.

Second, with the crumbling of economies and breakdown of trust in business leaders due to the series of scams starting with Enron and going on to Satyam Technologies and many others, the demand for CSR, which had already taken root, was reinforced.

The growing size of businesses and their globalization also made it necessary to make them both more accountable and conscious of their obligations to society. Because of increased wealth and changed ideology in favour of the market, there were increased expectations from business. The government, facing a shortage of resources, wanted it to contribute more to society and also be more responsible in its operations. That business had a role to play in development was officially recognized in the 11th Plan, and was followed up in the Companies Act.

Increased environmental consciousness, as well as greater consciousness of human rights, especially rights of tribals, Dalits, and women, led to pressure on business from the civil society, which saw making business more responsible in its operations as one of its roles. It confronted erring businesses more frequently, especially in connection with waste recycling, more conservative exploitation of natural resources, new environmental and human resources accounting systems, and violation of tribal rights in land acquisition. The Act, by making companies conscious of these concerns, was a step to meet these demands.

Finally, globalization ensured that global good practices were followed not only by MNCs operating in India but by Indian companies as well, who aspired to markets abroad.

What the Companies Act, and especially Clause 135, has done is to move CSR from a peripheral to a passionate involvement of top management; from ad hoc CSR expenditure to planned strategic investment; from a single bottom line culture focused on profit to a triple bottom line focus; and from a standalone CSR function dependent on the whims of one or two top leaders, to one where CSR is internalized and accepted by all in the company.

Aftermath of the Act

Though the Companies Act and even its concern with social development is broader than Clause 135, it is the financial aspect of CSR which led to a major discourse in the aftermath of the Act. The media has played a major role in spreading consciousness of the need for CSR, in keeping companies informed of the provisions of the Act, and the many new possibilities for making a social contribution. It is tracking not only the CSR spending under the Act but also whether the guidelines and procedures for deciding on CSR policy are being met or not. For instance, a feature in the paper *LiveMint* on 23 December 2015 pointed out that CSR committees at some of the top 100 firms, including TCS, HUL, and Maruti Suzuki, had met only once in a fiscal year, and only 24 per cent of companies surveyed for the purpose saw the committees meet more than three times. What is encouraging, however, is that many companies have assigned the chief executives or group heads as the head of the CSR committees as well.[5]

Though the exact amounts donated will become known only by the end of 2016, when one year of compulsory reporting on the contributions will have been completed, first results show that the top seventy-five companies have spent rupees 40 billion in financial year (FY) 2015, against the expected 90 billion. The top spenders are Reliance Industries, Oil and Natural Gas Corporation (ONGC), Tata Consultancy Services (TCS), National Thermal Power Corporation (NTPC), Infosys, and WIPRO. As always, education, health, and skill development have attracted the most funds.[6]

Inevitably, the Act has come in for its fair share of criticism and praise. Many question whether clause 135 is a way whereby the state is passing on its responsibility for social development to NGOs and the

---

[5] Arundhati Ramanathan , 'Firms' CSR Panels See Few Meetings in FY 15', *LiveMint*, Bengaluru, 23 December 2015.

[6] *The Economic Times*, 'Top 75 Companies Spent Rs. 4,000 Crores on CSR in FY 15', New Delhi, 3 September 2015.

private sector. It is also not clear as to who will monitor compliance, and how. But on the whole, the reaction to it has been positive, the greatest criticism being directed to the compulsory nature of the contributions. Many philanthropists like Ratan Tata think making CSR contributions mandatory is akin to paying a tax, whereas philanthropy is an act which must come from within; compulsion is not appropriate for charity. The Tata Group companies, according to him, have in any case been devoting up to 5 per cent of their profits for many years before it became mandatory to devote 2 per cent of the average profits.

Though not in favour of compulsion, many, including business leaders like Kiran Mazumdar Shaw, think it is a positive measure, making companies sensitive, and opening a major source of funds for social action groups. They accept that most companies would not care about the good of the larger community without being forced.

At the same time, it is widely agreed that paying a sum of 2 per cent of profits will not, by itself, make a company a good social citizen. Too much attention has come to be focused on the financial contribution and not enough on the governance or ethical behaviour aspect which is contained in the other parts of the Act. CSR policies must articulate a moral vision of development since law cannot, by itself, promote normative values. Business leadership, not government, must articulate a moral philosophy applicable to business.

There are also fears that it may lead to creative accounting and unproductive allocation of resources, and more, not less, unethical behaviour. Since the amounts to be spent are very big, approximately rupees 300 billion to 400 billion according to some estimates, it is questionable whether they will be spent wisely, as companies may not have the bandwidth for social development, and partner NGOs may not have the capacity or capability for spending large amounts.

Ratan Tata feels that the contributions can be better utilized if the government can clearly identify projects or sectors which need funds.[7] The government has taken one step in this direction by amending Schedule VII of the Companies Act 2013, so that many more avenues for spending money wisely become eligible. One of these new additions is to allow contributions to technology incubators approved by

[7] Ratan Tata, reported in *The Indian Express*, 'Mandating CSR Spends Akin to Taxation', 7 December 2015.

the Central government as CSR contributions, effective from 2014. This broadening of the understanding of what constitutes CSR is a very positive step, given that creating social businesses is likely to create more employment and incomes and meet social needs at the same time, on a larger scale than pure charitable handouts for health and education.

Mahindra and Mahindra Financial Services Ltd (MMFSL) has already set aside a portion of their 2014–15 CSR funds for funding two social startups—SustainEarth Energy Solutions, which aims to provide affordable bio-gas technology for rural areas, and Sickle Innovations, a startup making handheld cotton picketing machines using a patented technology which enhances labour productivity. Some other companies have followed suit.[8]

An analysis of the first full year's CSR spending by top companies indicates that a majority are spending on expected social matters such as education, health, vocational training to unemployed youth, environment, sanitation, drinking water, and women's empowerment, with little possibility of what is being attempted leading to disruptive social change, which is the goal of philanthropy, though there is also some effort being made to spread the contributions to non traditional areas such as preservation of traditional knowledge and funding of startups. There is also some indication that at least a few companies may not spend only to achieve targets. Indications are that at least some, like Bharat Petroleum, may opt for carrying over the amounts to the next year, if in their judgement the proposed projects are not sustainable or not delivering results.[9]

The Act is still a work in progress and hopefully experience will lead to improvements.

Philanthropy vs CSR

Because the Act has given a somewhat greater emphasis to financial contributions and less to ethical behaviour as is the intention of the

---

[8] *The Times of India*, 'Cos Act Amendment Allows Use of CSR Funds in Startups', 5 May 2015.

[9] *The Indian Express*, 'Healthcare to *Swachh Bharat*, How Firms Spent CSR Funds', 23 November 2015.

original concept of CSR, many tend to look upon it as synonymous with philanthropy. Though the other clauses are directed to making companies more responsible in terms of good governance, those other provisions are not considered as part of CSR, which is considered largely in terms of Clause 135. The emphasis of CSR has come to be totally on the permissible CSR *activities*, spelt out in the annexures to the Act and in later amendments and rules, rather than on the *non-tangibles of responsibility*.

Though the CSR envisaged is far from the totally impulsive and short-lived response to need that is called charity, and is akin to the rationalized and strategic response of philanthropy, it, nevertheless, is not philanthropy.

For one, philanthropy is purely voluntary, springing from compassion and good will to fellow beings, whereas CSR, as now practised in India, is a compulsory activity for companies above a certain size. In effect, mandatory CSR is regulated or induced philanthropy. CSR is very specifically seen as the business contribution to the nation's sustainable goals, not something to be spent at the donor's whim, which could well lie outside the listing in the Act. As mentioned, many see it as another tax, but instead of a direct levy, the government is achieving its objective indirectly. The only advantage to companies is that they get a choice and a say in how they would like their money to be used.

Besides, CSR applies very specifically to companies, and does not apply to individuals or families.

Second, CSR is not philanthropy because there is an expectation of a quid pro quo. Companies are motivated to be socially responsible because of the possibility it offers of promoting their brand, and by the benefit it offers for better labour relations and a good corporate image in society. The move to align CSR activities with a company's core competence makes good business sense, but does not spring from pure altruism. The underlying attitude is 'let us do some good and make money at the same time'.

Careful planning and impact measurement has to accompany the decision to give. While this is common to good philanthropic practice and sets it apart from impulsive charity, and while it was no doubt necessary as a corrective to the totally whimsical manner in which companies approached social benefit giving, giving by companies is now so regulated as to almost remove the passion and conviction which characterized the actions of great philanthropists like Jamsetji Tata and his sons, Ratan and Dorab, Andrew Carnegie, and John D. Rockefeller, and which led to advances in society.

Some of the major social change work of our lifetimes came from major corporate foundations like Ford, McArthur, Hewlett, and Kellog in America and the Tata Group in India. They were behind the civil rights movement, the green revolution, and much of the human rights work of the past decades in America, and the building of niche institutions such as the Tata Institute of Fundamental research, Tata Institute of Social Sciences, and so on in India.

Though this 'old-style' corporate philanthropy has not gone away entirely, being present in a new generation of entrepreneurs like Gates and Soros in the West and Azim Premji and Shiv Nadar in India, the present CSR does not belong to this genre, where giving and brand value are inextricably linked. Making a distinction between the short-term brand-oriented CSR, with an emphasis on meeting targets of spending, and the long-term investments in social, political, and technological change characteristic of philanthropy, is important. Today's corporate philanthropic activities are guided less by what is deemed good and necessary for societies in the long run, and more by short-term compulsions and interests of a company.

CSR is the result not of a personal philosophy or interest of the founder of the company but a considered decision of the Board, and part of corporate policy and action. By having to take a common view it may not lead to the most optimum use of money.

On the other hand, it must be admitted that in the short run, the outreach of CSR is likely to be far broader than individual philanthropists endowing institutions, only some of whose philanthropic investments may be path breaking. Moreover, in CSR there is likely to be far more direct involvement of the company donors in development of communities.

Impact of CSR on Philanthropy

After the passing of the Companies Act, corporate foundations are being set up to act as the CSR arm of the company. Unfortunately, some of these are misusing the public charitable trust form for laundering black money. One of the malpractices is to give the trust a cheque out of the CSR budget. The trust, after deducting the commission discreetly, returns cash to company officials or promoters. The actual expenditure is met with black money of the promoter of the trust or a middleman, thus helping to turn black money into white. At the end of the year the trust gives a report to the company, which is incorporated in the annual report the company has to file for its CSR commitment.[10]

As to whether spending on CSR will reduce individual philanthropy, the signals are mixed. Many progressive companies with noted philanthropists as their heads are separating their company CSR from their personal philanthropy and ensuring resources for both.

The Azim Premji Foundation, for instance, is separate from WIPRO's CSR wing. One reason for separating personal philanthropy from the company CSR is, in the case of WIPRO, that WIPRO's global customers also expect them to be involved in social action since many MNCs abroad are into CSR activities themselves. They naturally look for partners who are similarly engaged and expect that WIPRO would be engaged with the community in some way.

The WIPRO company and its promoter Azim Premji have carved out distinct, though linked, ways to engage in social action. The company launched an initiative called WIPRO Cares. It is managed by WIPRO employees who contribute resources to it, which are then matched by the company. They began by contributing to the Gujarat Earthquake relief, and then to the Tsunami rehabilitation efforts. But then they turned to seeking longer, more lasting solutions to poverty around them, through the WIPRO Applying Thought in Schools Initiative, to improve the quality of schooling in urban areas.

Similarly, Kiran Mazumdar Shaw's company Biocon has its own CSR activities while she pursues her passion for cancer research from her personal funds (see Chapter 7 on women and philanthropy).

While mandatory CSR has made many companies sensitive to social concerns and has led to the establishment of company

---

[10] *The Economic Times*, 'In CSR Trusts, Black Turns White and Vice Versa', New Delhi, 21 October 2015.

foundations to undertake or guide the CSR work, one negative fallout is that in some cases CSR has displaced voluntary family philanthropy.[11] This is undesirable because family or individual voluntary philanthropy has a different origin and purpose than CSR, which is essentially to ensure responsibility to all stakeholders in society and to aid the government's own social development work with funds. A foundation is based on a philanthropist's vision for a society, and is successful or not because of the founder's passion, whereas CSR is driven by board decisions, which are not necessarily driven by a social vision or passion but business concerns.

The Gates Foundation, for instance, has much more money and flexibility than CSR at Microsoft. The Tata Trusts are driven by different vision and goals than the CSR of Tata companies.

To conclude, it is too early yet to pass judgement on CSR and how it will add to social well-being. All that can be said at this stage is that CSR is not philanthropy per se. But, as in the case of charity, there is place for both CSR and philanthropy since they fulfil different needs in society.

[11] UBS-INSEAD, *Study on Family Philanthropy in Asia* (Singapore: UBS-INSEAD, 25 August 2011).

PART II

THE ECOSYSTEM

The only thing that saves us from the bureaucracy is inefficiency. An efficient bureaucracy is the greatest threat to liberty.
— Eugene McCarthy, US Senator (1949–59),
Time Magazine, 12 February 1979.

4

The Carrot and the Stick

The State and Philanthropy

Ronald Reagan has famously said, 'The nine most terrifying words in the English language are: I am from the government and I am here to help'.

To flourish, philanthropy requires freedom of association and expression, tolerance of diversity, societal acceptance of the role of private actors in public life, and a supportive legal and regulatory framework. These can either facilitate or restrain the generation, retention, and disbursal, as well as the manner of disbursal, of wealth and business profits.

Determinants of Philanthropy

Philanthropy necessarily requires the ability to hold private property. If there is no possibility of having legal rights over private property, as in rigid communist regimes, there can be no philanthropy, though charity may still be possible. But if private property is allowed and is protected by the state, it is believed that more people in that state will, on their own initiative, help others. Conversely, when the state expropriates all the wealth and takes on a public benefactor role, there is no moral necessity for individuals to be charitable.

Second, creation of wealth has to precede its distribution. Capital accumulation and the availability of an economic surplus is the most fundamental requirement for philanthropic giving. For these two reasons, modern philanthropy is essentially the product of a capitalist system. Whether philanthropy would be necessary if capitalist production did not in the first instance produce the ills which philanthropy seeks to address, is another question but it is discussed elsewhere in the book. For the present, one has to accept that an economic surplus is necessary for philanthropy.

But in addition to a surplus, sustained philanthropy, as mentioned earlier, also requires the passage of time and confidence in the security of one's fortune, whether personal or corporate. This in turn requires confidence in the stability of the political and economic environment. Owners of wealth need to feel assured that they will be able to retain their wealth and do whatever they want with it. The ability to own property and to dispose of it in any manner desired, the rate of economic growth, the general economic and political environment, taxation policies and how stringently they are enforced, are all important determinants of philanthropy in a society, as are the nature of government–business relations. In short, state attitudes and actions have a vital influence on philanthropy.

Philanthropic amounts (not charity) will be smaller in economies which, while following private market principles and allowing private property rights, have policies in place for wealth redistribution, either directly through laws (e.g., land reform laws), or high levels of taxation. The reason in both cases is the same—citizens are left with no disposable assets to donate to public well-being.

Conversely, the state can encourage philanthropy through an enabling legal framework which allows for surplus to accumulate in private hands, and which also makes the registration, reporting, auditing, and accounting of income and wealth devoted to philanthropy easier. Though absence of restrictions may enable one to create and retain profits, it need not necessarily lead to giving for public welfare. Here the state can encourage giving or not, by offering or withholding incentives through taxation of income, wealth, and inheritance, or by bestowing awards or other forms of recognition.

The 2007–10 Labour government in the UK, for instance, took many measures to promote giving. It both reduced the barriers to giving and provided motivation for giving by more favourable regulation of non-profits, and tax incentive policies including Gift Aid. It also set up new organizations and strategic partnerships, such as Philanthropy UK, to promote more effective giving. It funded research initiatives and established awards such as The Beacon Awards to encourage individuals to donate time and money. The Prime Minister, Gordon Brown, demonstrated a personal commitment to philanthropic giving with the appointment of Dame Stephanie Shirley as the ambassador for philanthropy—an idea now gaining traction around the globe.[1]

Essentially, the Indian policy framework for encouraging and regulating philanthropy was established during colonial rule, and based on and interpreted according to British law. The Independent state largely added and amended the basic structure as and when necessary.

The Indian Framework

Under British rule, the State played an active role in moving the wealthy classes towards new ideas of philanthropy, giving formal and informal encouragement through awards and conferment of status, a favourable tax policy, and regulation of charitable activity. The last was aimed especially at religious trusts to ensure proper utilization of charitable funds, and after the 1857 mutiny, to control religious funds which could be used for seditious activities.

The British rulers of the nineteenth century believed it the duty of the colonial government to bring 'moral and material progress' to the subject race, and therefore encouraged the building of schools, colleges, hospitals, dispensaries, public libraries, and museums by Indians. Because a laissez faire approach was the order of the day, self-help and voluntary action was preferred to state intervention to meet social needs. In this picture, charity held a vital place and it was assumed to be a permanent and indispensable element in a civilized social system, and was therefore encouraged.

After Independence, India adopted a socialistic pattern of society as the principal objective of social and economic policy in 1954,

---

[1] Cheryl Chapman, 'The Role of the State', *Philanthropy U.K.*, Quarterly Issue, Summer 2010: Promoting Philanthropy, 41: 12–14.

and a great deal of attention came to be focused on income distribution. Because of the enormity of the problems, as also for ideological reasons, the state came to play a dominant role in both the social and economic sphere. Less space was given to private initiative. At the same time, whatever the political colour of the government in power, and in keeping with the nation's faith in democracy, the government was, on the whole, supportive of civil society and philanthropic organizations, allowing them freedom of association for common action, and offering other forms of encouragement. Equally, it did not hesitate to step in and regulate charitable activity when it felt necessary.

Principally, the framework affecting philanthropy consists of legislative and other regulation of non-profit activity, administrative and other measures taken by the government, and the tax policy. It is discussed below under these heads.

The Legislative and Administrative Framework

History

In the early twentieth century there grew a demand for reform of traditional practices of charity, as a consequence of important debates by Hindu reformers, but also among Muslims and Sikhs. These were critiques of wasteful giving.

Among the reforms advocated were registration and listing of Hindu and Muslim charitable institutions, so that they could be more efficiently scrutinized and managed. The Government of India had in fact passed a new Charitable Endowments Act in 1890, but it had limited application and a new law was deemed necessary.

This resulted in new legislation to ensure proper utilization of charitable funds. The English used their own jurisprudence to interpret charity and charitable purpose, and the concept of 'public good'. According to this, 'charity' and 'charitable purposes' included many items not narrowly directed to relieving poverty, such as repair of bridges and roads, education, advancement of religion, and other purposes beneficial to the community. The essence of charity, for legal purposes, came to be giving which was for *public*, as against *private*, benefit. These principles were enforced through judicial interpretation and through new enactments to regulate the use of huge charitable funds with religious bodies and others.

In the South particularly, temples had huge endowments, but till the nineteenth century, British rulers had not interfered with religious institutions and customs. Under pressure from Christian missionaries, such practices were abandoned, and the government actively intervened in temple affairs to curb perceived misuses of temple and religious trust funds. Through various Regulations and Acts beginning in 1817, government began appointing non-official trustees on religious endowments, defining their roles and duties, and diverting funds belonging to religious institutions for secular purposes such as education and construction of roads and bridges.[2] The social meaning of endowment took on British values, focused around ideals of Christian religion and secular philanthropy. Religious gifting came to be considered, by extension from British norms, as transcendental, access to the deity a public right, and endowments to it as public trusts.

The colonial reinterpretation of religious endowments as a form of philanthropy separated the interests of the deity and trustee, whereas earlier no such distinction was being made. The trustee could not claim a share of the trust fund over which he had control, or use it in his business dealings as had been done earlier. Worship was interpreted by law as either 'private' or 'public', as distinct from the pre-colonial distinction of 'individual' or 'collective'.[3]

A sharp distinction between private and public interest was made for other trusts as well, and trusts were prohibited from using public charitable funds for personal business interests.

The new regulations extended to Muslim endowments called *wakfs*. *Wakf*, unlike *zakat*, is not obligatory philanthropy but a voluntary gifting of property for community welfare. In response to a demand for creating a *wakf* department to facilitate enquiries from the Muslim public about how *awqaf* resources were used, the late-nineteenth century colonial government increasingly tried to bring *awqaf* under government control, because they suspected that many such endowments were being used to hide taxable monies from the government. The *Wakf* Validating Act 1913 consolidated state control over *wakf* institutions.

[2] See Chandra Y. Mudaliar, *The Secular State and Religious Institutions in India* (Wiesbaden: Franz Steiner Verlag, 1974), pp. 3–26.

[3] See David West Rudner, *Caste & Capitalism in Colonial India: The Nattukottai Chettiars* (Delhi: Munshiram Manoharlal, 1995).

But there was Muslim resistance to state regulation because such funds were an important source of patronage for crucial Islamic institutions and the practice kept the institutions safe from the state. There was also concern among both Hindus and Muslims that state regulation would adversely affect Indian educational initiatives and other undertakings supported by charity.[4] Nevertheless, some regulation of trusts was imposed and accepted. *Wakfs* became minority institutions where the state has the sole authority to legislate and supervise its functioning.

State control over *wakfs* continued into the post-Independence period. *Wakfs* became state-run philanthropy run by *Wakf* Boards all over India, which in turn were under the Central *Wakf* Council, created by the *Wakf* Act of 1954, to advise the government on the proper functioning of *Wakf* in India.

Many believe that by controlling *wakfs* the state has weakened the beneficial impact of Muslim philanthropy on the community, because several abuses have crept into *wakf* administration.[5]

Contemporary Position

After Independence, Trust laws were enacted or amended for other trusts to create a legal framework which formalizes the space, and the rights and obligations of non-profit organizations (NPO), including foundations. It consists of five main laws, each of which is administered by an agency specifically created for the purpose. These are:

- The Registration of Societies Act of 1860, a Central Act, and its versions enacted by different states, with a Registrar of Societies in each state to register and regulate organizations registered under this Act.
- Before Independence, the only Act applicable to trusts in the whole of India was the Indian Trusts Act of 1882, whose provisions

[4] Carey Watt, *Serving the Nation: Cultures of Service, Association and Citizenship in Colonial India* (New York and New Delhi: Oxford University Press, 2005), pp. 73–5.

[5] For a more detailed exposition of Muslim philanthropy in India and the role of the state, see Mathew Cherian, *A Million Missions: The Non-Profit Sector in India* (Delhi: Authors UpFront, 2014), pp. 50–92.

related only to private trusts. The Central government did not enact any all-India legislation for *public* trusts but, charity being on the concurrent list, various states enacted a variation of the 1882 Act. Bombay enacted the Bombay Public Trusts Act soon after Independence (1950). It applied to Maharashtra and Gujarat. Later Madhya Pradesh and Rajasthan enacted similar Acts, and Andhra Pradesh and Tamil Nadu enacted the Charitable and Hindu Religious Institutions and Endowments Acts in 1966 and 1959 respectively.

Maharashtra and Gujarat have offices of the Charities Commissioner, created under the Bombay Public Trusts Act, 1950, to oversee charities in these states; Tamil Nadu has a Department of Religious and Charitable Endowments, and other states have some similar organization for public charitable trusts.

- Section 25 of the Companies Act 1956 allowed the formation of non-profit companies. It has now been replaced by Section 8 of the Companies Act of 2013. The relevant authority is the Registrar of Companies.
- The Income Tax Act, 1961, again a Central Act applicable all over India, provides fiscal benefits to NPOs such as NGOs, foundations, and trusts. The administrative agency is the Department of Income Tax Exemption.
- The Foreign Contributions Regulation Act (FCRA) of 1976 was enacted to regulate foreign contributions to NPOs. It was initially a measure directed at political parties to prevent them from forming shell trusts. Non-profit organizations were not the prime target. But today, after the 2010 amendment, it is most applicable to NGOs and political parties receiving funds from foreign sources, and has become an instrument for the state to control unwelcome political activism. Though NGOs doing pure 'charity' are not targeted, those involved in semi-political activism frequently are.

Till the Central Budget of financial year (FY) 2016–17, CSR rules under the Companies Act 2013 made it difficult for companies having over 51 per cent foreign shareholding, or those which are subsidiaries of foreign owned companies, to give to NGOs without getting FCRA clearance, since their contribution was to be treated as coming from a foreign source. They could only donate or partner with NGOs that have FCRA registration with the Home Ministry. It did not apply to such companies donating to beneficiaries directly, but applied to donations by such companies to their own foundations, who also could not receive funds from abroad without FCRA permission. Companies argued that this limited the options for them and for non-profits. They could not fund not-for-profits of their choice, and instead had to opt for those which are eligible as per the law, even though these may not be the best for the purpose.[6] Taking this into account, an amendment to the FCRA rules introduced in the budget of Financial Year 2016–17 frees donations by firms with substantial foreign holding from the 'foreign source' tag with retrospective effect from September 2010, so that they are now free to donate where they will. Many of the larger corporates in India have more than 50 per cent foreign shareholding and they were earlier compelled to work with FCRA registered organizations only. As FCRA registered organizations constitute a small portion of the not-for-profit universe, this amendment will promote wider and greater reach of corporate grants to not-for-profit organizations.

Charities Administration

During a hundred plus years of growth, rapid economic and social changes have changed the conditions under which the non-profit sector operates but the institutional framework has not changed commensurately, though some attempts at change have been made sporadically. The non-profit sector includes non-governmental organizations (NGOs), that is, organizations which provide social services, as well as donor organizations, such as foundations which provide the funds. In the following section, non-profit organizations, apart from being referred to as NGOs, are also referred to as charities following popular usage, and civil society organizations (CSOs).

---

[6] Moyna Manku, 'The CSR–FCRA Contradiction', *LiveMint*, 23 December 2015, www.livemint.com.

Administrative reform of the charities administration is needed for two main reasons. One, the misdeeds of a few charitable organizations have brought the integrity and accountability of the whole non-profit sector into question and there is a need to rebuild public confidence in charitable organizations through effective regulation. While self-regulation is better than legal regulation, it cannot, by itself, ensure good governance of the sector, and needs to be supplemented by the authority of government. Two, the further growth of the sector is dependent on being able to mobilize private charitable resources to supplement government and foreign funds. Whether charities are able to do this depends on public trust in their integrity and efficiency, which in turn can be helped by a good regulatory framework.

One recent effort at reform of the charities framework was the establishment in October 2000, by the Planning Commission, Government of India, of a Task Force to review, analyse, and suggest ways in which the present acts, rules, and procedures can be modified or simplified to facilitate the growth and development of the voluntary or charitable sector. The problem, the Task Force noted, is not only of lacunae in the laws, but also of the way the laws are interpreted and implemented by the various administrative agencies created to enforce them. Unfortunately, in spite of many sound suggestions by the various expert committees, there was very little change on the ground.

Later, in 2004, the Sampradaan Indian Centre for Philanthropy (SICP), New Delhi, was requested by the Planning Commission to undertake a comprehensive review of the administrative framework, including the laws, applicable to the non-profit sector. Its findings were submitted in a report to the Planning Commission the same year.[7]

Four overwhelming conclusions emerged from the study. One, though it is not as efficient, user friendly, and facilitative as it ought to be, the charities administration has at least not proved a barrier to the growth of charities. Compared to many other countries, the Indian legal framework has allowed space for CSOs to emerge without

---

[7] Sampradaan Indian Centre for Philanthropy (SICP), *A Review of Charities Administration in India* (New Delhi: Sampradaan Indian Centre for Philanthropy, September 2004).

restrictions. There has not been any denial of legal protection, or even of right of protest to redress a wrong decision. In spite of its many flaws, such as cumbersome procedures, delays, and corruption, there have not been major impediments in the way of functioning of CSOs. The income tax provisions to encourage charity are about as encouraging as in most progressive countries, and better than in others, though there is always a demand for more tax concessions to incentivize givers.

Two, if there are no major impediments, certainly there are several roadblocks, and several irritants in the agency/charities interface. For instance, the multiplicity of laws governing charity for different religions, for different types of organizations, and for different states, with no uniformity in the laws across states, and no consistency between laws, makes for confusion. There are long delays, corruption, and red tape, due to inadequate staff and budget allocations for regulatory agencies, as well as poor public information and education.[8]

If the work of the agencies was streamlined, the time and money saved by charitable organizations on unnecessary paperwork, and trips to the agencies, could be more fruitfully spent on substantive work. More important than the procedural and other irritants is the failure of the administrative agencies in performing two major roles. One, they have not been effective in regulating the sector and securing compliance with the laws to ensure fiscal and management discipline in the sector so that public confidence in the sector is maintained.

Seldom are charities visited, their work properly understood, and notice taken of the returns filed. A soft state has hardly ever applied any sanctions for misdemeanour; except in relation to receipt of foreign contributions, though many analysts believe that the tightened norms of the FCRA are being applied selectively to suppress dissent against government policies. Besides, firm regulation needs to go hand in hand with education and facilitation to help charities to be legally compliant. This, too, has not happened at all.

Three, better regulation is required because all is not well with the charities sector itself. Even as it is being given an increasingly important role in national development, its higher profile has also

---

[8] For details of the deficiencies in the administration system, see SICP, *A Review of Charities Administration in India*.

thrown light on indiscipline, lack of professionalization, and unethical behaviour within the sector. Even though the public is willing to assist charities in their laudable work by supporting them with funds, it is beginning to lose confidence in the integrity of the organizations and particularly in whether the contributions reach the beneficiaries for whom they are intended. A section of the charities sector has cynically manipulated the provisions of the law to their own personal ends.

That the problem exists in other countries and they have also felt impelled to take stern action is borne out by the fact that the Financial Action Task Force (FATF) in G8 countries mentioned that trusts are the ideal form of organization for money laundering and have been so used. In the USA too, the Revenue Service had to issue guidelines recently for stricter monitoring of 501(C) (3) (charities) organizations.

Even when there is no overt misuse, charities are guilty of non-compliance either out of ignorance of the law, or sheer indifference, knowing that there will be no consequences. At the same time it must be stated that if the attitudes of the law enforcers were more helpful and less heavy-handed than they are, compliance would improve.

Finally, an overarching cause of the present hopeless drift is the lack of political will. More than anything else, charity administration suffers from the fact that charity or voluntarism comes way down in the priority list of the government, both at the central and state level. Though the government expects a lot from the non-profit sector for assisting it with nation building, it is yet to create commensurate conditions to enable it to play its proper role. As a result, charity regulatory agencies suffer not only from poor budget allocations, but overall neglect. Charity is also being used for political reasons, both because of the huge pool of funds represented by some of the big trusts, and the potential the laws offer for political control. Influential people running schools and hospitals for profit are able to get politicians to waive action against them. Hence, reform is possible only if the administration and the public perceive a will to act. As mentioned earlier, several committees and commissions and task forces have made recommendations, and very few have been adopted. Unless the charities sector is seen to be of importance in national life and resourced with funds and people accordingly, reforms will remain on paper. In sum, action is required from both the charities sector and the Establishment.

Apart from several short and medium-term measures to improve efficiency and user friendliness of the agencies such as a single incorporation law, the report recommended the creation of a new institutional framework such as a Charities Directorate on the lines of the Charities Commission of UK, at the central and state levels, to be the overall authority to handle all matters related to charity.

Though a few steps have been taken to streamline the non-profit sector, such as tightening the administrative mechanism for charitable institutions by introducing stricter reporting of activities, funding patterns, and income,[9] much remains to be done to check misuse of charitable funds. While better regulation is certainly needed to restore public confidence, it must also be admitted that it is a double edged sword, which can be, and has been, used to stifle dissent and protest.

Tax Policy

In the context of philanthropy, a government's tax policy has two contrary strands. On the one hand, taxes are considered as a way of reducing inequalities which make philanthropy both possible and necessary. On the other, the tax policy is also used as an instrument for encouraging philanthropy.

Essentially, the argument about using the tax policy for either purposes boils down to who is the better spender of public money, the government or private individuals. This is a debate which is ongoing in almost every society. In the USA people have generally distrusted the government to spend their money well, due to the *politicized nature of decision-making in government*, the low calibre of people who work in government, its large size, and bureaucratic structure. In this view, the argument against inheritance or any other tax for that matter on grounds of rising inequality is that there is no guarantee that the extra revenue gained through higher taxes would be better used by the government.

[9] *The Business Standard*, 'Charitable Trusts Under IT Scanner', 26 May 2011.

It is further argued that even with government spending, it is the preferences of a handful of bureaucrats and politicians who assist select groups whom they consider suitable (read politically advantageous) to receive that help. And experience has shown that the state typically spends wastefully, unproductively, and at the worst possible value, and not necessarily on the most needy.

In socialist or socialistic countries like India, on the other hand, state spending on social provisioning is considered essential not only to reduce inequalities but because private initiative will not provide the necessary development inputs for all the people. Leaving more money in the hands of the rich, and encouraging them to give in philanthropy through tax breaks, will result in their spending only on what interests them, and very often on what benefits their own class, such as on art galleries, libraries, and the like. It will not be spent on what the poorer classes need; nor will it necessarily be spent where there is the greatest distress, that is, in backward parts of the country. The state would then still have to step in and make good the deficits, for which it will have to raise money by taxation. It is a tension which is yet to be resolved.

Meanwhile, the following sections looks at the history and present position of tax policies in India in the context of philanthropy, and the arguments for and against giving tax incentives.

A Brief History

To help the wealthy to invest in philanthropy, the colonial government began giving tax concessions. For reasons of expediency, the taxation policy of the years before the First World War favoured the business and landed classes, and was highly regressive, particularly in regard to direct taxation. The income tax was introduced in 1860, but till the First World War, the wealthy in Bombay were lightly taxed in comparison to the rural classes of the other non-industrialized provinces.[10]

However, this light taxation conflicted with the second major goal of imperial policy, namely to bring 'moral and material progress' to

[10] For more details on the 'Asiatic Revenue Policy' of the Raj, see A.D.D. Gordon, *Businessmen and Politics: Rising Nationalism and a Modernising Economy in Bombay, 1918–1933* (New Delhi: Manohar, 1978), pp. 11–39.

the people. It meant that the government lacked the resources to support social welfare activities while the wealthy retained a large surplus in their hands. So, in return for the low taxation, the government induced them to part with a portion for philanthropic activities. When the income tax was introduced in 1860, 'income from the property solely employed for religious or public charitable proposes' was exempt from the tax. Since then, the income derived from property held for charitable or religious purposes has enjoyed exemption, though the quantum of exemption has varied, with amendments to the Income Tax Act from time to time, to ensure that only those charitable and religious institutions which deserve them receive the benefit.[11] For instance, the Finance Act of 1948 gave companies and individuals 100 per cent tax exemption for charitable contributions for approved causes. The Companies Act of 1956 introduced Section 25 to enable individuals and corporations to set up non-profit companies for charitable purposes.

In contrast to the tax policy of the colonial government, however, the overall tax policy of the post-Independence government did not encourage genuine philanthropy because the effects of incentives given in one part were cancelled out by other tax and non-tax policies.

After the fifties, along with controls imposed on private enterprise through measures such as industrial licensing,[12] and an encroachment on private turf by the state which reserved certain fields for itself, heavy taxation was imposed on the wealthy to finance planned development and to bring about a more equitable distribution of income and wealth. The incidence of tax increased steeply by about 47.3 per cent between 1960–1 and 1972–3 for priority industries

---

[11] A study, *Taxation of Charitable Trusts and Institutions,* by the Direct Taxes Committee, The Institute of Chartered Accountants of India (New Delhi, First edition January 1978, Sixth edition February 2009), p. 20, mentions that sections in the Income Tax Act dealing with exemptions underwent major changes in several respects, principally in 1939, 1952, 1961, 1966, 1970, 1975, 1983, 1989, 1998, 2000, 2001, 2003, 2006, and 2008. The Finance Act of 1948 gave companies and individuals 100 per cent tax exemption for charitable contributions for approved causes.

[12] Industrial licensing was introduced by the Industries (Development and Regulation) Act of 1952.

and by about 54.3 per cent for non-priority industries. Personal rates of taxes at the margin went up from 77 per cent in 1960–1 to 97.75 in 1972–3, to become one of the highest in the world; and the ratio of tax revenue to national income went up from 6 per cent in 1951 to about 15 per cent in 1973.[13] Compulsory distribution of dividend till the measure was withdrawn, coupled with corporate taxation which took no account of the need for internally generated resources for expansion, made businesses divert available funds into working capital and development, rather than into philanthropy.

The consequent deceleration of economic growth, as well as changes in the easy relationship between the wealthy classes and government to one of distrust, had several adverse consequences for philanthropy. Paying heavy taxes for the sake of planned development and anti-poverty programmes came to be perceived as an alternative to charity and having to contribute anything additionally to charity was considered double jeopardy. High tax rates and the license-permit raj led to the growth of administrative and political corruption and a huge black money economy. The Wanchoo Committee, or The Direct Taxes Enquiry Committee (1972) estimated the income on which tax was evaded for 1968–9 to be rupees 14 billion.[14]

The presence of black money, as well as the changed outlook of the new generation of businessmen, encouraged conspicuous consumption rather than investment in productive activity or charitable institutions; at the same time, donations of large cash amounts, dropped anonymously into temple *hundi*s (donation boxes), became more common.

In a seeming paradox, there was simultaneously a spurt in the establishment of charitable trusts. But this reflected the presence of black money rather than a desire to give for public welfare.[15]

[13] S.V. Ghatalia, 'Taxation of Industry', in C.N. Vakil (ed.), *Industrial Development of India: Policy and Problems* (New Delhi: Orient Longman, 1973), pp. 227–9.

[14] Government of India, Ministry of Finance, *Report of the Direct Taxes Enquiry Committee: Final Report* (Wanchoo Committee Report) (1971), p. 107.

[15] Pushpa Sundar, *Beyond Business: From Merchant Charity to Corporate Citizenship* (New Delhi: Tata McGraw-Hill, 2000), p. 152.

For every genuine trust and foundation set up, there were several others which were mere names and tax dodges. The Direct Taxes Administration Enquiry Committee of 1958–9, under the chairmanship of Mahavir Tyagi, noted that loopholes in the provisions relating to charity in the Income Tax Act had helped the formation of pseudo charitable trusts which appropriated trust funds for their own business. Though the trust funds were invested and utilized for furthering the donor's business interests, the income of the trust fund continued to enjoy exemption from tax. It cited the case of the Walchand Diamond Jubilee Trust, in which an industrialist had created a trust for charitable purposes but stipulated that for a period of eighteen years the trust funds and the income there from were to be invested in the shares of a company through which the donor controlled other companies in which he was interested, and still continued to enjoy tax exemption.[16]

Similarly, by using the loophole relating to the interpretation of the word 'property', a trust could carry on business which had nothing to do with the primary object of the trust itself and still get exemption of tax for the income from this business. Another loophole allowed the trust to give priority to the relations and family members of the donor in carrying out its charitable activities and still enjoy tax exemption.

By and large, the Courts too interpreted the provisions allowing the loopholes in favour of the business donors.[17] This led the government to amend the Income Tax Act in 1961 on the lines suggested by the Inquiry Commission.

The most important change it brought was that 'charitable purpose' was more broadly defined as relief of the poor, education, medical relief, and the advancement of any other object of general public utility not involving the carrying on of any activity for profit.

---

[16] Government of India, Ministry of Finance, *Report of the Direct Taxes Administration Enquiry Committee, 1958–59* (New Delhi, 1959), pp. 179–81.

[17] As in CIT vs. Walchand Diamond Jubilee Trust (1958), 34 ITR, 228; J.K. Trusts Bombay vs. CIT (1957), 32 ITR, 535; and so on. Quoted in Government of India, Ministry of Finance, *Report of the Direct Taxes Administration Enquiry Committee, 1958–59*, pp. 179–81.

Second, it plugged the loopholes relating to expenditure of the income of the trust, and investment of trust funds, which could now only be in prescribed securities, and so sharpened the distinction between public and private benefit. To claim tax exemption, none of the authors, trustees, managers, or their relatives could enjoy any direct or indirect benefits from the trust income or property.

Further streamlining of trust management came after the Wanchoo Committee (The Direct Taxes Enquiry Committee, 1972) noted that misuse of tax incentives continued. On their recommendation, later Finance Acts incorporated the requirements that trusts above a certain minimum size must register themselves with the Income Tax authorities; furnish annual income tax returns; and have their accounts audited in a prescribed manner. Trusts were also banned from investing any of their funds in any business concern; and tax exempt status could be denied under certain conditions.

Simultaneously with curbing misuse of tax concessions, the government also dangled the carrot of further tax concessions to motivate industry to take up developmental work as well as to assist the growing voluntary sector on its own. In 1977, Section 35CC was introduced into the Income Tax Act to provide for 100 per cent deduction to a company in respect of expenditure incurred by it on approved programmes of rural development, which included construction and maintenance of rural roads, drainage and sanitary systems in rural areas, construction and maintenance of hospitals, dispensaries, and family planning centres, drinking water facilities, and so on.

This induced many companies to enter the field of rural development. But from 1983, such deductions were allowed only for contributions made to the Prime Minister's Rural Development Fund, and finally, pleading misuse, the tax incentive was withdrawn in 1983–4, and along with it, those whose reasons for community involvement were purely mercenary, also stopped their contribution.

As environmental issues came to the fore, Section 35CC (b) was introduced to allow 100 per cent deduction for conservation of natural resources; and Section 35AC was inserted to give 100 per cent exemption to donors who contribute to associations or institutions carrying out projects approved by the specially constituted fourteen-member National Committee for Promotion of Social and

Economic Welfare. The eligible projects covered a wide range of social development subjects including provision of drinking water, construction of housing for the economically weaker sections, promotion of sports, and so on.

In sum, the government's continuous effort has been to encourage philanthropy by providing incentives, but to simultaneously regulate public charitable trusts to ensure that funds meant for public benefit were not misused.

The Present Incentive Structure

Presently, Sections 11, 35AC, and 80G of the Income Tax Act provide varying degrees of encouragement.

- Section 11 exempts income of philanthropic organizations such as foundations from income tax, provided it is used for charitable purposes (as defined under the Act) and meets the conditions under Sections 12 and 12A.
- Section 80G and different sub-clauses of Section 35 allow donors to NPOs tax deductions ranging from 50 per cent to 100 per cent. Under Section 80G (of the Income Tax Act, 1961), donors to NPOs can offset 50 per cent of the donation from their taxable income, while under Section 35AC, which is more difficult to obtain, and available only for certain types of charitable activity, donors can offset 100 per cent of the donation.
- The government is also using different levels of tax deductions to steer philanthropy towards desired goals; for example, permissible deductions for donations to organizations doing research range from 125 to 200 per cent; statistical or social science research qualifies for a deduction of 125 per cent of the donation; scientific research for 175 per cent; and donations made to approved national institutions for an approved scientific research programme can claim 200 per cent deduction, with effect from 1 April 2011.[18]
- Sections 35CCC and CCD permit 150 per cent deduction for notified agricultural extension programmes or skill development

[18] http://www.randdcentre.com/benefits.htm.

projects. There is also 100 per cent deduction for contributions to projects for conservation of natural resources and environment, under different clauses of Section 35.

In all cases, the receiver must be tax exempt under Section 12A and have a certificate under any of the sections mentioned, that is, 80G or 35AC, or the other clauses of Section 35.

However, under 80G a donor can get an exemption only for a donation up to 10 per cent of his income, though there is no such restriction to claim under 35AC. A donor can give away 100 per cent of his income and claim exemption.

The National Policy on the Voluntary Sector had recommended encouragement to private giving by considering the option for tax rebates on donation of stocks and shares, but this has not been implemented. Nor is there any tax deduction for non-money contributions, that is, donations in kind.

Many HNWIs and analysts have argued for more tax incentives beyond those described. In the opinion of this author, however, India does not seem to be deficient in the giving of incentives. As the then Director of Charities Exemption in the Income Tax Department in Delhi said, in an interview with this author, 'If you have true charity in your heart, why do you need tax incentives to give?' Of course, not all will agree.

Behind the demand for more tax incentives and resistance on the part of the government to accede to the request is a trust deficit between the government and wealthy individuals, with the government inclined to suspect tax-evasion as a motive behind individuals establishing trusts on the one hand, and a belief on the part of HNWIs that they can make better social use of their money than the government, and should therefore be allowed to retain more wealth in their hands.

The Role of Inheritance Tax

Other than income tax, one other tax is believed to influence philanthropic giving, and this is inheritance tax. Estate duty or inheritance tax is primarily seen as a way of levelling wealth and opportunity, especially within each new generation, because inherited wealth increases inequality in society, and inherited economic power is inconsistent with the ideals of democracy. In particular, it is considered a way of preventing concentration of landed property in a few hands, also business interests. Though some analysts have argued that such levelling of wealth can reduce capitalist growth, most democracies, such as the USA and UK, have had such taxes without any evidence that it has impaired their growth.

But apart from its effect on inequality, inheritance tax is also seen as a way of encouraging philanthropy, because since most jurisdictions exempt gifts of charity given before death, this encourages the testators to give their assets in charity rather than have these taxed in the hands of their heirs. The high level of inheritance taxes which prevailed in the USA till recently is said to have actually encouraged large bequests to escape the high taxes and led to the establishment of the big foundations which have had a great impact on society, especially on research and development. By extension of this argument, since India does not have an inheritance tax, its absence is cited by many as the reason why Indian philanthropy is not as high as it should be given the volume of wealth in India.

A 2004 study done by the US government concluded that a permanent repeal of estate duty would reduce overall charitable giving by 6 to 12 per cent and that of charitable bequests by 16 to 28 per cent. It was therefore not considered desirable to do away with estate duty altogether. Instead the current low estate duty was adopted, inspite of the global trend to do away with it altogether. In India, the V.P. Singh government abolished estate taxes in 1985, which were absurdly pegged at the rate of 85 per cent.

One exception to the view that inheritance tax increases philanthropy is that of Raghuram Rajan, the former Governor of the Reserve Bank of India, who strongly disapproved of the idea of an inheritance tax. In his keynote address at the Festival of Ideas in February 2015, in Panaji, Rajan argued that it benefited only lawyers in society, and a better way than bringing people down was to take people up, by giving opportunities to many more people. According to him, it would be better to bring about a cultural change which pulls the rich towards philanthropy and makes them give back to society voluntarily. Rajan feels a better alternative is to 'incentivise' people to *create* wealth, which in turn has a spillover effect in the form of job creation, and then to encourage them to give it away for worthy causes which increase opportunities for the underprivileged. This is a view to which this author also subscribes, especially since an inheritance tax may increase tax evasion and compliance costs may far outstrip the amounts collected. Given the strong family and kin networks in India, such a tax is likely to be strongly resisted, and if enacted, evaded.

In India it is not only inherited business wealth which is a problem. Wealth and politics reinforce each other, and a pernicious form of rentier capitalism is in evidence, which an inheritance tax alone will not address.[19] While concentration of wealth is evident in business families, so also is large scale philanthropy. But there is less evidence of dynastic wealth accumulated by politicians, since Independence, going into genuine large scale philanthropy, though several of the politicians have set up trusts which, not infrequently, are used to dispense patronage.

For lack of empirical evidence it is difficult to say where the balance lies, pro- or anti-inheritance tax. Even though in his opening remarks on his taxation proposals in the 2015–16 budget of the Government of India, the Finance Minister acknowledged that taxation is not only a measure to raise revenues but an important instrument of social and economic engineering, he not only did not introduce an inheritance tax, but also abolished the wealth tax with effect from 2016–17. The reason given was, it would reduce the compliance burden, given its high cost of collection and low yield. At the same time, in order to reduce economic inequalities, the existing surcharge was increased by 2 per cent on the super-rich with a taxable income of over rupees 10 million. The surcharge may dip into the pockets of the very rich who give to major philanthropic initiatives, so there is not much hope that the abolition of the wealth tax will lead to more philanthropy.

At the same time, the new budget introduced new incentives for philanthropic giving in the form of tax exemptions for donations to two new endowment Funds set up by the government—the Swachha Bharat Kosh and the Clean Ganga Fund—which are now eligible for 100 per cent deduction under Section 80G of the Income Tax Act. In

[19] See Ashoka Mody and Michael Walton, 'Story of a Fraying Capitalism', *The Indian Express*, 14 May 2014.

a way, this amounts to the state competing with private organizations for philanthropic funds and again raises the question of whether the state is the better spender, or private agency. Moreover, as has been mentioned elsewhere in this book (see Chapter 11, on education) and in other works by me,[20] experiments by the state to set itself up as a philanthropist, as in the case of the Bharat Shiksha Kosh, where the Central government created an endowment to attract private charitable funds for education, have not been very successful. The Chhattisgarh government too had stated its intention to pool all the mandated CSR contributions into a Development Fund to be allocated by the State, but the idea had to be aborted after opposition to it from many quarters.

Tax Incentives as Drivers of Philanthropy?

By and large, tax incentives are favoured as encouraging philanthropy. The *World Wealth Report 2010* documents a growing trend for 'giving while living', as a result of which there is greater emphasis on incorporating giving strategies into donors' ongoing wealth accumulation and capital-preservation plans. This, the report argues, may lead to more interest in tax incentives.

In the Barclays Wealth report, 2013, 52 per cent of those surveyed said that the most effective way for the state to increase donations would be to increase tax breaks to offset charitable giving. However, it also says, many believe that the state's role should be restricted and that it should avoid intervening in philanthropic activities. Some of this is based on a lack of trust in the political process, with 59 per cent of the wealthy agreeing that this distrust 'has prompted them to give

[20] Pushpa Sundar, 'No Government Business In Philanthropy', Web Outlook India, 19 March 2015, http://www.outlookindia.com/article/No-Government-Business-In-Philanthropy/293764. Pushpa Sundar, 'Putting Bharat on Firm Foundations: Decentralized Financing of Rural Development', *Financial Express*, Monday, 30 July 2012, http://epaper.financialexpress.com/49627/Indian-Express/30-July-2012#page/9/1.
Pushpa Sundar, 'State Philanthropy: A New Paradigm for Financing Social Development?', 8 May 2006, http://pushpasundar.blogspot.in/2006/05/state-philanthropy-new-paradigm-for.html#more.

directly to charities', where they feel their money can make a bigger impact, rather than indirectly through taxation.[21]

In India too, the Bain and Company Report 2012 found that many of the donors surveyed have asserted that tax incentives are necessary. A blanket 100 per cent deduction on contributions to registered charitable organizations would, it is said, incentivize more donors, as it does elsewhere.

Though businessmen themselves, in personal discussions, generally disclaim tax incentives as a major reason for engaging in philanthropy or social responsibility, they also simultaneously complain, especially through their associations, about the inadequacy of such incentives. In a recent survey (the Times Foundation—TNS Survey, 2008), a little over half the eighty-two companies surveyed stated that they were *not in favour* of the government's proposal to abolish Section 80G, granting tax benefits to funds allocated to development projects. They felt this would discourage CSR spending. The rest did not think the proposal would have any impact, or were not very concerned about it.

In India, tax incentives appear to have played an important role in moving the corporate world into certain socially desirable activities, especially in the context of high tax regimes. As one second generation industrialist from a leading business house in the South admitted candidly, he personally would not have gone into backward areas or done any rural development but for the government's pressure and encouragement via tax concessions. Opinion is divided on whether this is a good thing or bad. Some argue that giving tax incentives distorts or vitiates what business wants to do or can do best. For instance, some believe that rural development was artificially thrust on industry and did not come spontaneously. Without the lure of tax incentives, companies might have preferred to invest in some other social project, and that that is the reason why very few companies have been successful in their rural development projects.

Though the larger number seem to favour tax incentives, there are also others, including President Barack Obama, who are against tax incentives for philanthropy on the ground that if you are really charitable, you do not need incentives.[22]

---

[21] Quoted by Chapman, 'The Role of the State'.
[22] Obama, quoted in Chapman, 'The Role of the State'.

A study, 'Richer Lives: Why Rich People Give', 2013,[23] on what drives rich people to give to charity, based on new research with over eighty wealthy UK donors, found that only a third (32 per cent) of all the donors interviewed cited tax reliefs on charitable donations as an incentive behind their giving decisions, with matched funding schemes seen as a better incentive. Rich donors acknowledged that many important issues in relation to tax reliefs for philanthropy remain to be addressed, including donors' ability to redirect tax to their favoured causes, or 'hypothecation'.

This indicates that there is no agreement that tax incentives are an important factor in giving. Though many countries including the UK and the USA have generous tax regimes, the fact is, how effective tax incentives *really* are in stimulating philanthropy is unknown because there is as yet no international research comparing the precise effects of different tax reliefs on levels of giving.[24]

Tax deductibility does not appear to be a major consideration in responding to requests for small donations; the cause or the need to oblige the person making the request is more important. Tax deductibility becomes significant, especially for companies, only when major donations to outside organizations such as a university, a management institute, or arts centre are under consideration, or when major resources need to be committed for a company's own project.

For companies, more important than tax incentives, or as important, are policies which affect corporate earnings and the ability to retain profits. In America, research showed that giving by the country's wealthiest people began to decline as a proportion of their income when the falling tax rates of the 1980s meant that they had less incentive to make donations.[25]

As far as responsible behaviour towards the environment is concerned, proper pricing of scarce goods, especially public goods like water, so that it reflects the true and not the subsidized value to society, is more important.

---

[23] Breeze, Beth and Theresa Lloyd. 2013. *Richer Lives: Why Rich People Give*.

[24] Chapman, 'The Role of the State'.

[25] *The Economist*, 'Philanthropy in America', 30 May–5 June 1998: 17–18.

The lowering of personal and corporate tax rates in India is too recent to assess the impact it will have on charitable giving. And since tax incentives have been misused in India, it is unlikely that the quantum of incentives will be increased. Hospitals, schools, and colleges are established as charitable concerns to gain tax and other benefits rather than as a purely altruistic gesture, and are then used as commercial concerns. Government attitudes towards incentives have, therefore, hardened.

Clearly, the last word is yet to be said on whether tax incentives in fact encourage philanthropy or socially responsible behaviour. Unfortunately, there is no research or evidence to show whether any of India's great philanthropists like Jamsetji Tata or his sons, Lala Sri Ram, G.D. Birla, and others were at all seduced by or ever availed of tax incentives. But it appears unlikely.

More than tax policy, a greater influence on philanthropy would appear to be whether the society has a culture of giving or not. Every year, the Giving USA Foundation publishes 'Giving USA: The Annual Report on Philanthropy'. According to the 2011 report, even in 2009, when the global financial and economic crisis reached its peak, Americans spent US$ 291 billion on charity, that is, they continued to donate because of compassion, and without thought of tax breaks. Some one million charitable organizations operating in the United States collectively raised nearly US$ 1.5 trillion in revenues during the 2010 calendar year. This amount is higher than the total amount of income tax revenues collected that year by the US government.

Overall, it appears that non-economic considerations may matter more than tax incentives to those for whom philanthropy is a mission, and that even for others, may matter only at the margin. Sometimes recognition, or some other non-material consideration such as a vision of national greatness, or the need to memorialize a beloved person is more important to a donor than tax incentives. The British, recognizing this, had knighted philanthropists or conferred titles such as Dewan Bahadur and Rai Bahadur on those who had contributed liberally to officially approved projects. After Independence, however, official awards ceased to recognize philanthropy as an endeavour worthy of honour, and few philanthropists have figured in the prestigious Padma Awards, for philanthropy. Nor have there been any private initiatives for recognizing outstanding philanthropists. One small beginning has been made in the annual publication of the Hurun List of Philanthropists. It acts not only to recognize generosity but also uses peer pressure or the name and shame tactic to encourage more giving. Many more such initiatives are necessary. Giving without expectation of reward is entirely laudable, but who can remain unpleased by the recognition of their generosity?

What all the above argues for is not a scrapping of incentives but a more systematic investigation into the connection between tax incentives and philanthropy, into malpractices by charitable organizations, and into how the positive effects of incentives can be enhanced.

5

Give, Give Wisely

Promoting Philanthropy

There is no doubt that philanthropy needs publicity. As we have discovered, tax relief, public recognition or personal satisfaction are not the main reasons why people give to charity. At its core, philanthropy is underpinned by humanity's inability to be indifferent to other people's suffering. Acknowledging and promoting these elements of human nature in all of us will produce the best possible publicity for philanthropy.[1]

In 1995, a workshop brought together thirty-two representatives of funding agencies, corporations, and civil society in New Delhi to discuss Indian philanthropy. It noted that while the voluntary sector and civil society had grown exponentially in the last few decades, the resources for their work had not kept pace. Most funds for their work came from government and foreign donors. Each of these sources had their own drawbacks. Government funds were often insufficient, inflexible, and subject to red tape, while foreign funds were dependent on geopolitical considerations and therefore unstable. There

---

[1] Olga Alekseeva, *History of Trust in Distrustful Times* (Moscow: Ekksmo Publishing, 2007).

was, therefore, a need to promote plural sources of funds for social development outside the aegis of the government to supplement government and foreign assistance and to provide social action agencies choice and independence of action.[2]

It further noted that traditionally, such funds came from philanthropy though there was inadequate public knowledge of the need for, the potential of, as well as appreciation of private philanthropy. Moreover, it had been dormant for several decades since Independence and needed to be stimulated once again. The amounts contributed were also far less than what a country of India's size and wealth could give. Worse, the impact of what was donated was below par because of inefficiencies in the philanthropic ecosystem. Philanthropic attitudes and practices needed a reorientation to incorporate new developments and meet the needs of the time. There were several constraints (listed in Chapter 3) which restrained philanthropy from reaching its full potential. The principal among these was lack of knowledge of and exposure to emerging social issues among donors, and a lack of trust in social organizations' integrity and efficiency.

Eight years after the above-mentioned workshop, Mr Narayana Murthy, while delivering the Maulana Azad Memorial Lecture in March 2003 on the 'Travails of Philanthropy', made essentially the same points about what is holding back Indian philanthropy.[3]

The Bain and Company's *Annual Philanthropy Report* 2012, based on a 2011 survey of HNWIs, reiterated many of the same points, particularly the lack of accountability and transparency among NGOs being the most serious obstacle to increased giving, indicating that little progress had been made in over fifteen years in overcoming the constraints. The other reasons mentioned by Bain and Company's survey included unfriendly tax laws for donation, low awareness of ways of routing money, peers influencing amount of contribution, capital requirements of own business, and the need to focus on wealth creation before wealth distribution.

---

[2] The workshop was organized by Pushpa Sundar and Dr M.B. Athreya in collaboration with Partners in Change, New Delhi, in December 1995.
[3] Dr N.R. Narayana Murthy, 'Travails of Philanthropy in India', Azad Memorial Lectures, Indian Council of Cultural Relations, New Delhi, 2003.

The Institutional Infrastructure Deficit

What is significant is that though separated by long gaps of time, all three analyses of constraints to philanthropy and its optimum use indicated that the problem lay in the absence of an institutional infrastructure to support, coordinate, and promote philanthropic effort. Though chambers of commerce and industry are well established and play an important role in the corporate world, there are virtually no parallel agencies to assist, coordinate, and improve the philanthropic role of the corporate world.

The 1995 workshop had in particular noted that the impact of what is being given was less than optimal because of the absence of such an organization which would collect and disseminate information of all kinds, promote professionalism in donor organizations, and act as a forum for interaction among those engaged in philanthropic activities. It felt that building of alliances or networks among donors was absolutely necessary. While there were associations of voluntary organizations and intermediary organizations to network and service NGOs with information, training, and advocacy support, such as Voluntary Action Network India (VANI), Association of Voluntary Agencies in Rural Development (AVARD), Voluntary Health Association of India (VHAI), and Society for Participatory Research in Asia (PRIA); and private business had chambers, there were hardly any organizations directed at donors to motivate and assist them in giving and to ensure efficient utilization of funds; which would promote interaction between donors and NGOs, between donors themselves, and between the government and donors. It concluded, therefore, that there was an urgent need for a national organization to promote not only a culture of giving but informed giving.

In the speech mentioned above, Narayana Murthy too emphasized the need to bring all philanthropic organizations into a network to share ideas and resources. In India, he said, there is no institution within the private philanthropy world which is systematically looking at issues of public policy and linkage between the government and private philanthropy, like the business chambers do.

Finally, Arpan Sheth of Bain and Company, in an interview to a newspaper, also underlined the need for the development of philanthropic organizations which will spend more time nurturing givers, working with them, advising them, and improving their competence.[4]

The fact is, India needs not one, but several different types of organizations to address the several aspects of the problem. One lacuna to be addressed is the lack of authoritative knowledge of various aspects of philanthropy because of a lack of research. Though philanthropy enlists only a small portion of a society's resources, and operates at the margin of the economy, its performance will improve only if one understands how it works, and why it does not, and how this can be changed. Though research will not by itself promote giving, research on philanthropic motivations, interests, practices, and impact will increase an understanding of how philanthropy works and improve the practice.

It is difficult to see how appropriate promotion strategies can be identified, developed, or implemented without a concrete understanding of existing attitudes, perceptions, and practices in the field. Equally, surveys to provide quantitative data as well as qualitative case studies are needed.

However, those engaged in philanthropy and those who wish to promote it must consider how such research may be financed as a public good. It is one of the biggest challenges facing the promotion of philanthropy.

Other kinds of organizations in the philanthropy space must be:

- Motivational organizations, engaged in creating a culture of giving
- Advocacy organizations, for securing from government an enabling environment for philanthropy, as well as policies to enhance social sector work
- A Clearing House of Information—organizations which collect and disseminate information relevant to philanthropic organizations
- Organizations to improve the credibility as well as capacity of NGOs, since that is one of the biggest constraints to giving

---

[4] Malia Politzer, 'Arpan Seth: Organizations Need to Spend More Time Nurturing Givers', *LiveMint*, 20 March 2012.

- Networks or associations of donors, including a national body as well as regional associations, which would also play a convening role for peer exchanges, as well as a donor education role
- Finally, an independent regulatory body which would oversee not only foundations and trusts but also NGOs, on the lines of the Charities Commission of Britain; a quasi-judicial independent body to adjudicate on legal problems of the philanthropic sector, and ensure discipline and accountability to it

Admittedly, the Indian context is very different from that of the USA, and something which has been successful there may not necessarily succeed in India. Nevertheless, it is instructive to take a brief look at the infrastructure for philanthropy in the USA, and how it developed.

Development of Infrastructure in the USA

The USA has several organizations working to promote and oversee philanthropy, such as the Council on Foundations, the Foundation Centre, Business Committee for the Arts, Centre for Corporate Public Involvement, the Conference Board, National Charities Information Bureau, Regional Association of Grantmakers, and others. Several universities also have centres for research on philanthropy, such as the City University's Centre for the Study of Philanthropy.

Many of these organizations were a response to a crisis facing either the donor community or the society at large, which in turn threatened the long-term business interests of the donors. Equally, the associations became necessary because of the increasing complexity of national political and economic life, which made it necessary to organize such associations to obtain relevant information to keep abreast of events, and to lobby at the national level. The state did not play an encouraging or promotive role in the formation of associations. In fact, it was the potential confrontation with the state which acted as a catalyst.

As philanthropic foundations and non-profit organizations expanded exponentially, and the demand for funds from business increased, businesses began to look for organized and federated fundraising, as well as to new kinds of organizations to help them respond appropriately and effectively to the flood of appeals for charity. Sometimes existing trade associations took on the role, and at other times new organizations were established.

After the Great Depression of the Thirties, there was a spurt of foundations due to tax incentives offered, and as the number increased, so too did their clout in public policy. There was a conviction in the business community that the growth of federal power could only be curbed by a concerted effort to marshal the financial and cultural resources of the private sector. This led to many more associations, such as the National Conference on Solicitations, to provide opportunities for businessmen to meet and discuss their donation problems and related issues, as well as broad considerations of public policy. The Council on Financial Aid to Education, established in 1953, became a major influence in fostering interest and support to education among business executives.

However, as their clout increased, the foundation world came under attack from Congress and others. The organizational consequence of such attacks was to bring the foundations closer for common action, leading to the formation of the Council of Foundations in 1949.

Later developments led to the emergence of new intermediary organizations to address new issues and challenges, and to give voice to particular types of constituencies such as women, minorities, and international funders.[5]

Arguably one of the most significant investments in philanthropic infrastructure globally has been the creation of associations of grantmakers and donors. Such membership organizations seek to support giving through the promotion of best practices and the development of members' knowledge and giving skills. Today, grantmaker associations exist in over sixty countries, although many are still in their infancy.

In sum, three main factors played an important role in the development of a promotional and coordination infrastructure: one,

[5] Pushpa Sundar, mimeo, 'National Organizations of Business Donors in the USA: Growth and Development', Paper prepared for the Johns Hopkins International Fellowship Programme in Philanthropy, Baltimore, May 1995.

threats and opportunities posed by legislative or regulatory actions, such as congressional investigations; two, the need for networking and coordinated action to meet the challenges of proliferating fund-seeking organizations; and three, the need for special groups to find a voice and get a hearing in a larger grouping.

Professor Paula Johnson of Harvard University sees four important 'waves' of promotion activity in the United States. The first wave focused primarily on improving the legal and regulatory environment for philanthropy; the second employed a broad-based public awareness campaign aimed at substantially expanding the portion of the population active in philanthropy and volunteering; the third was characterized by a concerted effort to grow the number, reach, and size of community foundations; and the fourth wave sought to promote philanthropy around the enormous anticipated 'intergenerational transfer of wealth'.[6]

Indian Experience of Building Infrastructure

In contrast to the US, the Indian experience in building an infrastructure for philanthropy has been very recent and very meagre. Of the three factors mentioned above, it is largely the second factor, namely the need for networking and coordinated action to meet the challenges of proliferating fund-seeking organizations, which has spurred these efforts.

One of the first experiments at creating an organization to promote philanthropy was the outcome of the 1995 Workshop on Philanthropy, mentioned above. The Indian Centre for Philanthropy, later renamed Sampradaan Indian centre for Philanthropy (SICP), was established in May 1996, under the Societies Registration Act of 1860, as a national non-profit organization for promoting and strengthening philanthropy. There were at the time two somewhat similar organizations, one in Mumbai—the Centre for Advancement of Philanthropy—and one in Delhi—the Charities Aid Foundation.

[6] Paula D. Johnson, Stephen P. Johnson, Andrew Kingman, 'Promoting Philanthropy: Global Challenges and Approaches,' The Philanthropic Initiative, *Allavida,* December 2004, International Network on Strategic Philanthropy, Bertelsmann Stiftung, Gütersloh, Germany.

Both were new, small, and feeling their way around. The Workshop had taken note of these organizations but felt that that should not deter the formation of Sampradaan, for a country like India needed not one but many such organizations. The experience of Sampradaan is given here in some detail to illustrate the problems of creating a promotional infrastructure, but more importantly, because its demise holds useful lessons for future efforts.

But before that, one must acknowledge that such efforts as have been there at infrastructure building have been due to the initiative and financial support of foreign donor organization such as the Ford Foundation, the Aga Khan Foundation, and the Asia Foundation. The Ford Foundation in particular played a convening role to bring different actors together to discuss the need for such organizations, and financially supported fledgling efforts such as Sampradaan, Centre for Advancement of Philanthropy, Credibility Alliance, Charities Aid Foundation India, and others. The Ford and Asia Foundation played a part in exposing Indian civil society activists and organizations to developments abroad, and the Asia Foundation in particular helped to bring such intermediary organizations in South and South East Asia into a network of philanthropy organizations called the Asia Pacific Philanthropy Consortium. The only Indian organizations which have taken an interest in promoting indigenous philanthropy and philanthropic organizations have been the Tata Trusts.

Where these donors faltered was either in providing short-term project funding rather than sustained long-term commitments which would have allowed the emerging shoots to mature, or in making too premature judgements about impacts. Sampradaan exemplifies the shortcomings of such an approach.

Sampradaan

Sampradaan's logo embodied Kalidas's verse, 'Noble men, like clouds, acquire goods [wealth] only to redistribute them, just as the sun draws water from the sea, only to return it in the form of rain.'[7] Recognizing the need both to promote giving and to

---

[7] From *Raghuvamsa* by Kalidas, India's classical poet and dramatist of fifth century AD.)

professionalize the practice for better impact, it adopted the motto 'Give, Give Wisely'.

Its mission was threefold: to promote a philanthropy movement in the country which encourages organized, informed, effective, and regular giving of time, talent, and other resources to meet important societal needs; to secure and maintain an environment conducive to philanthropy by increasing awareness and appreciation of its role by people, corporations, and the state; and to improve philanthropic practice by offering professional inputs.

Over time, it defined three interlinked sub-roles for itself in pursuit of its objectives, namely:

- A Resource Center role: SICP would do research, documentation, publication, and dissemination; act as a clearinghouse of information on national and international philanthropy; and be a catalyst for promotion of new ideas and concepts.
- An Advocacy role: to secure an enabling environment, especially through related tax and law reforms on behalf of the voluntary sector in India as a whole, and
- A Donor Advisory and Convening role: to undertake motivational campaigns, workshops, and conferences to disseminate ideas, to build skills in strategic giving, and to promote networking.

Its primary constituency was to be organized donors (foundations, trusts, and companies with an interest in social development), and the government, though the ultimate constituency was NGOs, and through them, the community as a whole. As it happened, Sampradaan fell between two stools: it started out to be a donor's forum on the lines of grantmaker associations in the USA, but could not muster support among donors. In spite of a concerted membership drive to attract donors, very few of its members were major philanthropists. In any case, grant making was not very common in India.

On the other hand, NGOs found its services of information and advocacy more useful and wanted to become members. But here it was in competition with networks of NGOs such as VANI and VHAI, which were playing the coordination and assistance role for NGOs. Ultimately, instead beceoming a network of donors, it assumed the character of an intermediary organization mediating between NGOs and donors, as well as undertaking a number of activities useful to both.

Between 1996 and 2014 it undertook five major types of activities, namely:

- Promoting a culture of giving by raising the awareness of the need for philanthropy
- Advocacy with the government to secure a more enabling environment
- Research, documentation, and dissemination
- Resource centre activities
- Promotion of community philanthropy through the establishment of community foundations.

One of the first tasks it set for itself was to build a solid corpus of knowledge on sources of Indian philanthropy. And this turned out to be its strongest contribution. It brought out eight monographs on leading Indian foundations of the time, including the Sir Ratan Tata Trust, The K.K. Birla Foundation, the Rashtriya Gramin Vikas Nidhi (RGVN), and others; a Directory of Indian Donor Organisations, updated several times; an online compilation of donors funding women and child issues; and A Manual of Good Giving. Small Occasional Papers on different themes were brought out, as were Fact Sheets and pamphlets on social issues needing urgent attention. They carried information on the organizations dealing with those issues, and opportunities for funding. A series of thirteen Fact Sheets, titled 'Laws and NPOs', gave information on how to start a trust, on tax incentives available, and on the legal and fiscal requirements under different Indian laws applicable to Indian non-profits.

It researched on different important sources of Indian philanthropy, such as business, religious institutions, individuals, and so on, and presented the findings in the form of books and reports. The research on evolution of business philanthropy in India resulted in the book *Beyond Business, From Merchant Charity to Indian Citizenship*; case studies on religious giving were published as *For God's Sake: Religious Charity and Social Development in India.*

To understand the patterns of individual giving in India, it conducted the first ever survey in India on individual giving and published the results in a book titled *Investing in Ourselves: Giving and Fundraising in India,* which also included case studies of the methods used by different NGOs to raise money for their work.

Other research included a survey of volunteering, and a Reader on Community Foundations to familiarize people with community foundations—a concept of philanthropy new in India. Perhaps the most seminal piece of work was on charities administration in India for the Planning Commission, which reviewed all the agencies involved in regulating philanthropy, such as the Charities Commissioners, the Income Tax department, and so on, and made recommendations for improvements.

There were plans to do research on topics such as philanthropy for education, disaster relief funds—how utilized?, national funds for education and for culture, and to develop Indian case material for training in grant making on subjects such as programme design; strategic planning; project/grantee identification; grant appraisal; grant monitoring and evaluation, and so on.

As part of its research programme, Sampradaan also built up a small information resource centre for those interested in philanthropy. For many years it was the 'go to' organization for information on Indian philanthropy, offering advice and guidance to NGOs and potential donors, national and international. It marked its presence on the national and international non-profit scene, participating in a variety of international fora, conferences, and study tours, making presentations on Indian philanthropy to bring visibility to it.

Its monthly print newsletter, 'Sampradaan', which later became online, reported on events, research, good practices, and developments in Indian as well as global philanthropy and civil society—a niche which needed to be filled.

On the advocacy front, it organized or coordinated meetings on policy issues related to philanthropy and submitted memoranda to the government, advocating changes in tax laws, orientation programmes for Income tax Officers, and for setting up a National Charities Commission. It collaborated with other organizations to advocate a new Societies Registration Act, reform of the FCRA Act, and so on.

For donor education and networking, it organized workshops for trusts: several annual conferences on different themes for donors, such as Making Partnerships Work; conducted the first ever NGO–Donor Dialogue to discuss issues related to funding; and again organized the first and only one of its kind workshop called 'Giving Wisely' for training professional staff of donor organizations in grant making.

To improve the credibility and efficiency of NGOs, it ran several workshops in UP, Bihar, Maharashtra, and Jharkhand on good governance, titled 'Effective Boards for Effective Governance'.

To create a culture of giving, it had planned a motivational campaign for giving—which unfortunately never took off—as well as a school motivational programme to encourage values of giving among children, which also was short lived.

In recent years it concentrated its energies on promoting community philanthropy by popularizing the concept of community foundations. It partnered with ten emergent community foundations in seven states of India, among them the Valley Dew Community Foundation (VDCF), established by the people of Mukkodlu village in Kodagu district of Karnataka, the Sainik Foundation (SF), Uttarakhand and Uttar Pradesh, and the West Bengal Community Foundation (WBCF), West Bengal. These organizations have succeeded in establishing thirty-one local funds soon after their emergence.

But alas, the big plans and dreams it had could not all materialize. After eighteen years of solid contribution to the field in the face of heavy odds, it rang down the curtain in December 2014. It was a sad end to a brave experiment which failed due to three major interrelated issues: one, it was ahead of its time; interest in philanthropy was yet to take off as it did with the beginning of the twenty-first century; two, lack of sustained funding, which was related to the first issue; and three, inability to find committed and capable management and professional staff willing to work for the kind of salaries it was able to afford.

The initial funds came from donations from founder members, and grants and donations from the Sir Ratan Tata Trust, the Sir Dorab Tata Trust, Housing and Development Finance Corporation (HDFC), and Gujarat Ambuja Cement, among others, but it was not till it received a grant for $60,000 from the Ford Foundation in December 1996, to be spent over three years, that it was able to begin operations. Later donors included the Asia Foundation, the Aga Khan Foundation, the Japan Foundation, as well as government, who recognized the good work it was doing. The Ford Foundation and the Tata Trusts repeated their grants once more. Yet it could manage an average annual budget ranging around rupees 3 to 5 million per annum. Most of the support it received was for particular projects, with little left to meet administrative costs and to pay good salaries. Its corpus of approximately rupees 2.6 million in 1999, grown to about rupees 6 million when it closed, was not sufficient to support a big organization. The self generated funds like sale of publications and fees from some of the workshops did not add up to much.

Intermediary organizations which play the roles, and undertake the activities described above, are in a particularly unfortunate situation as far as securing funding from the government is concerned because they work on cross-sectoral issues of importance to the whole sector, and are therefore not considered under various departmental schemes of different ministries; do not fall under any one state jurisdiction; and are not grassroots service providers and therefore not NGOs as interpreted by Government agencies. While mother NGOs are recognized as necessary for enhancing NGO capacity, the value of the kind of organization described above, an intermediary organization which enhances the ability of private donors to contribute to social development, and of the whole voluntary sector, is not recognized.

It is difficult for such organizations to raise money from the public through donations because their work is not easily understood by the general public. The role of research and advocacy is not appreciated by most individual donors, especially because there is no emotional content to the work, such as obtains in NGOs for children, or the disabled, or even the environment, where the end result is more readily visible to the public.

Though Sampradaan managed to get project support from institutional donors, what was required was core organizational support for a long time, because there is no other way in which these organizations can support themselves.

For this reason it is important that government or enlightened donors extend support to such national apex organizations working on behalf of the whole sector to improve and strengthen charitable practice. Funding of such organizations to promote and help the healthy growth of charity is in the interest not only of private donors but also the government, which does not have enough resources itself to undertake all the social development work that is necessary. Since it offers inducements in the form of tax incentives to promote charity, it is surely the government's responsibility to see that charitable resources are used wisely and for maximum impact.

Unfortunately, the few foundations who supported SICP had a short horizon and judged results and impact in a time horizon of three to five years, whereas social change, especially when one is operating in green field areas such as this, requires a longer time horizon.

The problems that SICP faced with funding are in fact a critique of the new 'philanthrocapitalism' (see Chapter 11), with its emphasis on quick results and strict guidelines for impact measurement. It also shows why the older model of philanthropy, whether under the control and guidance of an experienced philanthropist patron or the arms length method of the older Ford Foundation, which was more relaxed about the timelines and outcomes, was better.

The difficulties faced by Sampradaan are endemic to the social sector, but with somewhat better funding, many organizations soldier on, though all too often they cease to be effective. Few have the courage to close down and transfer their funds to another organization as SICP decided to do. In 2015 it turned over its corpus to Dasra, a philanthropic intermediary in Mumbai.

One of the key problems in attracting membership from donors was that Sampradaan was established by professionals and not by philanthropists themselves. Even the Board did not have a heavyweight philanthropist, and hence could not use peer pressure to bring donors to the table. It set out to be an organization to support donors without any donor interest or support. At the time, donors felt that if they needed any advice they could hire a consultant for the purpose. There was no need to interact with peers to learn from each other. Without any buy-in from the constituency for which it was supposed to exist, its programmes lacked demand. A key lesson, therefore, is that for a promotional infrastructure organization to be successful, peer pressure is very important in drawing like minded individuals to an organization. Had the organization been led by a Ratan Tata or a Narayana Murthy, it would have had a better chance of survival.

Another weak link was in finding personnel with the right managerial capabilities who also had a good understanding of the social sector. Even more than just managerial capability, an organization of this sort, starting up in an uncertain terrain, needs entrepreneurial skills, and one or two angel investors or godfathers who both mentor and support the venture until it becomes self-supporting. From hindsight, it is clear that its leadership was not entrepreneurial, and for the most part it was led by professionals with strong academic interests, which is why it built up a strong research programme, but could not go to scale.

Another lesson was that any organization which deals with public goods, such as advocacy and research, faces a problem of free loading—beneficiaries cannot be identified and made to pay. The key question, therefore, is how to make such intermediary organizations sustainable.

Finally, though India needs a large mega organization to promote and coordinate philanthropy on different fronts, the time was not ripe for it. A new organization, working in an uncertain terrain with limited funding, cannot afford to have an ambitious scope and must limit the things it will do, however important all the other tasks are. It must work thematically with clarity of objectives. Sampradaan tried to do too much at a time when society was not ready for it. There needed to be a focused and phased approach and clarity of goals.

Biswajit Sen, an independent consultant, who was called in at the instance of one of the donors in 2003 to review SICP's work remarked, after noting that it had done remarkable work in a short time and against many constraints, that Sampradaan was ahead of its time. He said, 'As seen in the environmental analysis, the private philanthropy sector in India is still in the early stages of institutional evolution and needs to evolve to doing several new things in innovative and futuristic ways. Hence an organisation like Sampradaan has to look to the future possibilities rather than present service demand.' He added that though the need for such a role may not be immediately appreciated by funders, 'when one views a sectoral, promotional and development organisation, such as Sampradaan, the role chosen by it cannot be restricted to the current demand for services by different organisations in the sector'.

He recommended that for the immediate future, SICP should position itself as a think tank, working on policy research, taking up donor/government funded research projects on issues of policy planning and inter-linkages in the areas of charity, philanthropy, NGOs, and related issues. It should also strive to position itself as an advocate of the civil society world with the government.

But before it could do that, it needed to find the funding which was hard to come by. And so, sadly, the curtains came down in January 2015.

How visionary and how necessary such an organization was can be seen from the fact that even today, in conversations with donors, and in the annual surveys on philanthropic trends in India conducted by Bain and Company since 2010, one of the reasons most often cited for a less than optimal level of philanthropy is the lack of organizations which can provide information on emerging development issues; who, if anybody, is addressing them and how; and lack of credible organizations with integrity to support. It was these very concerns which brought SICP into existence and which it tried to address. What it set out to do remains an unfinished agenda, since there is still no national organization which is doing all that SICP set out to do. Fortunately, a few more organizations have emerged to fill some, if not all of the gaps.

Other Initiatives

As mentioned earlier, Mumbai has the Centre for Advancement of Philanthropy (CAP), whose strength is legal advice, especially to would-be donors and the smaller trusts. It also keeps its members informed of policy changes, especially in the taxation field. Together with Samhita, a philanthropic initiative that aims to create an enabling ecosystem for NGOs, donors, volunteers, service providers, and other support organizations, it is preparing to create a network or association of donors.

Bain and Company is filling some of the information and data gap with its annual surveys of philanthropy since 2010, which hopefully will build up good trend data on Indian philanthropy, as well as sectoral knowledge.

The Give India Foundation, also Mumbai based, has been instrumental in promoting collective philanthropy, helping all the donors, however small, who would like to donate for social change through NGOs, to find the right match and to channel donations online. Most notably, it has actualized Sampradaan's idea of a national campaign to promote giving through its Joy of Giving Week—a nationwide campaign to promote giving. It has also started the First Givers Club (FGC), a platform to bring together likeminded individuals interested in philanthropy. Its membership as well as the amounts donated are going up steadily with the greater interest in philanthropy today.

The FGC has helped its members move from ad hoc giving to more structured giving for greater impact. Apart from personal giving, some members have turned champions for a cause, and they leverage their networks to raise funds for particular causes. Many of the members are first time philanthropists who find the support services of FGC, like audits, annual and monthly budgets for their giving and releasing funds when required, very valuable, unlike the big philanthropists who have been in the game for long. The FGC helps professionals who want to give to find a cause and/or follow through with significant engagement of time and money. As a result, individuals and professionals are getting together to seed and fund initiatives in a collaborative manner.

Also Mumbai-based is Dasra, which means 'enlightened giving' in Sanskrit, established in 1999 as a membership organization. Its main constituency is HNWIs, and it is motivating them to give strategically for issues that matter.

Philanthropic acts of giving are very network-based and dependent on who one knows or who one trusts. Moreover, the challenges in giving in India, such as the absence of a centralized data base of NGOs and lack of transparency of many potential recipient organizations, not only NGOs, make due diligence unduly complex and challenging for HNW individuals and genuinely committed philanthropists. Dasra addresses itself to this problem, as well as that of low impact of giving.[8]

[8] Neera Nundy, quoted in 'Creating a Community of Givers', *Business India Interview*, 3–16 March 2014, p. 130.

According to Arpan Sheth, author of the Bain and Company's *Annual Philanthropy Report* of 2012, ' ... philanthropic organizations need to spend more time nurturing givers, working with them, more time advising them and getting their competence up'.

Dasra's Giving Circles and the Indian Philanthropy Forum address these concerns. The Giving Circles allow members to pool funds, thus leveraging resources with others for result-oriented giving around special themes like livelihood for crafts persons, or sport for youth development. A member commits resources and Dasra provides managerial and strategic guidance to the selected organization.

The Indian Philanthropy Forum was launched in 2010 to encourage a dialogue on giving and to generate funds. It exposes and inspires HNWIs-cum-philanthropists to relevant issues and places in India where funding could have an impact, by bringing them in dialogue with organizations and leaders that are bringing social change.

The fact that it is Mumbai-based is a factor in Dasra's favour, since Mumbai has traditionally had not only more business wealth but also a more dynamic culture of giving, and higher levels of social consciousness and activism than Delhi.

Concern over lack of accountability among NGOs remains a serious obstacle, preventing donors from giving more. It was cited by 53 per cent of HNWIs and emerging HNWIs surveyed by Bain and Co. for their *Annual Philanthropy Report* 2012.

Unfortunately, there are very few organizations attempting to tackle the problem at its root. One of these is the Delhi-based Credibility Alliance (CA). It works to motivate its NGO members to adopt transparent practices such as publishing annual reports with their balance sheets, and also screens and rates credible NGOs on the basis of select parameters. As with many such initiatives, CA has a problem of scale due to paucity of funding.

There are three online portals—GiveIndia, Samhita, and GuideStar India—which are also encouraging accountability and awareness by screening NGOs for credibility. These developments have helped to combat the notion that NGOs are unreliable recipients of philanthropy.

A few other initiatives are adding to the philanthropy infrastructure. One is the emergence of Philanthropy Advisory services specifically directed to promoting giving among HNWIs. Philanthropy is estimated to be a key beneficiary of the $41 trillion intergenerational transfer of wealth globally between 1998 and 2052, and the challenge is to convert at least a percentage of this wealth into social investment. Abroad, wealth advisors are beginning to play a key role in helping their clients expand their responsive social capital investment by wealth and succession planning, including setting up of charitable foundations. One of the few such initiatives in India is Stanchart's Investing for a Better Future, a three pillared philanthropy programme which includes advisory and education services.

The media is also doing its bit to promote giving: the Bloomberg channel has programmes on philanthropy and social entrepreneurship. This is partly a cause, partly a result of a willingness among philanthropists to talk about their philanthropy and to be seen as role models, unlike in previous years, when giving quietly was the cultural norm. But now, after the visits of Buffet and Gates, and their publicized Giving Pledge, philanthropists are becoming conscious of the value of publicizing their giving. It provides role models for others to emulate and also creates peer pressure to give more.

Future Steps: Creating an Effective Infrastructure

Philanthropy presupposes a culture of giving. The distinction between philanthropy and charity has to be publicized and there has to be a public understanding of the difference. So one of the first tasks of an association is to create a culture of giving to organized philanthropy, in addition to charity. Creating a culture of giving requires, among other things, a continuing debate in society, based on good research, and one needs to work on the beneficiary side as much as on the donor side to make the impact wide and deep and sustainable.

For donor associations to become a reality in India, there must be a consciousness of common interest and a common challenge. The creation of such a consciousness through debate and peer interaction must be a first step.

Second, any effort to promote philanthropy must take into account the fact that giving is strongly influenced by historical, cultural, and religious trends. For instance, while community foundations have become the fastest growing philanthropic model in the world, in India they have failed to make a headway and one must go deep into the cultural environment to seek reasons for it before wasting money and effort on such promotion.

Third, according to Paula Johnson et al, efforts to promote philanthropy must acknowledge and engage the multiple constituencies that are both the shapers and stakeholders of philanthropy's role in society. Such constituencies include the general public, HNWIs, corporations, government, and the institutions of civil society. Many conversations about philanthropy today tend to engage constituencies horizontally, that is, bringing together those in similar professional and peer groups. More 'vertical' conversations that represent a range of constituent voices could generate new and potentially powerful approaches to improving the quantity and quality of philanthropy.[9]

Mostly, philanthropic promotion efforts target only the very wealthy. Luckily in India, given the potential for collective philanthropy, organizations such as GiveIndia Foundation, Child Relief and You (CRY), and others are also exploring the potential of lower and middle income individuals.

The Challenges

The most significant and the most basic challenge facing almost all philanthropic support organizations is funding. In their start-up phase, such organizations often rely almost entirely on foreign funding. Charities Aid Foundation (CAF) India was actually started by the parent organization, Charities Aid Foundation UK, and received the bulk of the funding from it in the initial years.

Very seldom has the government supported such organizations. But, as has been argued here earlier, the government must also share some responsibility for building an effective infrastructure for foundations and civil society. A heavy reliance on foreign donors is not desirable partly because foreign funding will and has already started

[9] Paula D. Johnson, Harvard University, Stephen P. Johnson, The Philanthropic Initiative, Andrew Kingman, *Allavida*, 'Promoting Philanthropy: Global Challenges and Approaches', International Network on Strategic Philanthropy (Bertelsmann Stiftung, Gütersloh, Germany, December 2004).

to come to an end, but also because it can raise issues of legitimacy, agenda setting, and public perception. The priorities of foreign institutions and local organizations, and particularly of local governments, are not always fully congruent.

Therefore, it is of the utmost importance that Indian philanthropists see the creation of an effective ecosystem for promotion of philanthropy as of equal importance to creating hospitals, colleges, or other institutions. Because, it is not enough for donors to give. They must give wisely.

PART III

THE CHANGING FACE
OF PHILANTHROPY

There is something about philanthropy that seems to go against the democratic grain—we expect rich men to be generous with their wealth and criticize them when they are not; but when they make benefaction, we question their motives, deplore the methods by which they obtained their abundance, and wonder whether their gifts will not do more harm than good.

—Robert Bremner (1977).

6

Donors Old and New

I don't know what the future may hold, but I know who holds the future.[1]

—Ralph Abernathy

Indian philanthropy, no less than others, has been touched by the winds of change blowing within India and across the globe. The new developments have impacted not only the quantum of philanthropy but also the sources of philanthropy. The profiles of donors, their caste–class background, their age, gender, their education, their motives and attitudes to philanthropy, and their philanthropic preferences too have changed, as has the location of the new philanthropy. In many ways the changes have more to do with the nature of new wealth than the fact of economic growth per se.

The Changing Landscape

Signs of change in the landscape of Indian philanthropy were visible by the end of the Eighties. Nineteen ninety one can be taken to

---

[1] Quoted by N.R. Narayana Murthy in his Maulana Azad Memorial Lecture, 'The Travails of Philanthropy in India', 29 March 2004, Delhi. According to him it is the privileged few, who have enjoyed the fruits of growth, who hold the future.

mark the watershed between the old economy and the new economy, which would begin India's march to become one of the economic powerhouses of the world.

The liberalization of the economy from 1991 onwards, the technological revolution, the opening of markets, and the stock market boom led to the generation of new wealth on an unprecedented scale, so that today we are witnessing a second wave of wealth creation, with many globally ranked billionaires and millionaires of Indian origin.

The distribution of the new wealth is highly skewed, and has increased the inequalities in society. Social need continues to be at a high level with the government unable to meet the economic and social expectations of a growing population by itself. The result is that the attitudes to social responsibility and obligations of the individual have changed.

The fall of communism, leading to a rapid spread of the idea of democracy round the world, and the wider acceptance of the free market ideology has meant that governments are no longer considered the first and only solutions to socio-economic problems. The private sector has been given a bigger role not only in the economic but also the social sphere in the space vacated by governments.

Not only does the government and society expect more of private actors, but the new rich themselves have a changed attitude towards the role of the state. They do not believe that it is the duty only of the state to deliver welfare. As in the UK and elsewhere, the Indian rich are defining new roles for individual and foundation philanthropy, and as will be seen in the next chapter, are joining hands with the government to solve social problems like nutrition and primary schooling.[2]

Just as the rapid globalization of business and industry has meant that whatever happens in one country—climate change, diseases, economic crisis etc.—impacts on all for good or bad, so too, global concepts such as sustainable development, social responsibility of business, and ethical investment also play a part in influencing donor behaviour everywhere.

---

[2] Beth Breeze and Theresa Lloyd, *Richer Lives: Why Rich People Give* (London: Directory of Social Change, 2013).

As mentioned earlier, the media too has begun to play a proactive role in motivating donors, and in educating the public on development issues.

Finally, many business schools have introduced courses on philanthropy, CSR, and development, influencing a new generation of wealth creators.

The outcome is both an increased potential for, and interest in, engaging in philanthropy. Whereas only 29 per cent of all legal philanthropic entities in India were established before 1990, the number of trusts and foundations has doubled in the decade 1990–2000, following economic liberalization, and an even more significant growth was noticed between 2001 and 2011, when 42 per cent of all trusts and foundations were established.[3] Similarly, the number of non-profit institutions has also boomed in recent years, resulting in approximately one NGO for every 400 people.[4]

The New Wealth

Traditionally, wealth was concentrated largely in four major economic groupings: the princely and aristocratic order, the landed elite, major religious organizations like the Tirupati temple, and the business community. These were the groups who contributed most to philanthropy, as distinct from charity, which was practised at all levels of society.

[3] Formal legal entities to manage family philanthropic activities increased from 4 per cent in the 1930s to 13 per cent in the 1960s, and to 42 per cent in 2000–11. Source: *UBS-INSEAD*, 'Philanthropic Unit, Decade of Establishment—India', *Study on Family Philanthropy in Asia* (August 2011), p. 42.

[4] Out of a total of 3.17 million registered societies or non-profit institutions (NPIs), only 875,000 NPIs had registered up to the year 1990, while 2.25 million NPIs registered since 1991. As there is no procedure for de-registering a society, a notable percentage of the 3.17 million are likely defunct: Government of India, Ministry of Statistics and Programme Implementation, *Final Report on Non Profit Institutions in India* (March 2012), p. 94, http://mospi.nic.in/Mospi_New/upload/Final_Report_Non-Profit_Instiututions_30may12.pdf.

After Independence, due to land reforms, and the abolition of privy purses of rulers and their other perks, the first two groups no longer counted for major philanthropy. Religious institutions, *with a very few notable exceptions* like Tirupati, Satya Sai Baba Trust, Sri Dharmasthala Kshetra, and others have used most of their wealth and income from devotees for religious purposes and ad hoc charity. It was largely the business community which, either directly or through the foundations and trusts that it had set up, was the site of philanthropy.

However, after 1991, sources of philanthropy changed due to the pattern of new wealth creation, which was also reflected in the social composition of the wealth-creating class. Many of the new entrepreneurs have come from non-traditional social backgrounds.

A unique feature of Indian capitalism has been that it has always been dominated by private dynastic family businesses, and while this continues to a large extent, the business sector has been enlarged by the addition of state-established public enterprises, new entrepreneurs with no previous background in business, and foreign businesses. To those from the traditional business communities—Marwaris, Jains, Banias, Chettiars, and Parsis—which occupied the middle rung in the caste hierarchy of India, have been added entrepreneurs from a range of peasant castes—Marathas, Nadars, Reddys, and also Brahmins. The founders of the pioneering Infotech group, NR Narayan Murthy, Nandan Nilekani, and N.S. Raghavan come from a middle-class, Brahmin, non-business background.

Equally, several Dalit entrepreneurs have also emerged though, understandably, they are yet to open their philanthropic account.

A few successful industrialists have also come from among the Muslims, such as Azim Premji. And there are more women entrepreneurs creating wealth in their own right, like Kiran Mazumdar Shaw of Biocon industries. Though the numbers of women entrepreneurs are increasing steadily, very few of them have become philanthropists for reasons explored in the next chapter.

While manufacturing has continued to contribute to growth post 1990, the new growth has come from Information Technology, telecom, and the service industry—legal and financial services, health care, air travel, and hospitality. The most dynamic among these was the indigenous software industry located around the southern metropolises of Bangalore, Hyderabad, and Chennai, and the tele-com industry, largely located in Mumbai and Delhi.

Wealth has been generated in humungous amounts in the sports and entertainment fields too. Many of the new rich in these fields come from Punjab, Bihar, and from Muslim families, traditionally not associated with wealth creation or philanthropy. This new wealth is again concentrated in Mumbai, Chennai, and Delhi.

As a consequence, Mumbai has 30 per cent of the super-rich, fol-lowed by Delhi and Bangalore. Not surprisingly, they have become the new centres of philanthropy, though not in the same order. As before, Mumbai takes the lead, but Bangalore has become the new hub of philanthropy, not Delhi. While Chennai had several philan-thropists of note, such as Pacchaiyappa, Raja Annamalai Chettiar, and Kuppuswamy Naidu of Coimbatore in an earlier era, no big names immediately come to mind today.

Characteristics of the New Rich

A recent study conducted by Economic Intelligence Unit (EIU) and commissioned by Citibank claims that the number of the new rich in India will almost double by 2020. The New Wealth Builders (NWBs) represent a new breed of self-generated successes. Most of them have acquired their wealth in the past ten years, and almost none have inherited their wealth. Many are from humble backgrounds, and focussed on making progress for society.

Many of the new entrepreneurs are young, and it is predicted, by the study just quoted, that a majority of the NWBs in future will also be young, in their mid-20s and 30s.[5]

They are making money on an unimaginable scale at a younger age than their older counterparts. The average age of the rich has fallen and six of the richest in India are below forty. India has the youngest millionaires in all of Asia—and among the fastest-growing population of HNWIs in the world, according to the most recent Asia-Pacific wealth report published by Merrill Lynch. Today, most

---

[5] Reported in *The Times of India*, 'No. of New Rich to Grow Fastest in India, Says Study', 24 September 2015.

of India's billionaires are in the age group of 31–45, against the bulk of HNWIs in Hong Kong and Japan, who are mostly over 66.[6] Changes in the profile of donors and their motives are discussed in this chapter and the next, while the changes in philanthropic practice are discussed in Chapters 8, 9, and 10.

Today's Donors

Today's philanthropists come from one of eight main categories: one, donors from the older family businesses which have dynastic philanthropic traditions. Among the top ten richest individuals/families in India are some from the older business families like the Tatas (Ratan Tata), the Birlas (Kumar Mangalam Birla), Ambanis (Mukesh Ambani), S.P. Hinduja, and Pallonji Mistry (Shapoorji Pallonji). Almost all of them also figure in the list of top philanthropists, which further includes Anand Mahindra of the Mahindra and Mahindra group, and the Godrej family, led by Adi and Jamshyd Godrej.

Two, new entrepreneurs, from the Infotech and other fields. Those from the New Economy who are on the list of richest Indians are Dilip Shanghvi, L.N. Mittal, Azim Premji, Shiv Nadar, Sunil Mittal, and Gautam Adani.[7] Almost all of these new rich figure in the list of leading philanthropists too, which also includes G.M. Rao of GMR group, G.V.K. Reddy of GVK group, S. Gopalkrishnan, Nandan Nilekani, Shibulal, and Narayana Murthy, all Infosys founders; Naveen Jindal of Jindal Steel and Power, Airtel chairman Sunil Mittal, Shiv Nadar of HCL, Ronnie Screwvala and wife Farida, and many others.

Three, celebrities from the field of sports and entertainment who are using their new wealth to fund social causes or are lending their name to raise money for the same. These include M.S. Dhoni and Amir Khan, and others.

Four, non-resident Indians (NRIs) such as Vinod Khosla, Manoj Bhargava, and Gururaj Deshpande, who are using philanthropy to repay a debt to their motherland.

[6] Yogini Joglekar, 'Youngest Indian Millionaires Lead Asia, World HNIS', 14 October 2011, dnaindia.com.

[7] Source: *Hurun India Rich List*, Shanghai: September 2015, published by a China-based luxury and events group.

Five, professionals, whether CEOs of companies, or doctors, lawyers, or bankers, among whom are Hemendra Kothari and L.M. Naik.

Six, companies who have no previous record of giving for public benefit but are now compelled to give under the Companies Act of 2013, as for instance Maruti Suzuki, Vedanta, Axis Bank, and others.

Seven, foreign philanthropists and foundations working in India or giving to India, most notably the Bill and Melinda Gates Foundation and the Ford and the Dell Foundations.

Eight, community foundations like Bombay Community Public Trust and the Valley Dew Foundation, and hybrid foundations like Concern India, CRY, and HelpAge, which both raise and disburse money.

These categories are further discussed below.

Traditional Donors

Since the late nineteenth century some families have been at the forefront of philanthropy and have built up dynastic traditions. The new members of the dynasties are continuing the family tradition, but with a difference. Earlier, the younger generation took on the mantle of family philanthropy only after the retirement or passing away of the patriarch. Today both generations are involved in the family philanthropy together, and GenNext is taking on responsibility for the family philanthropies as well as branching out on their own at a younger age. Many members of GenNext are young women.

Anand Mahindra is representative of the new generation of the older philanthropic dynasties established during the early years of Independence. The Mahindra family, including Keshub and Harish Mahindra, the founders, has been known for their education initiatives. The K.C. Mahindra Trust, founded in the 1960s, has been giving scholarships for studies abroad, but now the education work has been consolidated and expanded by Anand, who in addition to the traditional responsibilities has added to the portfolio the Pune campus of the United World College (UWC), started Nanni Kali, an NGO working for education of girls, and the Mahindra Ecole Centrale, an engineering college in Hyderabad collaborating with Ecole Centrale of France. His donation to Harvard, for humanities, is well known.

The Godrej tradition of philanthropy is being taken forward by Nisaba Dubash, daughter of Adi Godrej, and the Thermax tradition by Meher Pudumjee, daughter of the late Rohinton Aga and Anu Aga, both known for their philanthropy.

The younger generation of other well-known philanthropic dynasties such as the Birlas, Singhanias, Murugappas, and others, follows a similar pattern in their philanthropy—consolidation and focusing of family philanthropy with expansion in new directions.

But there are some among the patriarchs who stand out for a lifetime of outstanding philanthropy. Prime among them is Ratan Tata.

Ratan Tata

Among the older philanthropists, perhaps none is so deservedly well known nationally or internationally as Ratan Tata. Born on 28 December 1937, he did his Bachelors in Architecture from Cornell University and then studied advanced business management at Harvard Business School. Both institutions have benefited from his gratitude with huge donations ($50 Million to Harvard Business School).

He led the Tata Group for five decades, and retired as Chairman of the Tata group in 2012. When Tata was anointed chairman of Tata Sons in 1991, he was assigned charge of the Tata Trusts as well, a traditional family responsibility. But even after stepping down from his business responsibility, Ratan Tata has continued as Chairman of the Tata Trusts. He has made them one of the most generous, most progressive, and best known philanthropic foundations, not only in India but in the world as well. In 2014 alone, the Tata Trusts together disbursed rupees 5 billion ($80 million at current exchange rates) to various causes and institutions. In dollar terms, this number would have been higher if the rupee had not devalued as much since then.[8] The figure for 2015 is estimated to be $100 million (approx. rupees 650 crores).

---

[8] See, Annual Reports of Sir Ratan Tata and Allied Trusts and Sir Dorab Tata and Allied Trusts, 2013–14 and 2014–15 for details; www.tatatrusts.org/upload/pdf/Annual_Report_2013_14.pdf, www.tatatrusts.org/upload/pdf/Annual_Report_2014_15.pdf, www.tatatrusts.org/upload/pdf/SDTTAR2013-2014.pdf.

For many years now, Ratan Tata has been part of a circle of people with philanthropy on top of their minds, including Bill Gates and Peggy Dulany, daughter of David Rockefeller of the legendary Rockefeller family and founder of Synergos, a non-profit organization. In the past, Tata has been on the board of the Ford Foundation as well. His learning from these experiences, as well as the historical legacy of the Tatas, have been instrumental in shaping his thoughts over the years.

Since his retirement as chairman of the group, Tata, as Chair of the Trusts, has been focusing his time and energy on transforming the way in which the Trusts function. (See Chapter 9 on foundations.)

Three areas which are all equally a passion with him are entrepreneurship, technology-led innovation, and philanthropy, and it is the intersection of the three which informs his philanthropy. He believes disruptive innovation can help the underdog and is searching for creative solutions to problems, moving beyond financial grants. He, like many of the new international philanthropists, does not keep his philanthropy and business interests in water-tight compartments but believes above all in innovations to solve not only India's problems but also the world's.

With a passion and respect for risk-taking, which is reflected in his philanthropy, and his engagement with researchers, it is not only his money that he is willing to put on the line but also his personal contacts and goodwill. He looks for people with big vision and then sets out to do what he can in every way to make the person succeed—the hallmark of the true philanthropist.

Interested in low-cost innovation which led to the Nano, the common man's car, he has funded the frugal engineering centre at Massachusetts Institute of Technology (MIT) where the research agenda includes his interests—nutrition, low-cost housing, sustainable energy, waste management, and clean water.

He has given rupees 950 million to its sister centre at IIT Bombay. His interest in innovation, unusual among Indian philanthropists, is also evident in his contribution to the X prize, a multimillion prize in the US for solving big problems.[9]

[9] Madhav Chanchani, Kala Vijyraghvan, and Hari Pulakkat, 'Ratan Tata and his Happy Space', *The Economic Times*, Special Feature, 11 June 2015.

In his acceptance speech for a Lifetime Achievement Award instituted by the Rockefeller Foundation, he said his life's work is not done yet because he has not been able to touch as many people at the bottom of the pyramid as he had hoped to, by building affordable products.

The New Donors

Whereas inherited wealth accounted for much of the philanthropy of the pre-globalization years, today new entrepreneurship is the dominant source of both wealth and philanthropy among the very wealthy.

The four main characteristics of these new philanthropists are that many of them are self-made, first-generation rich individuals from diverse backgrounds; they are younger than the traditional philanthropists; they are more educated; and their attitudes to life and society are also different.

The fact of being the first generation of wealthy individuals has made many of them think more carefully about the purpose of their wealth. They are thinking not only about investment but also about legacy, intergenerational wealth transfer, and philanthropy. Observers find a clear link between the rise of entrepreneurship and a growing focus on more active, engaged philanthropy that draws on business skills and commitment of time, as well as financial donations.[10]

With more than what they can spend on themselves, and inspired by stories of Western philanthropists like Bill Gates and Mark Zuckerberg who have given away their wealth at a young age, the more sensitive among them are following suit.

Bain and Company's *India Philanthropy Report 2012* shows, younger (under the age of thirty) HNWIs are emerging as key players in philanthropic decision-making. Interestingly, the participation of under-30s in family philanthropy in the US is much less, only 13 per cent being actively involved in family philanthropic projects. The Bains

---

[10] See Volume 17 of 'Wealth Insights' of *Barclays Wealth Report* 2013. Downloaded on 12 June 2015. https://wealth.barclays.com/en_gb/home/research/research-centre/wealth-insights/volume-17.html.

report, based on a survey of 398 Indian HNW families, indicates that not only are many of these younger donors keen to increase their involvement with philanthropy in the future, they are also keen to give more and want to change how they and their families engage with the organizations they give to. 57 per cent of young philanthropists say they will increase their charitable contributions this year, as compared with 49 per cent of those who are over thirty years old.

What is more, these philanthropists are *beginning* at a younger age. The average age of donors in the *Hurun India Philanthropy List of 2014* is seven years younger than in the previous year. There were twenty-seven new faces in the list.

Whereas the older wealth creators were, with the exception of the Tatas, not highly educated, their new counterparts mostly are, thanks to the heavy investments made by India in education. Many of them, especially the InfoTech entrepreneurs, have professional degrees from both Indian institutions as well as prestigious universities abroad, like Harvard, MIT, and Stanford. This has influenced their attitudes, expectations, and approaches not only to their businesses, but also to philanthropy.

By education, training, or necessity, many of the new philanthropists believe that the wealthy should give back to society, and favour more direct action at the community level to solve social problems, rather than old-style charity or institutional philanthropy. Moreover, they offer not only money resources but organization and management skills, vision, leadership, and an ability to take risks on new ideas.

Jayant Sinha, a minister of state with the present government, writing on philanthropy for a newspaper, observed that for purposes of philanthropy the real distinction is between old wealth and new. The old wealth comes from older established business families going back several generations. Though they often build hospitals and schools, they tend not to give away large chunks of money because they see it as needed to maintain their business dynasty and, in a sense, as held in trust for future generations of the family. The obvious exception here are the Tatas. The new wealth, by contrast, is by definition first-generation wealth. Its owners have made it themselves and see a corresponding right to dispose of it as they like. Most of them, notes Sinha, have also made their money very quickly. They are in their forties and fifties and see philanthropy as the next chapter of their career.[11]

Their attitude to philanthropy is also different than that of the older generation. According to Sinha, the new generation of philanthropists think India 'not only can solve its own problems, but *should*' (emphasis mine).

The preponderance of a younger, new wealthy class in India's still-nascent philanthropic space presents challenges, too. According to the Bain report, close to 80 per cent of those surveyed admitted that they were 'novice donors', with less than three years' experience in the sector. 'If 77% are self-reported novices, and it takes three to five years to become intermediate, then we have a real risk that a large percentage of those funds are not creating the significant impact that they could have, because novices lack the rigour and analytical approach of more experienced givers', says Deval Sanghavi, co-founder of Dasra, an organization that connects Indian philanthropists to worthy causes. There is a very real risk of newer philanthropists having a few failures with bad NGOs and giving up.[12]

New Entrepreneurs

Azim Premji

Among the new-economy philanthropists, the pride of place undoubtedly belongs to Azim Premji. Apart from being the thirteenth richest person in the world of technology according to Forbes magazine's list in 2015, with a net worth of $17.4 billion, he has occupied the top rank two years running as the 'most generous Indian' in the *Hurun India Philanthropy Lists of 2014* and *2015*. Premji (69) gave away rupees 275.14 billion for education to the Azim Premji Foundation in 2015, more than double the amount he had given in 2014 (rupees 123.14 billion). He, in fact, contributed about 80 per cent of total donations made by thirty-six top Indian philanthropists, who together gave away nearly rupees 350 billion.

---

[11] Deval Sanghavi, quoted in Alison Bukhari, 'Philanthropy in India today', *Alliance magazine,* 1 June 2013.

[12] Malia Politzer, 'Under-30s take centre stage in Indian philanthropy', *Livemint,* 20 March 2012.

He was the first Indian to sign up for the Giving Pledge started by Bill Gates and Warren Buffet, with rupees 90 billion pledged to the cause of education. In his commitment to the Giving Pledge, he wrote that he had been deeply influenced by Gandhiji's notion of holding one's wealth in trusteeship, to be used for the betterment of society.

Though Premji is a Khoja Muslim from Kutch, his motivation for philanthropy has come not from religion but from a modern, secular humanist ethic and a desire to make a difference. Premji felt he had wealth, an understanding of how large systems work, and credibility. He spent two years exploring the situation in education and found it shocking. He felt he could make a difference as an individual. The result was the Azim Premji Foundation.

For Premji, the inspiration has been his mother, who dedicated most of her life to building and running a charitable hospital in Mumbai for children affected by polio and cerebral palsy. 'My mother was the most significant influence in my life as I was growing up', he says.

According to him, his acts of philanthropy arise out of a sense of responsibility for the society he lives in, dissatisfaction with the inequity, injustice, and lack of human and environmental care that exists in India, and a desire to bring about social change.

In an inspiring acceptance speech at *The Economic Times* Lifetime Achievement Awards, 2013, Premji explained why he thought philanthropy was important:

To my mind that is the basic question that we need to ask ourselves: Do we feel connected to our country, to the people around us? Should not every Indian have the very basic, bare necessities of a life of dignity? This is certainly not hoping for too much; it's just basic safety, adequate food, a roof to sleep under, basic education and healthcare. Most of us would feel this way. I think we just need to act.[13]

Though he feels that the government needs to do more and better, he believes that that does not in any way lessen the responsibility of those who have the privilege of being successful. In his words, 'To

---

[13] Azim Premji's Speech at *The Economic Times* Lifetime Achievement Awards function on 7 December 2013.

me philanthropy is the connection that we can have if we are not indifferent to all these issues that face us. It is the mechanism for us to contribute to making some positive change. And I think the greater our success, the greater the responsibility for us.'[14]

As to why he chose to devote a large portion of his personal wealth to education, he said 'Education is a powerful vehicle for social change'. Aware that trying to improve education is a very long process, he added 'I think that basic education is the basic route to building a better society'.[15]

A vocal critic of mis-governance, he is against ostentation as well. Premji drives a Toyota Corolla, is known to avoid staying in five-star hotels, and leads a generally frugal life. He leads from the front, by example, and is today an acknowledged role model for many of the young rich. For V.G. Sidhartha, founder of the Cafe Coffee Day chain and the biggest investor in the software company MindTree, he is an icon as much for his large donations to good causes, as for the time and effort he puts in to craft a well-thought-out plan of action to ensure maximum return on investment for every philanthropic rupee he gives.

In the speech mentioned above, he also talked of the lessons he had learnt in twelve years. He said that though he had then been engaged in philanthropy for twelve years, his one regret was that he had not started earlier. He said, 'There is so much to do, and this kind of work takes so much time that the earlier we try to contribute, the better it is'. Involving your family early on in philanthropy is also very important. Their understanding, involvement, and endorsement may eventually be the most determining factor. Referring to women, he said some of the smartest people are those who have chosen to become homemakers, and they can play an important part in starting their families' philanthropic efforts.

According to Premji, the key to scaling up philanthropy and doing good work is getting good people in the team, exactly as in businesses. He acknowledged that the work in philanthropy is perhaps more complex than business, because social issues are more complex, and therefore needs really good people who have the intent,

[14]   Premji's Speech at *The Economic Times* Lifetime Achievement Awards.
[15]   Premji's Speech at *The Economic Times* Lifetime Achievement Awards.

empathy, and ability. Philanthropic work also needs patience and tenacity. One has to change one's mind set significantly if one has to make a difference.

Among the new wave of philanthropists are also the Infosys founders, each of whom has either donated to a cause or started his own philanthropic institutions. Among them are N.R. Narayana Murthy, who led the new philanthropy movement with the founding of Infosys Foundation, now run by wife Sudha Murthy; S.D. Shibulal, 59, who founded the Samhita Academy, which runs an inclusive school bringing together economically under-privileged kids and regular applicants; K. Dinesh, 60, who backs social entrepreneurs in healthcare and education, and whose ancestral land is home to a hospital project; N.S. Raghavan, who has funded and mentored healthcare and life sciences entrepreneurs through his Nadathur Investments, and founded the NSR Centre for Entrepreneurial Learning at IIM Bangalore; Nandan Nilekani, who set up the New India Foundation for funding social science research on India, and wife Rohini, who has set up Arghyam, a non-profit for optimizing India's water resources, among other initiatives.

Azim Premji's views on involving the family in philanthropy and starting early in life obviously find resonance among other business leaders.[16] Without their giving becoming dynastic as yet, husbands and wives and/or the children of the new generation of philanthropists are all engaged in philanthropy. Thus, Nandan Nilekani and wife Rohini, Sudha and N.R. Narayana Murthy, Shibulal and wife, all work together on common philanthropic initiatives; at other times, independently on their own interests.

In three other wealthy families—the Nadars, the Kotharis, and the Jindals—both generations are working together to create impact. Shiv Nadar, wife Kiran, and daughter Roshni, Hemendra Kothari and daughter Aditi, are all engaged in philanthropic enterprises,

---

[16] Ahona Ghosh, 'Act of Giving: Giving across Generations', *The Economic Times Bureau*, 4 October 2011.

Also, 'Parent-child Duos at Indian Philanthropy Forum Highlight Generational Approaches', *Alliance* magazine, posted by Aditi Kothari, 12 August 2011.

sometimes each one having their own initiative and at others jointly managing the common venture. While the children are starting early and playing a central role, their parents, who came in late, are helping them with funds and direction.

Shiv Nadar

Shiv Nadar was born in 1945, in a village in the Tuticorin District of Tamil Nadu. He started HCL Technologies in 1976 with five other promotors, and currently owns around 62.1 per cent in India's fourth largest IT company, with a market cap of rupees 470 billion. With an estimated net worth of around $5.6 billion, he figures in the Forbes list of billionaires. For Nadar, 'Philanthropy is not just about giving but also enabling. It's about placing bets on the future'.

In 1994, Shiv Nadar started the eponymous Shiv Nadar Foundation with a windfall gain. It is one of India's largest philanthropic foundations today. Like Premji's foundation, it is created out of personal wealth and not from company funds; he has committed 10 per cent of his personal wealth to the foundation.

Like Premji, the inspiration behind Nadar's philanthropic work was his mother who, though immensely pleased over the fact that he was doing well in his business life, wanted him to start thinking right away about others less fortunate than him. Though he was then only in his forties, she said that if he keeps waiting for the right age, he may never get started. According to Nadar, 'she was part of the older generation in whom the thought of sharing was ingrained in their mind. She used to support the local village school even during hard times in our family'. It was her advice to choose education.

Again like Premji, he feels that he should have started earlier, and the rural work of the foundation, especially, should have come much earlier, though according to him the expertise for undertaking such activities did not exist then. But now his mantra for philanthropy is 'Thoughtfulness, patience and thoroughness'.[17]

Among the younger entrepreneurs from a business background are Naveen Tiwari of a start-up InMobi and his colleague Atul Satija,

[17] See http://www.shivnadarfoundation.org/news.aspx for more on Shiv Nadar.

both of whom quit InMobi to launch a non-profit foundation—
Nudge Foundation—sinking rupees 12.7 million of personal money
to help upskill people.[18]

Many of the new wealth creators are from non-traditional backgrounds and fields as divergent as finance and medicine, and so too,
many of the new donors.

Asit Koticha, 54, is the founder and chairman of the ASK Group,
a financial services company, who donated $7 million to his alma
mater, the University of Mumbai, in 2010 to build an international
convention centre. He gave 10 per cent of his income to charity since
starting the firm in 1983. Now he is helping to build homes through
Habitat for Humanity, and also supports non-traditional causes
such as the Olympic Gold Quest, which works to motivate India's
medal aspirants.[19]

Ashish Dhawan (45) of Central Square Foundation is the youngest philanthropist on the Hurun list of philanthropists for 2014, the
oldest being Pallonji Mistry (85) of Shapoorji Pallonji. The transition of Ashish Dhawan from a hedge-fund manager to philanthropist
demonstrates the new wave of philanthropy in India, as does that
of cardiologists Vijay and Khushman Sanghvi, who have donated
rupees 120 million towards medical research.

Some new donors are CEOs of non-family businesses such as
L&T, who as CEOs of their companies make CSR contributions,
and engage in philanthropy on their own behalf. For instance,
L.M. Naik, CEO of L&T, oversaw the contribution of rupees 730
million or 1.5 per cent of the net profit of the company in 2012–13,
apart from giving ESOPs to its employees. As part of its CSR programmes, L&T supports 147 schools and fifty learning centres; nine
health centres, eight mobile vans; and eight training institutes for
construction skills.

Not satisfied with company philanthropy, Naik himself is supporting a Radiation centre in Surat and hospitals for the poor

---

[18] Reported in 'Angels of a Different Stripe, Flocking to Charity Startup',
Economic Times, Delhi, 11 June 2015.

[19] Naazneen Karmali and Anuradha Raghunathan in Forbes online,
20 June 2012, http://www.forbes.com/sites/johnkoppisch/2012/06/20/
2012-indian-philanthropists/.

elsewhere in Gujarat; skilling centres for several professions; and secondary and higher secondary schools in Gujarat to give free education and boarding to the underprivileged. He reportedly sets aside rupees 500 million to 1 billion every year, depending on what the projects need.

Several of the new donors are to be found in the sports and entertainment fields. Among the celebrities who are into philanthropy is M.S. Dhoni, India's cricket captain for many national and international matches. He has set up his own foundation, an educational institute, a cricket academy, and a leprosy rehabilitation centre, among others, and also supports charitable events.

Those from the entertainment world who help raise money for charitable causes by endorsing the causes or raising funds for them are Lisa Ray, Rahul Bose, Farhan Akhtar, and many others. The causes supported range from gender-based discrimination, legal fees for prisoners, global warming, crimes against women, and others. Film star Amir Khan has raised money for several causes through his popular TV show *Satyameva Jayate*.

NRI Donors

New philanthropy has also been enriched by the addition of NRI donors and international donors. Many NRIs have gone from rags to riches. Many of them still cherish fond memories of their corner of India, and want to give back something to help those who have not been as lucky as them. Some professionals who have made good, thanks to an education heavily subsidized by the Indian taxpayer, are conscious of this, though unfortunately, not too many.

They are thus looking for ways in which they can give some money or skills to some needy cause. Hence, 'diaspora philanthropy', as this giving by NRIs is called in international circles, is growing. In recent years it has become a significant source of funds for non-profit organizations engaged in development and welfare. How to raise money abroad has become an important part of any training in fundraising; and online giving through the internet is catching on. At the same time, the potential is far greater than is being tapped, principally due to lack of information and proper mechanisms through which this money can be channelled.

Amongst the noted NRI philanthropists are several such as L.N. Mittal, Gururaj Deshpande, Vinod Khosla, Romesh Wadhwani, and Bharat Desai who, though based abroad, are deeply engaged with Indian philanthropy.

Some of them, like Silicon Valley venture capitalist Vinod Khosla and his wife Neeru, with a net worth of $1.4 billion in March 2011, have signed the Giving Pledge initiated by Gates and Buffet.

Khosla,Gururaj Deshpande, and several others like them use their philanthropic capital to invest in companies that focus on the poor in India. Khosla's firm focuses on clean technology and info-tech start-ups. He is therefore keen to fund technologies that can be widely adopted in India and China. One of his investments to benefit the poor was in SKS Microfinance, a lender to poor women in India.

NRI philanthropist Ramesh Wadhwani, who is ranked seventy third on the Forbes list of the richest entrepreneurs in the world of technology, has a net worth of $2.8 billion. An IIT alumnus, he has been endeavouring to improve the research ecosystem in India through funding of centres of innovation. He is supporting research in biosensors and cancer cell motility at IIT, Mumbai, and cardiac and neural research at the Institute for Cell Biology & Regenerative Medicine. The focus is on low-cost solutions with high global impact. In July 2015 he announced he would commit up to $1 billion to fund entrepreneurship in India.[20]

NRI billionaire entrepreneur Manoj Bhargava, also one of the few Indians to sign the Giving Pledge, is set to announce a plan to give rupees 5 billion over six years for a development programme in Uttarakhand. Bhargava, who is one of the richest Indians in America, has already given more than rupess 3 billion to over 151 organiza-tions across India, with 406 completed or ongoing projects in the areas of healthcare, education, disability, livelihood, water, and sani-tation in the past five years, through The Hans Foundation (THF), a grant-making foundation. His proposed project, called Uttarakhand 2020, is a village development project with a focus on education, healthcare, forest regeneration, with a budget of rupees 5 billion. So

---

[20] 'Premji, Nadar Among 20 Richest Techies : Forbes', *Indian Express*, Delhi edition, 13 August 2015 .

far, this is all par for the course. But it is his views on philanthropy which are interesting.

He says, 'Charity is very difficult to do right, way more difficult than doing business',[21] a view shared by Premji as well as Andrew Carnegie, patron saint of philanthropy. He goes on to say, 'Everybody has this misconception that this [philanthropy]is about money. That the more money you give the more things happen. That's nonsense.'[22]

For Bhargava, philanthropy is about understanding people and communities in a heterogeneous manner and within a particular context, and finding common-sense solutions to their problems. In his foundation, the problem is the starting point, and then innovation and technology are used to solve that problem. He feels recruiting, and not funding, is the biggest challenge in philanthropy. For those who want to work in social sector projects, there is always a conflict between idealism and wanting to help the poor, and building a career.

Unlike many of India's celebrated philanthropists, he does not like to give to educational institutions abroad which are already rich. '"If you don't improve the lives of the poor it's not charity. How is putting your name on a building charity?' In his Giving Pledge he wrote, 'My choice was to ruin my son's life by giving him money or giving 90% plus to charity. Not much of a choice.'[23]

Luckily for him, his son Shaan shares this view. He is director of special projects of the Foundation and divides his time in the USA and in India, while a full time CEO runs the Foundation on a daily basis.

Foreign Donors

Though they cannot be counted as Indian philanthropists, they have nevertheless made valuable contributions to Indian development, and since they work in India or for India, some mention of them is necessary here. Apart from the older foreign donors like the

---

[21] Saumya Bhattacharya, 'A Giver and His Grudge Against Fellow Givers', *The Economic Times*, 11 November 2014.

[22] Bhattacharya, 'A Giver and His Grudge'.

[23] Bhargava, quoted in Bhattacharya, 2014.

Ford and the McArthur Foundations, the field has been widened by noted individual philanthropists like Bill Gates, Pierre Omidyar, and others. The Dell and the Clinton Foundations are some of the new overseas donors to India.

Apart from supporting several other causes, the Ford Foundation and the Aga Khan Foundation have uniquely given support for research, advocacy, and communication to promote philanthropy itself.

Bill and Melinda Gates have given $22.8 billion-and-still-counting from 1994 onwards, of which $1 billion is for causes in India, including drug research and low-cost production and delivery of vaccines and drugs through partnerships with research organizations and domestic pharmaceutical companies. The Gates Foundation's goal is to go beyond prevention and treatment of neglected diseases to nutrition, mother and child health, and agriculture.

The Omidyar Network has been promoted by eBay founder Pierre Omidyar, who gave up his executive role at eBay while only thirty. His wealth is around $8.5 billion. He has since deployed $1 billion of his fortune for philanthropic causes. The Omidyar Network is a global philanthropic fund that makes for-profit investment into social ventures, and also gives grants to non-profits such as Janagraha, the Bangalore-based NGO working on civic issues .

Dell Inc., as part of its philanthropic efforts in India, recently announced over $2.57 million for organizations promoting education, a move that will directly benefit one lakh children up to seventeen years of age. Dell said the amount would be marked to ten Indian institutions working toward child labour rehabilitation, educating daughters of sex-workers, and an initiative to impart information on climate change.

Space forbids mention of the work of many other foreign donors contributing to India.

Companies and CSR

The pool of philanthropic funds has been enlarged due to the mandatory provisions of the Companies Act of 2013, which has brought many more companies into contributing to the social sector. While this will definitely benefit Indian society, whether it is philanthropy or not has already been discussed in Chapter 3.

Community Philanthropy

A new kind of philanthropic organization—the community foundation—has made an appearance in India though it is yet to become popular. Community philanthropy refers to the act of individual citizens contributing money and goods, or volunteering their time and skills to improve the quality of life of the geographic community or area in which they live. Community philanthropy arises both from the impulse of generosity as well as shared values of self-reliance and social cohesion. In the West, and in some other countries of the world, a vehicle which has become very popular for the practice of community philanthropy is a community foundation, which as a concept is almost unknown in India.

A community foundation is a tax exempt, independent, publicly supported philanthropic organization, established and operated as a permanent collection of endowed funds for the long-term benefit of a defined geographical area such as a city or a village. It is a means to build, over time, substantial funds for the community, through large and small contributions. These are not spent but invested to secure a steady stream of income to help meet the community's charitable needs—from primary education to vocational training to art. In a sense, the community foundation serves as a savings account for the community.

Typically, a community foundation serves three constituencies:

- Donors, who are offered a variety of options through which they can achieve their charitable objectives, such as Named Funds, Discretionary Funds, Donor Advised Funds, Field of Interest Funds, and so on;[24]

---

[24] In a Named Fund, a separate fund is created under the main endowment, named after the donor and his wishes; in a Discretionary Fund the donor creates a fund in the community foundation and allows the foundation's trustees discretion in using the fund's income for a broad range of community issues; while in a Field of Interest Fund the donor identifies a particular area of interest, such as health, youth, the arts, or the environment, and gives the Foundation's trustees discretion to use the annual income within the specific geographical area covered by the community foundation. Many such variations are possible.

- Communities, which benefit from the assets created by the use of the community funds and from actions aimed at improving the quality of life in the community; and
- Charitable organizations which work in the community, and who receive grants from the community foundation for their development and welfare work.

The concept of pooling community resources for community betterment has existed in some form in both rural and urban areas of India from ancient times, but only recently has it taken the formal institutional form of a foundation in India. Community philanthropy seeks to harness local resources and local traditions of giving, and blends them with new institutional forms. In India, community philanthropy largely consists of donations to NGOs working on social issues, rather than donation to community foundations, as described.

Globally there are more than 1,800 community foundations, almost three-quarters of them created in the last twenty-five years, but only sixteen or so community foundations in India, in addition to about a hundred community funds established by small local rural communities. Amongst the few comunity foundations in India are The Valley Dew Community Foundation (VDCF), established by the people of Mukkodlu village in Kodagu district of Karnataka, the Sainik Foundation (SF), Uttarakhand and Uttar Pradesh, and the West Bengal Community Foundation (WBCF), West Bengal. Many of these were promoted or supported by the erstwhile intermediary organization Sampradaan .

Motives

Apart from a change in the profile of the donors, a second discernible shift is in the motivation for giving. The underlying motivations, such as an instinctive desire to help the less fortunate, passion for a cause, wanting to make a difference, and to pay back a debt to society, as well as to have one's name or that of some dear one memorialized, remain unchanged. But giving out of a nationalist fervour, which was evident in the pre- and immediate post-Independence period, has more or less disappeared. So has the religious motivation even for secular purposes, especially in the case of large scale giving, whereas in traditional philanthropy religion was a powerful motivating force. While privately the rich may give to religious organizations in charity, the public face of their giving is secular. Only occasionally will mention be made of a wealthy HNWI giving to build a temple, though it still happens. But Indian philanthropy is no longer equal to temple building, as the Birla philanthropy was wrongly accused of being in an earlier era.

The giving by the super-rich is also less out of guilt, though in some cases it is to expiate some wrong committed.

The main motive for large-scale giving seems to be a desire to pay back to society for having enabled the donor to succeed. This is especially visible in the case of NRIs giving to their alma mater in India and of Indian donors to their alma maters abroad.

A recent study by the Centre for Emerging Market Solutions (CEMS) at the Indian School of Business, Hyderabad, and FSG Social Impact Consultants, a global non-profit consulting firm, which looked at the patterns and trends among India's big philanthropists, concludes that philanthropic activity among India's UHNWIs reflects the infancy of the field, because 60 per cent of survey respondents said the main force behind their philanthropy was 'giving back to society'. Only 25 per cent cited 'effecting meaningful and measureable social change' as their main motivation. The study concludes that while India's largest givers are driven to philanthropy by a heightened sensitivity to social inequities in the country, it is only a minority whose giving is aimed at solving social problems.[25]

Pressure from the government is also not so important a driver of philanthropy now, since the government is in any case compulsorily making the rich pay for social development through the 2 per cent CSR contribution.

[25] Nidhi M. Reddy, Lalitha Vaidyanathan, Katyayani Balasubramaniam, Kavitha Goraopali, Sharad Sharma, 'Catalytic Philanthropy in India: How India's Ultra-high Net Worth Philanthropists are Helping Solve Large-scale Social problems', Centre for Emerging Market Solutions (CEMS) at the Indian School of Business, Hyderabad, and FSG Social Impact Consultants, February 2012.

In the UK giving by the rich is growing, because in a context of increasing wealth disparity, some of the wealthiest people are said to be deeply uncomfortable with a situation of massive wealth-holding by a few in the face of increasing need, and have responded accordingly. In India too, this is a motive for some, though not all of the rich. Many do not appear to feel uncomfortable at all. In fact, the attitudes of the new business class as a whole are different. Gone is the austerity and simple living espoused by business leaders of the older era, when Lala Sriram and others advocated simple living on the part of the well-to-do in order to reduce discontent among the poorer sections.

In its place has emerged a hedonistic lifestyle and open flaunting of wealth, with conspicuous consumption on weddings and other functions, instead of spending on social causes. The richest industrialist in India is known less for his philanthropy than for his very visibly lavish lifestyle.

While in the USA many of the richest donors like Warren Buffet and Bill Gates are concerned about leaving an over-large inheritance to their children, and see philanthropy as a solution to that problem, this is not as yet a concern for the rich in India, given India's strong family and kin ties.

But at least for some of India's rich, philanthropy is coming to represent *a way to enrich their own lives*. This also perhaps explains why many like Shiv Nadar, Hemendra Kothari, Nandan Nilekani, and Ronnie Screwvala are now approaching it as a second career. Having made their money at a very early age, they have energy, time, and desire to devote themselves to doing good for the public.

In traditional philanthropy, donors gave for a cause or an institution out of a sense of identity or belonging to a place or community. For instance, G.D. Birla created the Birla Institute of Technology (BITS) at Pilani out of a sense of belonging: it was the Birla home land. Similarly with many of the other big donors such as the Chettiars, who enriched their homeland Chettinad and Chennai with numerous institutions. Either the identity was with a place— their birthplace, their college, or their community—or because they identified with the cause, such as the freedom struggle or women's emancipation. Such motives are not entirely absent among the new donors either. Certainly, as we have seen in the case of donations to

Harvard by Ratan Tata and others, and to the IITs by their alumni, a desire to pay a debt of gratitude and identification with a place or institution counts as much today as it did yesterday.

But giving is no longer limited to one's place of origin or domicile. It has become pan national and even pan global and for causes which may not have any personal connection but which are believed to benefit humanity at large.

Many affluent middle-class Indians are now giving to formal organizations working nationally, instead of only to their immediate community. A common thread in such giving is a strong family influence and a desire to achieve scale in order to solve society's problems. Saving taxes is a motivating but not a primary factor in the giving decision, though with the intergenerational transfer of wealth likely to be on a very large scale, and wealth managers playing a greater role in the management of such transfers, tax planning and tax incentives for charity will definitely count for more.

Finally, one of the motives for philanthropy, namely to have one's name immortalized in the institutions endowed, may no longer work if a trend now becoming visible in the West spreads to India. In the West, even some well-known institutions are replacing the original donor's name with that of a later larger donor, or out of political correctness (expediency). For instance, a $100 million gift from Hollywood producer David Geffen toward the rebuilding of Lincoln Centre in New York led to the renaming of Avery Fisher Hall after him. Students of the University of Cape Town agitated to remove the statue of Rhodes from the university on the ground that he was an oppressive colonizer. In similar fashion, Princeton University is apparently riven by demands that the university rename buildings that honour Woodrow Wilson, on the ground that he advanced segregation in Washington DC.[26] Who knows, but revisionism may catch up with the JJ School of Art on the ground that Jamsetjee Jeejibhoy, after whom the school is named, was an opium trader!

[26] Christopher Caldwell, 'Donor Beware', *The Wall Street Journal Review*, 12–13 March 2016.

7

Less than Half the Sky

Women as Philanthropists

If non violence is the law of our being, the future is with woman.
Who can make a more effective appeal to the heart than woman?[1]

Mao Zedong famously proclaimed that 'Women Hold Up Half the
Sky'. Though true in other spheres, it does not fully apply to women
as philanthropists. Though women's philanthropy has existed in
India through the ages, given the underlying fact that creation of
wealth was almost exclusively a male preserve till very recent years,
the story of Indian philanthropy is mostly a His story. This is now
changing, albeit very slowly.

Though women have been the object of philanthropy, and in
some cases, prime movers themselves, the field of women's studies
has so far taken little note of this aspect of women's lives. Recent
studies of the Indian women's movement have touched on the role of
women as 'doers', and some historians of social work have glanced at
voluntary social work by women, but there are no historical studies,
theoretical analyses, or empirical surveys of women as 'givers', that

[1] Mahatma Gandhi, *Young India* (Bombay: Pragjee Soorjee and
Company, 10 April 1930).

is, as philanthropists. Nor have studies on philanthropy in general analysed how much of philanthropy is directed specifically to women and in what form and for what issues.

The role of women as donors raises several questions which are yet to be answered. Perhaps the most fundamental one is, does women's philanthropy deserve separate treatment? If yes, is it because the factors affecting it are different in some way from those affecting philanthropy in general? Is the practice of philanthropy, in terms of the issues chosen for focus, the instruments or methods deployed to address them, and the outcomes, different because women are at the helm? The answer to the first two questions is a definite yes; the answer to the last is not clear, given the absence of detailed micro-level data, and is the reason why women's philanthropy needs more systematic study. There are no surveys offering quantitative estimates about the amount of philanthropy which flows *to* women; nor of what comes *from* women, on which to draw for definitive conclusions. The following attempts to open some windows on the issue in the hope that it may lead to a more systematic and comprehensive work on the subject. In what follows, it is almost axiomatic that the focus of attention is on middle and upper class, and urban women only, for historically only these women have had money, education, or time for philanthropy, as defined.

In general, the same factors which encourage or constrain philanthropy apply to giving by women: a culture of giving, an enabling legal and political environment, government policies which allow or discourage the accumulation of wealth and its disbursal according to one's inclination, the level of education in society, and the level of societal consciousness. But there are some factors which singularly affect women's ability to give and to manage their philanthropy. Prime among these is the status of women in society, as reflected in the level of their economic independence, educational opportunities, mobility outside the house, self confidence, and self assertion. A low status indicated by a deficit in any of these, either due to a patriarchal culture, and/or legal and customary barriers to possessing property, impinges on their ability to engage in philanthropy. None of these factors apply to men, to the same degree. It is primarily for this reason that women's philanthropy needs to be looked at separately. Even though their motives for wanting to give for social progress would probably be the same as men's, it is surmised that their choice of issues to focus on, or their approach to giving, would be coloured by gender differences.

Though charity requires no education and only a compassionate heart and enough means to share with others, philanthropy, as defined, requires education and social ability in order to understand what social issues need to be addressed and how, in order to get the best results; and substantial means and the ability to devote one's own wealth for the purpose. It is to their credit that despite their generally low socio-economic status, Indian women have made significant contributions to social progress even while remaining outside the formal power and profit structure. As will be seen below, lack of economic independence and an enabling socio-legal structure may have inhibited philanthropy by women, but socio-political movements have encouraged it.[2]

Women and Philanthropy before Independence

In pre-capitalist times, women, no less than men, were motivated by religious ideals to donate time and money in the service of the needy. That they did so is clear from legends and inscriptions and religious texts. While the charity of the average woman in pre-British times was probably limited to almsgiving to mendicants and students, there are several instances on record of wealthy women, especially queens, courtesans, and wives of wealthy merchants, giving wealth and houses to monastic orders, endowing temples, and building tanks and wells for public use.

While women enjoyed a high position in ancient India, with the beginning of the Christian era they were pushed to a subordinate status. Denied education, married off early, prevented from doing paid work, the women of the upper castes and classes had no economic independence and had limited property rights.

Even where women enjoyed some rights in property, they had only a life interest and did not have full ownership rights and could not alienate, sell, or mortgage it. After the death of her husband a

---

[2] Portions of this chapter have appeared earlier in Pushpa Sundar, 'Women and Philanthropy in India', *Voluntas* 7: no. 4 (1997): 412–25.

widow had only a right of maintenance and could not claim any other rights in joint family property. A woman's right of usufruct was also subject to her not re-marrying. In a Hindu undivided family (HUF), a woman could never be a *karta* or administrator of the family wealth or property.

But there was one class of property over which women had full control—the *stridhana* (woman's wealth), given at the time of marriage. A woman was considered the absolute owner of such property and could dispose of it any way she liked—theoretically. In practice, it was often managed by the husband or the male members of the family, for the family.

Muslim women, however, enjoyed full property rights, although their share in the property was limited to half the share of the male of the same degree, and a widow's share was limited to one-eighth. A woman was entitled to a dower from her husband that she could, theoretically, dispose of as she wanted, whereas she could dispose of her other property only up to a third. Although they had better property rights, Muslim women suffered many of the same disabilities as Hindu women—limited social mobility, lack of education, and so on, so that the property rights were more apparent than real.

With such restrictive property rights, it is not surprising that there were few women donors. Only women with a considerable stridhana could indulge their philanthropic impulses on any significant scale. In spite of this, several of them did devote their wealth to good causes. In the reform movements of the late nineteenth and early twentieth century, which were aimed at reforming religious practices and women's status in society, philanthropy *for* women was very much in evidence. Education was deemed to play a major role in improving the lot of women and so promoting women's education became a major plank of Indian philanthropy. It is worth noting that the reform movement for improving the lot of women was initially led by men like Ishwarchandra Vidyasagar, Dayananda Saraswati, D.K. Karve, and others but later several remarkable women like Pandita Ramabai, Kamlabai Hospet, and Parvatibai Athavale, some of them child widows themselves, set up women's organizations to improve the lot of widows and destitute women. Apart from donating to these organizations whatever they could of their own resources, these remarkable women raised funds from other donors.

Parvatibai Athavale, herself widowed early, travelled all over India to collect rupees 70,000 in twenty years—a large sum for the time. In Bengal and Punjab too, women set up women's schools and destitute women's homes by raising funds for them.

Prominent among the philanthropists of the nineteenth-century Bengal were two women—Rani Rasmani (1793–1861) of Janbazar and Rani Swarnamayee (1829–97) of Kashimbazar. They typify the new motives and expressions of philanthropy mingling with the old. Rani Rasmani built the Dakshineswar temple; but she also carried out many other works of direct social benefit and was one of the chief contributors to the city's development. Swarnamayee spent generously on education of women above all.[3]

Another notable woman philanthropist was Swarnakumari Devi of the elite Tagore family. In 1886 she founded the Ladies Association to promote a spirit of service among women, and to help widows and orphans by educating them. She raised money by holding women's handicraft fairs at which products made by women were sold to women. Later, she established the Hiranmoyee Widow's Industrial Home.[4]

In Bombay (Mumbai), a dynastic philanthropic tradition was set by the Wadia family, descendants of Lowjee Nusserwanjee Wadia, who left Surat to become a master shipbuilder and founded the Wadia shipbuilding dynasty. He and his descendants gave liberally to Parsi charity. Among them, the most outstanding philanthropist was Nowrojee Maneckji. Nowrojee was greatly influenced by his mother Motlibai, a philanthropist in her own right.

Widowed at the age of twenty-six, Motlibai, inheritor of a vast fortune, was herself from a very philanthropically oriented Parsi family, who donated liberally to charitable causes. In 1888 she gave a magnificent donation for the construction of an obstetric hospital.

Nowrojee's wife Jerbai continued the Wadia tradition. She used the money he had made in his lifetime to improve the living condition of the workers in the mills. She went from site to site, bought

---

[3] Pushpa Sundar, *Beyond Business: From Merchant Charity to Corporate Citizenship* (New Delhi: Tata McGraw-Hill, 2000), p. 119.
[4] Sundar, 'Women and Philanthropy in India': 417.

up land wherever she could find it, determined to build housing colonies that would improve the quality of life for the poor. She herself examined the plans of the buildings and created trusts for their upkeep. When her son died she used his estate to create Rustam Baug, a housing estate. Her work was continued and expanded by her sons, Sir Cusrow and Sir Ness Wadia. They built Cusrow Baug, a housing estate, hospitals for women and children, lent their support to the Wadia College, and set up funds for scholarships and help to the indigent.[5]

Lady Ratan Tata, a remarkable lady and a philanthropist in her own right, assumed the leadership and administration of the two Tata Trusts, the Sir Dorab Tata and Sir Ratan Tata Trusts, in the Twenties. Far in advance of her time in her approach to philanthropy, she invited F.S. Markham of the Museum Association, London to advise the Sir Ratan Tata Trust on how best to proceed to meet its objectives. In 1932, the Sir Dorab Tata Trust requested Dr Clifford Manshardt, a noted expert on social work, who had established the Nagpada Neighbourhood House to help mill workers, to study the trust and make policy recommendations which were then adopted.

Among other women of the period who endowed institutions for charitable causes was Maharani Chimnabai of Baroda State. She was actively involved in welfare activities for women and set an example for aristocratic philanthropy by founding several magazines on women's health, politics, and education.

The movement for setting up of the Benaras Hindu University began in 1911, spearheaded by Pandit Madan Mohan Malviya, and in February 1916 the foundation stone of the new university was laid in Benaras (now Varanasi). What was remarkable was that different social classes and groups were targeted by the fund raising campaign for the university. While the wealthy were of course a principal focus, the middle and lower castes and classes were pursued too. According to Carey Watt (2005), who studied the movement in detail, there were several donations from women too. Amongst the lists of donations published regularly in the *Central Hindu College Magazine* were some women donors—one a widow, and another who gave jointly

5 Sundar, *Beyond Business*, p. 136.

with her father.[6] From this one can presume that a small percentage of women were engaging in charity and philanthropy of the new kind on their own account throughout the twentieth century.

Women also gave donations to Kangri Gurukul and other Arya Samaj institutions for women, including the Kanya Mahavidyalaya (KMV) in Jalandhar. It is estimated that about 25 per cent of donations to the KMV came from women.

Women were also active in fund raising activities for the modern social service organizations. Watt mentions the name of Padmavati Devi, who was a key figure in raising funds for the Women's College in Benaras. He also cites the example of Lajjyawanti, who vowed to collect rupees 50,000 on her own and achieved her objective within a year, after extensive tours of the Punjab and other regions of India.

However, it is interesting to note that there were critical comments in various journals about women trying to usurp the functions of men in public life. Making donations to modern causes by women was more acceptable than active fund raising.[7]

A new category of social action called 'social work' or 'social service' had also emerged in the inter-war years. Earlier charitable work, though voluntary, was generally ad hoc and mostly ameliorative. The noticeable change was in the professional approach now adapted to doing good, with a thrust on prevention, rather than on relief.

Outstanding examples of the new approach were the preventive work done in maternal, infant, and child welfare fields by the Bombay Presidency Infant Welfare Society under the leadership of Lady Cowasji Jehangir and Sir Mangaldas Mehta, and the work for prevention of juvenile delinquency by the Society for Protection of Children in Western India, led by Sir Rustom and Lady Masani. Women of the business aristocracy, especially wives of leading Parsi industrialists, were in the vanguard of such social work, among them Lady Ratan Tata, Lady Cowasji Jehangir, and Jerbai Wadia of the House of Wadia in Bombay, and Swarnakumari Debi of the elite Tagore family in Calcutta, who gave both time and money to their causes.

[6] See Carey Watt, *Serving the Nation: Cultures of Service, Association and Citizenship in Colonial India* (Oxford University Press, New Delhi, 2005), p. 81.

[7] Watt, *Serving the Nation*, p. 86.

Janaki Devi Bajaj, wife of wealthy industrialist Jamnalal Bajaj, shared a close relationship with him, and had actively associated herself with all his activities. According to Mahatma Gandhi, the businessman who came closest to his ideal of 'trusteeship' was Jamnalal Bajaj. His philanthropic activities were widespread—in Bombay, Vidarbha, and his home district in Rajasthan; he gave for important causes elsewhere as well. After meeting Gandhi Jamnalal's life was completely changed. He put himself and his wealth at the disposal of Gandhi not only for the freedom movement, but also for his constructive programme of removal of untouchability, popularization of khadi and village industries, promotion of basic education, and Hindu–Muslim unity. Janaki Devi shared his interest in all these activities, and also surrendered her wealth after his death for the *Goseva* or cattle improvement programme in which he had been interested, and other causes.

Amongst the mill-owning elite, those who have left an indelible impression on Ahmadabad's social life is the Sarabhai family. Anasuyaben Sarabhai, who returned from Europe before the First World War, and was impressed by the new ideals of social service which she had witnessed there, committed herself to noble causes in Ahmedabad. She devoted her time to education and social reform among mill workers. She also organized them, and the modern trade union movement of Ahmadabad owes much to her. Her sister Mridulaben Sarabhai founded Jyoti Sangh, a women's welfare organization for destitute women.

In the North, Gujar Mal Modi (1902–76) established a major business empire. Along with business activities, Gujar Mal also devoted himself to social welfare activities. He built up several organizations such as the Shri Modi Eye Hospital and Ophthalmic Research Centre at Modi Nagar, and the R.B. Multanimal Modi Charitable Trust and Sainik Bhavan at Patiala. In much of his philanthropic work he was aided by his wife Dayawati Modi. She worked in refugee camps and provided victims with food, clothing and shelter, and took an active interest in education and women's welfare, arranging for widows' remarriage, and providing jobs and skills to helpless women.

What emerges from the above limited survey is that women of wealthy families played both a primary and secondary role as philanthropists. The foundation of several business dynasties was laid in the pre-Independence period, and these dynasties were often in the vanguard of philanthropy as well. The women of many of these families actively assisted their husbands or other family members in their philanthropic activities, but also went beyond assisting to endow or manage organizations or institutions in their own right, especially after the death of their husbands.

Until the late 1800s, women's agendas were largely welfare oriented and non-political in nature. Thereafter, women became interested in both welfare works as well as in struggle for political rights and social reforms through legislation. The early twentieth century saw a proliferation of widows' homes and orphanages to provide for education and training, and the establishment of several national organizations to provide a political platform for women. Most of these associations were privately funded by individual donations and gifts by the wealthy, and hardly any funding was offered by the state.

Mahatma Gandhi inspired several women both to participate in the national struggle and to share in the task of national development. For instance, Janaki Devi Bajaj, after becoming a widow, became a great worker in the *Bhoodan* movement, led by Gandhi's disciple Vinoba Bhave, for more equal land distribution in rural India. Gandhi cast his spell not only on wealthy aristocratic women but also on the average Indian woman. It is impossible to record the names of the many Hindu and Muslim women who contributed to or raised money to found charitable organizations for women in pre-Independent India.

Among the women whose philanthropic work spanned both the pre- and post-independence eras, and who both assisted their family in their philanthropic ventures and initiated some in their own right, was Sarala Birla, wife of industrialist B. K. Birla. Her collection of Indian art, including that on display at the Birla Academy of Art and Culture in Kolkata, ranks amongst India's most distinguished private collections. Academically well qualified, and more self-assured than many young women of the conservative Rajasthani Marwari community of the time, she partnered her husband on most of his ventures including some forty-five educational institutions like the Birla Institute of Technology & Science, Ashok Hall Group of Schools, Mahadevi Birla World Academy, G. D. Birla Centre for Education, B.K. Birla Institute of Engineering & Technology (BKBIET), and many more. The Sangit Kala Mandir, Kolkata and the Birla Academy of Art and Culture, Kolkata, owe their origins to the efforts of both Sarala Birla and her husband.

Paradoxically, all these women social entrepreneurs and philanthropists unequivocally accepted the Gandhian ideology that women's prime function and responsibility was to be housewife and mother and that while men and women had equal rights, their duties were different. Women philanthropists in the post-Gandhi era, however, have been swayed by a different ideology—of gender equality and empowerment of women on all fronts so that they fulfil their full potential, whether inside or outside the home.

To sum up, philanthropic effort in the pre-Independence period was largely concentrated in three areas: the education of women and girls; the relief of groups under distress, especially of vulnerable women such as child widows, unmarried mothers, and orphans or deserted women, through provision of shelter and schemes for economic independence; and the political and legal emancipation of women.

Women and Philanthropy after Independence

With the waning of the nationalist and Gandhian fervour after Independence, women's philanthropy too ceased to be a strong force. Centralized planning, the consequent high taxation needed to raise resources for development by the state, inflation, and rise of consumerism, all contributed to reducing donations. The consequent disinterest in philanthropy extended to women as well. However, trusts continued to be formed *in* women's names and *for* women, such as the Srimati Nathibai Damodar Thakersay (SNDT) university for women, endowed by Sir Thakersay in memory of his mother.

After the late 1960s the picture changed for general philanthropy. A slow growth rate and the government's ineffectiveness in removing poverty led to the growth of a strong civil society movement. Wealthy individuals once again began to support voluntary organizations with donations, especially once tax policy gave exemptions for philanthropy, and slowly philanthropy began to rise from its earlier slumber. While women, especially young women, entered the voluntary sector in much greater numbers, and also gave donations to civil society organizations, especially during times of calamity, the fact is that, till recent times, philanthropy by women has not been significant, even as philanthropy *for* women has been on the rise.

Thanks to the women's movement and greater awareness of gender issues due to the declaration of 1975 as Women's Year by the UN, giving for empowerment of women is on the rise, especially for better education and nutrition of girl children—for long a most neglected section of society—and to improve the livelihoods of women. Trusts such as the Chameli Devi and the Neerja Bhanot Foundations have been endowed by the relatives of these women for giving awards and scholarships to women, while non-profit organizations funded by prominent industrialists, such as Nanni Kali, established by Anand Mahindra of the Mahindra and Mahindra Group, focus on the girl child.

Women have also continued to manage their family trusts, if any. For instance, Shobhana Bharatiya of the Birla family, the late Manju Bharat Ram of the Shri Ram family, and Sita Subbiah of the Murugappa Chettiar family have, among many others, worked to further the philanthropic projects of their families.

But until recently few of them bequeathed their wealth for social causes on their own account, though there were some notable exceptions. For instance, Sumitra Charat Ram, from the leading Sri Ram family, established the Bharatiya Kala Kendra for art and culture promotion. Rajashree Birla, mother of Kumarmangalam Birla, Chairman of Aditya Birla Group of industries, has set up and is the driving force behind the Aditya Birla Centre for Community Initiatives & Rural Development, which has a presence in 3,000 villages. Additionally, she also oversees two family foundations, and has taken up the cause of widow remarriage, assisting 500 widows so far. Recent projects include a 325-bed hospital near Pune that is named after her late husband, Aditya.

Durgabai Deshmukh and Kamladevi Chattopadhyaya are other names on the role of honour of women contributing to philanthropy and social causes in their own right. They both dedicated their lives to building institutions for women such as the Andhra Mahila Sabha in the case of Durgabai, and for causes they believed in, such as revival of crafts, in the case of Kamladevi, giving both their own resources and time.

In most cases though, the top-level decisions were and are still being made by the male members in family concerns or male CEOs in corporations, though the day-to-day running of philanthropic projects is increasingly being relegated to women family members. These few exceptions apart, women's philanthropy remained lethargic till the end of the twentieth century.

Constraints on Women

In the funding of women's organizations, outright and regular donations or bequests from women count less than other means of funding, such as membership fees, special charitable events, sales of goods, and/or grants from government or foreign funders.

The reasons why women's philanthropy has remained on a low key until very recent times are not far to seek. Women's ability to earn incomes and to save and invest them for wealth creation remains low, as can be seen from the fact that the overall participation rate of women in the workforce is very low, at only 29 per cent, as compared to 80 per cent for men. This is partly due to the lower female literacy of only 62 per cent, as against 85 per cent for men. The general environment is also against self-assertion of women in any field, with discrimination in wages and lack of opportunities for greater upward mobility. Gender inequality in the workplace is also exhibited in occupational segregation. Working women have to constantly battle against not only horizontal segregation but also the separation of women and men into gender-specific jobs. Though Indian law stipulates equal wages for equal work by men and women, in fact, women's remuneration is lower. According to the Global Gender Gap Index 2009 of the World Economic Forum, women's estimated earned annual income (approximately rupees 55,790) is less than a third of men's income (approximately rupees 1,74,102). However, the perceived gap in wages for similar work is a little narrower, with women's incomes perceived to be roughly two-thirds of men's incomes.

Even where they are employed in significant numbers, such as in IT and hospitality industries, most women are employed in junior roles and there is a significant 'pipeline leakage' from junior to middle management ranks. They are estimated to hold less than one in eight management roles in Indian companies and this falls to one in twenty at executive levels. Advancement of women in management jobs has not kept pace with the corresponding increase in the number of working women. Their presence in senior management levels is negligible.

Though the numbers of women graduating is almost 50 per cent of the total number of graduates, only 10 to 15 per cent of students admitted to the Indian Institute of Management (IIM) or IITs, which would guarantee entry to senior management levels right away, are female. Consequently, though many are entering management positions, yet there is a bottleneck at middle management.

Women are even fewer when it comes to board-level positions in Indian companies. It is estimated that out of 1,112 directorships of 100 companies listed on the Bombay Stock Exchange, only fifty-nine positions, or 5.3 per cent, are held by women. This compares with 15 per cent in Canada, 14.5 per cent in the US, 12.2 per cent in Britain, 8.9 per cent in Hong Kong, and 8.3 per cent in Australia.

On average, women account for 6 per cent of seats on corporate boards, and 8 per cent on executive committees. The failure to reach top management positions makes many believe that a glass ceiling operates to prevent women advancing in their careers. The 'glass ceiling' comes in many forms: for instance, women's underrepresentation in the corporate hierarchy, gendered wage gap, occupational segregation, discriminative corporate policies, sexual harassment at the workplace, exclusion of women from informal networks, and so on.

A prime reason for skewed opportunities for women and why few women reach the top or are able to strike out on their own, is a patriarchal culture and socio-cultural practices in both society and corporate workplaces, which militate against more women in the workforce and also against their achieving their full potential.[8]

India is still very much a conservative, traditional society and a woman's role is seen primarily to be that of a homemaker, not a career oriented woman. Family responsibilities must come first and personal fulfilment later. In order for this to happen, they are

---

[8] See Pushpa Sundar, 'Czarinas or Girl Fridays', and other articles in *Interrogating Women's Leadership and Empowerment*, IIC Quarterly, Winter 2012–Spring 2013.

socialized into seeing themselves as subordinate to men who will make all the important decisions, especially related to the external world. Their self-perception, therefore, is one of a follower, not a leader. It thus becomes difficult for them to assert their rights or see themselves in leadership roles or to be visionary philanthropists, even though women have some inherent strengths which are ideal for philanthropy. They are more intuitive by nature, are more empathetic with the underprivileged, and can lead naturally without being authoritarian.

Finally, the socio-legal hurdles to holding property continue to constrain women from becoming significant philanthropists. The 1956 Hindu Succession Act greatly enhanced women's property rights but left important loopholes which perpetuated women's inequality. The 1975 National Committee on the Status of Women reviewed these loopholes and made proposals to remove discrimination, but the picture has not changed substantially. The net result is that women are still not able to inherit and bequeath family fortunes freely. Only recently, in a landmark judgement, has the Supreme Court ruled that women can become *karta*s in HUFs.

Whether women's charitable donations would have increased if property laws might have been more favourable for them is difficult to say. But an unfortunate fact is that the boom in property prices has led to investment of surplus family wealth in property and jewellery by women as well as male heads, rather than in social causes. Alienating family wealth for public benefit is generally unthinkable. What is more, the increasing spends on wasteful wedding expenditure, including jewellery and on other pomp and show, is being fuelled largely by women.

Philanthropy Post Globalization

The globalization and opening of the economy has not only brought growth to India and led to a new wave of wealth creation, but has also led to an upswing in women's philanthropy, principally because it brought more opportunities for women to strike out on their own as creators of wealth. Several women have taken advantage of the more liberal environment and have become entrepreneurs in their own right. These women at the top fall into three categories, elaborated below.

In the first are women entrepreneurs like Kiran Mazumdar-Shaw of Biocon, Deepa Soman of Lumiere Business Solutions, Shahnaz Hussain of Shahnaz Beauty products, Paru Jaykrishna, CMD of Asahi Songwon Colours, Meena Bindra, Chairperson BIBA, and many others. They have perhaps faced the hardest battle in making it to the top. Those who have opened up non-traditional fields such as biotechnology, as Kiran Mazumdar has done, have perhaps faced even more constraints.

A second category of women are part of family businesses and perhaps have had less of a struggle in reaching the top because they were often groomed for the positions by the family owners of the companies. Nevertheless, women such as Shobhana Bharatiya, Chairman and Editorial Director of HT media, Mallika Srinivasan, Chairman of TAFE, who also has the distinction of being head of a company dealing with agriculture-related engineering products, Roshni Nadar Malhotra, Executive director and CEO of HCL Corp., Priya Paul, Chairperson of Apeejay and the Park Hotels chain of boutique hotels, and many others have proved their own worth, while taking the family firms to new heights.

Perhaps the largest category of women who have reached the top is that of professional women, whose rise has provided a role model for countless women. Starting at middle rungs, they have risen to the top through merit to feature among Fortune 500's top global CEOs. They are found at the top of large banks, such as Chanda Kochar, CEO of ICICI Bank, Shikha Sharma of Axis Bank, and Arundhati Bhattacharya, CEO of the State Bank of India. At the head of an MNC is one of the most celebrated women CEOs—Indra Nooyi, Chairperson and Chief Executive Officer of PepsiCo. Other well known women CEOs and directors in Indian firms include Sminu Jindal of Jindal Steel Ltd, Radha Singh of Yes Bank, Renu Sud Karnad of HDFC Ltd., and Vinita Gupta of Lupin.

All these women have played an important role in India's economic rise, and have vindicated women's potential to be as good in business as men. They have inspired other women, providing them with role models, though there is no evidence, either positive or negative, that they have actively encouraged or given a hand up to other women. What is common to these women is the fact that they have broken stereotypes and traditional mindsets and have managed to think out of the box, while exhibiting great leadership qualities. Today's women philanthropists come largely from these three categories.

Today's Women Philanthropists

This rise of the new women philanthropists has been noted in the *Hurun India Philanthropy Lists* of 2014 and 2015, brought out by the Hurun Research Institute, which ranks the most generous individuals from India. The 2014 list mentions philanthropic donations by women entrepreneurs, both individually and through joint donations from their family concerns. Amongst the individuals mentioned are Anu Aga, who individually donated rupees 140 million, and in 2015 upped it to 30 per cent of her and family's income; and Rohini Nilekani, Zarina Screwvala, Yasmin Gupta, and Savitri Jindal, who jointly with their families donated rupees 9.87 billion.[9] Kumari Shibulal is also a philanthropist, jointly with her husband.

Anu Aga is known as much for her social work and activism as her business accomplishments. In 2004, she retired as the chairperson of Thermax Ltd, handing over the command to her daughter Meher Pudumjee. Thermax is a $1.1 billion engineering solutions provider in the energy and environment sectors, which was founded by Anu's husband Rohinton Aga in 1966. Anu launched the Thermax Social Initiative Foundation (TSIS) in 2007, funding it with 1 per cent of pre-tax profits till 2011. Then the contribution was increased to 3 per cent of the company's pre-tax-profits annually, because Anu was inspired by Warren Buffet's visit in the year 2011. The foundation adopts the municipal corporation's schools in urban areas for children of lower-income groups in order to improve them. Alongside, Meher also helps people further their interest in music. Apparently, after meeting Buffet, both mother and daughter overcame their fear of losing wealth and have increased their giving. There is a generational difference in their approach to philanthropy. While Anu

[9] Hurun India Philanthropy Report 2014. Retrieved from http://www.hurun.net/EN/ArticleShow.aspx?nid=9583. Reported in *Business Standard and Other Papers*, Delhi, 30 December 2014.

looks for the passion behind projects, Meher is more concerned with sustainability and credibility.[10]

Kiran Mazumdar-Shaw of Biocon Industries, Bangalore, is one of the few who has been truly path-breaking in her choice of product line (biotechnology) and as a leading woman entrepreneur. Unable to become a doctor due to high capitation fees to get admission, which her principled father refused to pay, she is passionate about health care, especially for poor and marginalized communities, and cares particularly about cancer prevention and treatment. She has given rupees 400 million from her personal wealth, through the Biocon Foundation, to set up a cancer hospital and research centre inside Narayan Health City in Bangalore. In order to improve the cancer research expertise in India she has also funded two fellowships in oncology for Indians at the Koch Institute for Integrative Cancer Research at MIT, for which she has committed $2.5 million. The Biocon Foundation set up by her in 2004 has pioneered a mobile phone-based health initiative (mHealth) to ensure that cost effective health care reaches remote areas, as also a Health Micro Insurance programme, Arogya Raksha Yojana (ARY). The Biocon Foundation is her personal contribution to philanthropy, and her company contributes to CSR programmes separately.

Talking about the influences which led her to philanthropy, she mentions first her father, who taught her that money is not a currency with which you buy favours, but a currency with which you create more value, and therefore must be used wisely. So in 2005, as soon as her company went public, she created the Biocon Foundation as a personal vehicle for her philanthropy.

More recently, she has been influenced by the example set by Bill Gates and Warren Buffet in pledging 50 per cent of their wealth to philanthropy during their lifetimes, and the power of networking represented by the Giving Pledge to increase the impact of philanthropy. It has led her to become a part of the global Philanthropy Initiative led by them.

If the wives of the big philanthropists abroad—Bill Gates' wife Melinda, Laurene Powell Jobs, widow of the founder of Apple Inc.,

[10] Ahona Ghosh, 'Act of Giving: Giving Across Generations', *The Economic Times*, 4 October 2011.

Steve Jobs, and Susie and Jennifer Buffet, Warren Buffet's daughter and daughter in law—are managing the family foundations, the women of India's wealthy business families are not lagging behind. The wives of three leading philanthropists of India, namely Azim Premji, N.R. Narayana Murthy, and Nandan Nilekani are equally involved in their husband's philanthropy ,but each has also carved a niche for herself. They all have their own views on how philanthropy should be managed.

Sudha Murthy, wife of Infosys co-founder N.R. Narayana Murthy, heads the Infosys Foundation, which works with schools in Karnataka and sets up orphanages. Her mission is to build toilets in rural areas, especially for women. She plans to build 10,000 toilets in northern interior Karnataka. Also author of two dozen books, Sudha Murthy dedicates a portion of her royalty to the project. Like other modern philanthropists, Sudha Murthy also researches the cause and the credibility of an organization before donating money.[11]

Yasmeen Premji is passionate about design, but keeps a distance from her husband's company as well as his philanthropy. As for approach, Yasmeen Premji believes that philanthropy should be quick and generous and decision taking should not take years.[12]

Rohini Nilekani, wife of Nandan Nilekani, another co-founder of Infosys, the company which pioneered the Infotech revolution in India, is a major philanthropist in her own right. In August 2013 she set aside rupees 1.64 billion to back the causes which she believes will make a difference to Indian society. Her philanthropic projects include her charity Arghyam, which works on water resources conservation and utilization, and sanitation. She has also established the Akshara Foundation and Pratham Books, which work for children and education.

Recently, she sold a portion of her shares in Infosys, and plans to use her money to back select social ventures in the areas of governance, legal services, environment protection, and new media. She plans to manage the money directly to give grant capital to individuals and organizations, without endowing a foundation, so that she

[11] Reported in *The Indian Express*, 'Three Women Behind India's Top IT Tycoons Step Forward to Tell All', 27 December 2012.
[12] *The Indian Express*, 'Three Women Behind India's Top IT Tycoons'.

has flexibility, without being bound by the rules that govern corpus spending. For the present, the grants will be rupees 50 million each, and below. She wants to give grants rather than make social investments, because she feels that though markets can be a force for social good if people so choose, they cannot do everything and there is a need for philanthropic capital as well, that does not worry about financial return. This is a very welcome development, as grant money is scarce in India and very important for work in areas such as transparency and governance, where there can be no business model.

Realizing that individual philanthropic capital can be but a drop in the ocean, she is interested in creating a network effect to draw more philanthropic capital to worthy organizations, and like the others, she first wants to understand the likely impact of her giving before committing to any cause.[13]

Two other women, mother and daughter, have made a mark in the field of philanthropy in recent times. Kiran Nadar, wife of technology czar and HCL founder Shiv Nadar, is a trustee of the Shiv Nadar Foundation, and has set up the Kiran Nadar Museum of Art as a philanthropic private museum.

Her daughter, thirty-one-year old Roshni Nadar Malhotra, came back from the US three years ago after a management degree in social enterprise from Kellogg Graduate School and brief stints at Sky News and CNN as a news producer. She joined her father's companies with stints in treasury, finance, brand, and corporate strategy, but soon decided to take the road less travelled, into philanthropy.

'I am not interested in the technology business, at least not in getting hands on. My involvement will be at the corporation level, in the preservation of wealth rather than direct involvement in HCL', says Roshni, now executive director and CEO, HCL Corporation, and trustee of the Shiv Nadar Foundation. She oversees school education, one of the three areas in which her father's philanthropic foundation plans to spend a billion dollars in the next five years.

Her special project is the Vidya Gyan Schools, the two free schools that the Shiv Nadar Foundation has set up in Bulandshahr district

---

[13] *The Indian Express*, 'Three Women Behind India's Top IT Tycoons'. Also, Archana Rai, 'With Rs. 164 Crore, Rohini to Open Kitty for Governance', *The Economic Times*, 8 August 2013.

of UP, with the objective of building future leaders from among the bottom of the pyramid. This school is running since three years. She believes this could do to poor students in UP what Doon School and other elite schools do for India's elite.

The foundation spends rupees 150 thousand per child and offers free education from class six to the 12th standard. Roshni claims that they take the brightest lot from the bottom of the pyramid and try to give them the best education that any child in India can get. Her plan is not to take philanthropy to the masses, but rather to focus on the brighter students among the poor.[14]

Like other women from prominent business families, Nita Ambani, wife of Mukesh Ambani, chairman of the petrochemical and refining giant conglomerate, and India's richest man, manages the family's philanthropies. She is the founder and chairperson of Reliance Foundation, Reliance Corporation's philanthropic arm. The Reliance Foundation is said to have invested rupees 7.12 billion in FY 2013–14, comprising about 3.24 per cent of Reliance Industries Limited's profits for the said year. Nita Ambani, who is also on the Board of Reliance Corporation, asserts that she would not be able to pursue her passion for philanthropy without the wealth creation of the Reliance Company. The Foundation is focusing on five major areas: school education, healthcare, rural development, urban renewal initiatives, and art and culture.[15]

Khatija Kazi is an unusual woman philanthropist for two reasons: one, she is a Muslim and if women philanthropists are rare in India, a Muslim woman philanthropist is even rarer; and two, she is an NRI who is making her philanthropic investments in her home town in India. Comparatively, there are fewer wealthy Muslim families in India and the women of the community, in particular, suffer from several constraints such as lack of education and lack of social mobility. Khatija has been able to overcome these because she and her husband Zubair Kazi moved away from the small port town of Bhatkal in Karnataka to America and made their millions there. They then

---

[14] Caroline Hartnell's Interview with Roshni Nadar, *Alliance Magazine*, 13 May 2015.

[15] For details see Suman Layak, 'Reliance's Better Half', *The Economic Times Magazine*, 12–18 October 2014.

decided to help their town overcome the terrorist tag it had acquired for being home to several notorious terrorists.

Though it is Kazi who has put in the money, it was Khatija who identified the need for development to overcome communal strife and decided to use their money for educating the women of Bhatkal, so that they can take care of their children better and prevent them from going astray. She has set up the Bhatkal Women's Centre to provide computer courses, Montessori and KG classes, and courses on English language, cookery, and stitching. There is a library and a gymnasium too. She is also training them in holding exhibitions of their work, and in customer services. Though she is based in the USA, she visits the Centre at least twice a year, for a period of two months at a time.

The latest to join the ranks of Indian women philanthropists, though based abroad, is Indra Nooyi, PepsiCo's India-born CEO who, in January 2016, gifted an undisclosed amount to her alma mater, the Yale School of Management, becoming its biggest alumni donor and the first woman to endow a deanship at a top business school. (Also see Chapter 10 on education.)

The above is not an exhaustive list of India's current women philanthropists, but the narrative serves to bring out a few points concerning philanthropy by women in today's India. One, that philanthropies started by the men of the wealthy business families are today being managed by women of the family. Philanthropy is considered to be 'soft power' and women are considered to have a special aptitude for dealing with this aspect of wealth management. Today daughters, if any, are taking up the mantle of the fathers in philanthropy as well as business.

Two, the number of women who are philanthropists in their own right is still miniscule. Though a number of women entrepreneurs and professional women have reached the top of their field in their own stream, they are, by and large, yet to open their philanthropic innings. One of the reasons for this is that managing their work and careers in a highly competitive environment leaves them little time and inclination to take on philanthropy as a responsibility. Given India's patriarchal culture, unlike male wealth creators, they do not have the same backup and support, that is to say, they do not have 'wives'! The other possible reason is that, as is well known, it takes at least one to two generations, apart from their own, for an individual or family to feel secure enough about their wealth to give it away. Women who are first-generation wealthy will need time to become adept at giving away money on a large scale.

Three, women as philanthropists may be few in number but, as was seen in the last chapter, their influence on philanthropy as mothers should not be overlooked. Two of the foremost philanthropists of India today, namely Azim Premji and Shiv Nadar, are on record as having been inspired to give by their mothers. Women as mothers have played an important role in countless generations in promoting a culture of giving.

The seeds which have always been there are today sprouting, given more favourable conditions, and hopefully will grow more vigorously in the future.

8

Making a Difference—Differently

To give money away is an easy matter and in any man's power. But to decide to whom to give it, and how large and when, is neither in every man's power—nor an easy matter.

—Aristotle

Doing philanthropy is harder than doing business. It's tough. The market system does not give you feedback on philanthropy like it does when you are running a business. It is a long cycle before you know whether you did the right thing or not.[1]

The story of Indian philanthropy is one of continuity as well as change. Recent developments in the ecosystem have not only changed the profile of donors but have also led donors to do different things, and to doing old things differently.

In the main, the philanthropic preferences continue much as before, with most donors giving for education and health. However, within these broad fields there are changes in emphasis and methods, and new fields and causes have gained traction. There is also a difference in donors' approach to philanthropy and its management.

---

[1] Warren Buffet, on a visit to India to promote the Giving Pledge, 'First Photos: Warren Buffett in India', *Rediff Business*, 23 March 2011, http://www.rediff.com/money/slide-show/slide-show-1-warren-buffett-in-india/20110323.htm#7.

Philanthropic Preferences

Traditional

The causes espoused by philanthropists in India have varied at different periods. But what is striking is that they have mostly adapted their giving to emergent needs fairly quickly, so that the response was appropriate to the needs of the time.

When the educational, health, and social infrastructure was non-existent or inadequate, donors gave liberally to build such infrastructure. In addition to the establishment of schools, colleges, and universities, related causes such as supporting journals, newspapers, historical research, and development of languages and literatures, and improvement societies of all kinds also received private money. So too did campaigns to support the freedom struggle, women's emancipation, and welfare institutions for the special needy, such as widows and orphans. The civic amenities and institutional facilities of most cities—parks, gardens, drinking water stands, auditoria and halls, hospitals, hostels, public benches, and museums and art galleries also benefited from private philanthropy.

After Independence, the horizon was further broadened to support new fields of endeavour such as cancer research, wild life conservation, and management education. Several wealthy individuals like Vikram Lal of Eicher, the Lalbhais and Sarabhais, as well as corporations like the Tatas and ITC provided patronage to artists, filling the gap left by princely patrons. By donating their collections of books, precious artefacts, and art collections to museums and art galleries like the Prince of Wales Museum, the Birla Academy of Art and Culture, the L.D. Institute of Indology, and Calico Museum, some of the super-rich have also made art available to the art-loving public.

Around the Seventies, supporting rural development, especially for creating new livelihoods and income generation, became a popular area for philanthropic support, not least because the government offered substantial tax incentives for giving to the field.

A noticeable change during the period was the shift of focus from purely urban concerns to include the rural, and from concentration on building mega institutions to grassroots development. However, the interest in grassroots communities round their operational areas was largely the preoccupation of companies rather than wealthy individuals.

Over time, population control, environmental concerns, consumer issues, experimental architecture, research into classical music, and development of journalism were added to philanthropic portfolios.

Preferences Today

From impressionistic evidence as well as surveys such as the Bain and Co.'s annual reports, it is clear that education, healthcare, and promotion of livelihoods remain the favourite causes. This fits into a wider Asian trend of prioritizing educational causes, followed by poverty alleviation and development, then health and disaster relief.[2] But new issues are also being taken up.

New Issues in Education and Health

Even in education, if we look at the disaggregated picture, it is seen that there is a definite movement away from establishing brick and mortar buildings named after the donor, to innovative solutions to spread mass literacy and improve educational standards and delivery of education by using online resources and digital technology. For instance, Tata Trusts, the philanthropic arm of the Tata group of companies, is seeking to break out of the traditional approach to education by joining hands with Khan Academy, an online American teaching provider that reaches 26 million students worldwide. It extends free education to anyone, anytime, anywhere, which can diminish illiteracy rapidly. The five-year partnership will provide free world-class education in math and science in local languages to anyone who seeks it in India. The aim is to improve the content for middle- and low-income students, first in urban areas and then for rural areas.[3]

A few philanthropists like Azim Premji and Shiv Nadar are addressing the systemic issues of inefficiency, poor content, and poor coordination in public education, instead of focussing only on brick and mortar, especially in primary education. Some technology companies such as NIIT and Microsoft are working to bridge the digital divide.

---

[2] *UBS-INSEAD Study on Family Philanthropy in Asia*, 2011, p. 9.
[3] 'Tata Trusts, Khan Academy Plan to deliver Edu Online', *The Economic Times*, 7 December 2015.

In healthcare too, there is some move away from building hospitals to devising cheaper and better healthcare delivery for neglected sections of society, through digitally aided clinics, health help lines, and so on.

Research, especially scientific and medical research, hitherto a neglected area, is beginning to receive more attention. For instance, the Infosys Foundation has committed rupees 300 million to the Chennai Mathematical Institute for support of the faculty and students. And the Infosys Science Foundation has instituted what is considered the Indian Nobel Prize for outstanding research work in the pure and social sciences.

Though some ecologists like Kanwal S. Bawa feel philanthropy in India has not given sufficient attention to the environment, the fact is that environment has become a favoured field for philanthropy ever since climate change came on to the global agenda. After health and education, it probably ranks as a major interest for philanthropic giving, especially for companies who have to meet their mandatory CSR contributions. It is worth pointing out that J.R.D. Tata was one of the first individuals, from the world of business or otherwise, to point out the need for environment protection and more attention to environment issues. Setting an example the Tatas funded the Tata Energy Research Institute in Delhi, though now, after diversification of funding, it has been renamed The Energy Research Institute (TERI).

Women's Empowerment

Interestingly, yesterday's women's emancipation has become today's women's empowerment, with a different set of issues receiving more attention: issues such as gender parity in employment opportunities and wages, education and nutrition of the girl child, physical safety, and sexual harassment and sexual abuse are taking the place of social and legal reform for widow's rights, abolition of child marriages, education for women, and equal inheritance rights.

Governance

Not surprisingly, governance has become a major concern. Globally, billionaire philanthropists Pierre Omidyar and George Soros are among those that are pushing the governance and human rights agenda proactively. These philanthropists are of the opinion that issues of governance, if left only to politicians and bureaucracy, will get stymied and all their efforts in trying to address social issues will remain stunted or result in sub-optimal outcomes.

The governance systems of many countries encourage dishonesty, with complex and too many laws providing many loopholes for cheating. The disclosure provisions are inadequately implemented, and regulations do not help in the absence of rigorous implementation. For philanthropy to make the maximum impact, the broad governance framework has to be right, with transparency and accountability as its key virtues. Therefore, many global philanthropists feel that governance, including reform of the political and administrative system to make it transparent and to eliminate corruption, should be an important philanthropic concern.

Because the governance agenda has become a global issue, India cannot afford to be left behind, not least because it itself has a serious governance deficit.

One aspect of the agenda is to enable citizens to access government data in public interest. For instance, anyone wanting to work on extractive industries which account for a lot of today's corruption would need data on block-wise revenues from oil and gas fields, and payments and profits made by petroleum companies, to enable the filing of public interest litigation (PIL). But it is not available in the public domain. India has a long way to go in giving access to open data, or in offering philanthropic support for such research and advocacy.

In spite of the fact that very often it is the emerging class of venture capitalists, rich technocrats, and professionals who bemoan the corruption and the irresponsive nature of government, the number of those who are willing to support work on governance and political reforms is very small. Clearly, government money will not come forth for such work. But neither are many philanthropists interested in backing such initiatives since the process of creating accountable governance can be long and tortuous, and involves challenging the might of the state. A backlash would mean hurting shareholder interests.

Fortunately, a few brave hearts like Anu Aga, former Chairperson of the Thermax group, and a Rajya Sabha Member, believe that one must go beyond company interests and do what is good for the country. Aga therefore supports the Association for Democratic Reforms, as do some other new philanthropists, especially in Bangalore and Mumbai, who believe that who is funding what and why is critical in national policy issues.

Narayana Murthy, founder of Infosys Technologies, funded the Right to Information (RTI) awareness campaigns in the early years, leading to the Right to Information Act. Now Rohini Nilekani supports Data Spend, a data journalism initiative. Rohini, who raised rupees 1.64 billion by selling her Infosys shares in late 2014, believes these new areas are important for India, and is therefore also supporting the Takshashila Institution, a pro-market think tank, though she disagrees ideologically with it on many development issues. According to her, 'The idea is to trigger healthy debates, to have a multiplicity of voices, of all hues and biases'.

For the same reasons, she supports the Spending and Policy Research Foundation, the Ashoka Trust for Research in Ecology and Environment, the Association for Democratic Reforms, the PRS Legislative Research, the Vidhi Centre for Legal Policy, Forum for Medical Ethics, the Economic and Political Weekly, and the Indian Institute for Human Settlements, which focuses on urbanization issues.

Luis Miranda of IDFC PE is also funding think tanks for the same reason—to get diverse views into policy making. He is backing the Centre for Civil Society in Delhi, and Gateway House in Bangalore, to get a more right wing perspective into decision making and to integrate foreign policy with business views.

Mohandas Pai, another of the Bangalore philanthropists, supports the Bangalore Political Action Committee (BPAC), which is also supported by fellow Bangalorean, Kiran Mazumdar Shaw of Biocon.

C.V. Madhukar, co-founder of PRS Legislative Research (PRS) and director for governance related investments at the India office of Omidyar Network, feels that working on or funding governance matters need not be confrontational or harm business interests. Safe issues can be looked at to begin with. For instance, the Omidyar Network plans to publish an annual 'State of the Judiciary' report on the lines of the state of the environment, or state of education reports already being done by some civil society organizations. It would shed light on judicial delays, types of cases, and number and nature of PILs.[4]

Some of the new philanthropists have established think tanks, or organizations supporting different ideologies to promote democratic reforms and data access, such as the Observer Research Foundation funded by the Ambanis and the Shiv Nadar-funded Centre for Critical Thinking. Instead of merely blaming politics and politicians, they, like others, feel that they have to help rebuild the institutions of democracy by cutting edge research, training, and advocacy for a new type of politics and politicians.

Mostly, the new progressive donors come from middle-class, professional backgrounds who understand the value of research and advocacy in getting the policy mix right for progress. Hopefully, this trend will gather strength in the coming years, and with better funding from private sources, research and advocacy will become more rigorous and objective.[5]

Media

Recognizing its power and outreach in influencing public opinion, a new avenue for philanthropic attention is the media. The mainstream media is hampered by the ownership pattern. Its need to make profits from advertising compromises its impartiality and independence, leaving it open to political interference. Some new philanthropists have therefore begun to support alternative media arrangements such as web portals. Pierre Omidyar, founder of eBay, has already committed $250 million to a radically new media platform called Look Media, which also works in India. Rohini Nilekani, too, feels media plays an important role in governance and she is therefore part of a joint initiative of several Bangalore philanthropists who have begun to fund new media initiatives, such as the online paper, *The Wire*.

[4] The above information is from Naren Karunakaran's report in *The Economic Times*, a Special Feature on Philanthropy: 'Why They are Giving to Deepen Democracy and Governance', 4 November 2014.

[5] Naren Karunakaran, 'Indian Money for Indian Think-Tanks', *The Economic Times*, 4 November 2014.

Civil Society

The dynamic expansion of Indian civil society has been one of the major developments of the twentieth century, and NGOs/CSOs are now said to number approximately 3 million, though many of them may be defunct. While a few foundations like the Tata Trusts, the Sehgal Foundation, and some others have been supporting civil society organizations (CSOs) for some years now, they have largely been funded either by government or by foreign donors like the Aga Khan Foundation, the Ford Foundation, and the like. But with declining foreign aid, and especially because of the restrictions placed by government on Indian NGOs accessing foreign grants, NGOs are turning to indigenous sources of support. Indian companies, on their part, are seeking assistance from NGOs to fulfil their commitments under the Companies Act of 2013, since not too many companies have in-house expertise in social development.

While there is a greater willingness on the part of companies and some Indian foundations to give grants for specific development projects where they can see immediate and tangible outcomes in indices such as number of children in schools, litres of water treated, and so on, very few foundations or companies are willing to invest in building philanthropic infrastructure, or to give funds for institutional support and organizational development of NGOs which would enhance their capacity to work better. Hardly any thought is given by Indian donors as to whether the NGOs are capable of delivering the desired outcomes on the scale required. Some Indian donors have provided money for a few training courses of NGO staff, but by and large it is foreign aid agencies which have provided support for capacity building in the NGO sector.

Now, at last, a few individuals and foundations have realized the need for such support. Amit Chandra, MD of Bain Capital Advisors (India), a prolific donor to many causes, sees capacity building of NGOs as a way of getting better returns on capital (grant or equity). He and Dasra, Bombay, are funding a few NGO leaders to learn leadership or other key skills for managing NGOs, either at programmes in India or abroad.

Hemendra Kothari, Chairman, DSP BlackRock, is another person who feels that philanthropy should not mean just creating institutions in one's own name, but should include supporting the good work of NGOs and helping them scale up. The number of such donors needs to increase substantially if civil society is to become efficient in its chosen tasks.

Human Rights

In general, either politically or socially sensitive or controversial issues such as human rights, ethnic issues, insurgencies, and legal aid are avoided by HNWIs in deciding on causes to support, due to their potential for conflict.

But there are a few such as the redoubtable Ratan Tata who are not shy of approaching them. Ratan Tata, chairman emeritus of the Tata group, believes India is still feudal in its mindset and that much of the inequity in society can be attributed to the debilitating caste system. Dalit issues are, therefore, integral to his giving. And now, his successor Cyrus Mistry too is experimenting with innovative platforms to drive Dalit entrepreneurship.

They are part of a distinguished cohort of Indian philanthropists that also includes Adi Godrej of the Godrej Group, Anu Aga of Thermax, and Farhad Forbes of the Forbes Marshal Group, attempting to act on complex issues of Dalit empowerment in their own companies and outside.

When the fledgling Dalit Indian Chamber of Commerce & Industry (DICCI) was struggling to hold a convention and trade fair a couple of years ago in Mumbai, it was Adi Godrej who helped stage it. His forebear Ardeshir Godrej's first donation, in 1926, was for a Dalit cause.

When DICCI was a small, ragtag bunch of entrepreneurs from Pune, some even reluctant to come out of the closet as Dalits, Anu Aga and her daughter Meher Pudumjee, with their personal resources, helped them showcase the community.

Farhad Forbes, who witnessed the black empowerment movement in the US as a student, is one of the most ardent advocates of Dalits, both within his companies and outside. He has institutionalized a successful skills programme for Dalits and the underprivileged. The heft and visibility that this small group of business leaders has offered to affirmative action in the private sector is much more than what money can achieve. Their giving to the Dalit cause, despite the raised eyebrows of peers, is understated, and transformational.[6]

Legal Aid

Legal aid, especially for poor under-trials, is not a sexy enough subject for most philanthropists. But given the fact that the judicial system's wheels turn exceedingly slow, many of the poor who have fallen foul of the law spend even up to ten years in jail, waiting for their trials for even minor offences, because they cannot afford bail or to hire lawyers. Now news comes that Sunil Mittal, whose Bharti group has done the usual 'supporting school education' routine, has actually decided to take a pay cut of rupees 50 million as part of his company's move to launch a rupees 100 million initiative called the Nyaya Bharti Foundation, to provide financial and legal assistance to under-trials involved in minor offences for the first time.[7] Though it is part of the group's CSR programmes and not individual philanthropy, it nevertheless is breaking new ground for others to follow.

Humanities and Social Sciences

Though education is a favourite of most philanthropists, one area of darkness is giving for education in the humanities and social sciences. Most favour giving for technical education. But as in other areas, a small niche is opening here too.

Like many of the other new rich, the Narayana Murthy family has invested deeply in school education and other anti-poverty programmes as the only way to bring long-term change in poor lives. But they also recognize that philanthropy cannot concentrate only on poverty removal, important though that is, and that more is needed for progress of society than economics and technology. Therefore, they have also included support to humanities in their portfolio, especially

---

[6] Naren Karunakaran, 'How India Inc's Top Names like Azim Premji, Ratan Tata, Others Are Driving Philanthropic Initiatives', *Economic Times Bureau*, 2 October 2014.

[7] Report in *The Times of India*, 'Mittal Takes Rs. 5 cr Pay Cut for Legal Aid Initiative', 27 November 2015.

to bring the rich Indian classical heritage to global attention. India's classical learning gets more attention in Western universities than in India because of the abysmal funding for research on classical learning in the life sciences, astronomy, philosophy, and literature. The Murthy classical library, set up in 2010 at Harvard University with a $5.2 million endowment from the family to Harvard, is an effort to partly address this gap. The Harvard University Press will publish five English translations of classic works in the Indian languages every year. Narayana Murthy's son Rohan is in charge of the four-year project. The first translations will include Surdas and Abul Fazl.[8] Of course, questions have been raised as to why the donation had to be made to a Western university rather than to an Indian one. The Murthys' defence is discussed in Chapter 10.

The Gaps

Though newer causes are slowly coming onto the Indian philanthropists' horizons, there are several critical areas which continue to remain unaddressed or underfunded. For instance, C.N.R. Rao, awarded the Bharat Ratna, India's highest award, for his work in solid-state and structural chemistry, has expressed dissatisfaction with the level of science funding in India. Not only is the level of funding provided by the government inadequate, but, according to him, industry too is not doing enough to help science. No private foundation has stepped in with funds.[9]

Sex trafficking, a problem that is huge and unattended, will probably not receive attention from philanthropists for a long time along with other contentious issues such as labour, environmental and resource rights, individual right to privacy, freedom from gender or identity-based violence, or right to sexual expression.

Each philanthropist has his own pet projects and causes, which is as it should be. But by and large, it is foreign foundations which are more inclined to support underfunded or challenging and sensitive

[8] 'NRN Becomes Bellweather for Indian Classics', *The Economic Times*, New Delhi, 21 February 2014.
[9] 'Science Needs Corporate Funding, C.N.R. Rao Says', *Times News Network*, 13 May 2014.

development issues in India, while domestic philanthropists, conscious of potential negative consequences, tend to steer toward 'safe' issues, when it should be the exact opposite. Otherwise, the government uses the foreign contributions issue to clamp down on legitimate civil society protests. The most optimistic view is that with time, domestic foundations will become confident and independent enough to move into sensitive sectors they have largely steered clear of up to now. For the present, the important fact is that more HNWIs are interested in philanthropy and are opening up to emerging issues. It is now up to infrastructural and intermediary organizations in the philanthropy space to educate the would-be donors as to where the need is the greatest.

Doing Things Differently

Generational Differences

A change in the pattern of giving—for what and how—is most noticeable among the younger generation of philanthropists. They are more inclined to give to progressive causes such as gender equality or civil rights, and to move toward more scientific, professional approaches in surveying areas of need and solving problems.[10] In the UK and elsewhere, there is reported to be an increased willingness on the part of younger donors to seek professional philanthropy advice to learn how to do it better. They are also more keen to consult their children and involve them in decisions. Donors are reported to revisit and re-evaluate their charitable affairs because the more effective their giving is, the more pleasure they get out of it.[11] According to a Bain and Company report of June 2012, this appears to be true of the younger generation of donors in India as well. The young, wealthy, socially conscious novice donors want to

[10] Ahona Ghosh, 'New Intent and Bold Innovation in Corporate Philanthropy', *Economic Times Bureau*, 19 June 2012.

[11] Theresa Lloyd and Beth Breeze, 'How Has UK Philanthropy Changed Over The Past Decade?', *Alliance Magazine*, 15 October 2013, http://www.alliancemagazine.org/opinion/how-has-uk-philanthropy-changed-over-the-past-decade/.

adopt Western practices that favour more structured ways of giving, with a focus on outcomes. It also observes that '… this growth [in philanthropy] is contingent on organizations demonstrating impact and raising confidence in the returns on giving'. Therefore, India's nascent philanthropic ecosystem will have to become more transparent, accountable, and outcome oriented.

The second generation philanthropists differ in their approaches from those of the earlier generation in that they tend to move away from an own-and-operate model, and are more strategic in their funding and push families to find existing organizations to scale up. They are also more focussed on impact rather than recognition. Sangita Jindal of Jindal Steel admits she seeks personal recognition, but her daughter does not. Likewise, though Meher Pudumjee, Anu Aga's daughter and the current Thermax chairperson, is involved with the company foundation, the Thermax Social Initiative Foundation, with her mother, she also likes to support her own causes, of which music is one, from her own funds. Both Aga and Pudumjee give away 30 per cent of their dividend income to causes of their own liking, in addition to those determined by Foundation policy.[12]

The younger generation is also starting sooner and with more focussed thinking. Aditi Kothari, an executive vice-president in DSP BlackRock, and daughter of Hemendra Kothari, investment banker, wants that professionals should run the family foundation independently and that it should not depend solely on family funds. Like many other New Economy philanthropists, father and daughter each have their own causes—the father's passion is wildlife conservation while the daughter's cause is education. Unlike the father who goes by his gut instincts, Aditi claims to be more academic in her approach to giving, doing a lot of research and interacting with the organizations before giving.[13] Whereas the older approach came out of experience and was more instinctive, the approach of the younger generation is more professional and cerebral, with due diligence and cost benefit analysis. While this is a gain in many ways, it may rob philanthropy of the passion and vision which characterized the earlier philanthropists.

---

[12] Ahona Ghosh, 'Act of Giving: Giving Across Generations', *Economic Times Bureau*, 4 October 2011.
[13] Ghosh, 'Act of Giving'.

Though there are exceptions such as the above, by and large even many new-generation companies and foundations still tend to channel their innovation within classic sectors like education, at the most developing a new approach to improving education, rather than move into sensitive or non-traditional areas, such as mental health. This merely affirms the need for developing a philanthropy infrastructure to guide would-be donors.

Broadening Horizons

A trend noticeable especially among new and younger donors is the broadening of their horizons not only in terms of causes, but also geographically. Globalization is weakening the ties that bound wealthy families and companies to the cities of their birth, and to which they gave so magnificently. The world is now their oyster, and no longer is philanthropy limited to one's own caste, community, city, or even country. Many of the wealthy today have been educated abroad and made their millions through professions and businesses abroad. It has therefore led many donors to think internationally, and on a bigger scale. While this is a good trend, the personal involvement which was evident when a donor engaged with his backyard is to some extent diluted when the cause is personally and geographically distant.

It will take a while for internationalization of Indian business philanthropy to reach any scale since domestic need will continue to claim prior attention, but even now, as companies seek to integrate their business operations vertically as well as horizontally and to develop core competencies to meet the challenges of globalization, many are moving their philanthropic focus from the cities to village communities around their production units on the one hand, and from India to foreign locations on the other.

Global Approaches to Philanthropy

In the West there have always been two approaches to doing philanthropy. The first one is what is called the 'arms-length approach', popular especially in America, where foundations independent of the donor family engage professionals to carry out the grant-giving according to well laid down procedures. The philanthropist or hired professionals decide what is needed for society from their reading of the situation and then decide which individual or organization is the most competent to achieve their vision. They then negotiate/agree with the individual/organization on how much is needed to implement that vision, how long it will take, and the manner of achieving it. This is a top-down approach, also called proactive giving, where it is deemed that the donor knows best as to what is needed to bring about change.

Reactive or responsive giving refers to grants made at the request of a beneficiary which meets what he/she perceives as his/her personal or organizational need. This could be considered the bottoms-up approach.

During the last few decades, however, there has been much global debate about the best ways to transfer charitable resources to get the 'most bang for the buck', and in some cases practice has changed accordingly.

The West is re-examining the grant making approach after billions of aid poured into developing countries have had little impact on poverty, disease, or peace. The US government alone has spent $30 billion a year on an average in the last several years, on aid to poor people in the world. But not only has it not made the poor better off, but has in some cases made them worse off.

Rich countries and philanthropists, it is now believed, should let the poor countries or poor beneficiaries determine what they need and give them the money to come up with a better solution, that is, be more responsive rather than proactive or top-down.

At the same time, there is also more hands-on interest by the philanthropists in the use of philanthropic funds, in contrast to the earlier 'arms-length' philanthropy of foundations such as the Ford and the Rockefeller Foundations, where there was complete separation of the founder philanthropist from those who make the decisions and manage the use of the endowed funds. In the new approach, donors want to exercise more control over the recipient and the project, and an assurance of outcomes and results which can be measured.

One reason for the change is that many of the new donors feel that a lot of philanthropic money has been wasted both by the charities receiving money as well as by inefficiency within foundations, and they want their money to work hard to produce results.

In the West, a distinction is being made between the old or traditional philanthropy, that is, of the older foundations and international NGOs, and the 'new' philanthropy, practised by the 'philanthrocapitalists' like Pierre Omidyar, the founder of eBay, the Google founders Sergey Brin and Larry Page, and Microsoft's Bill Gates. Defined as philanthropy that uses the principles, models, and techniques of capitalism, it implies a thorough businesslike assessment, close monitoring and performance measurement, and strategic and focused direction of resources to achieve impact. It also means choosing the best agency to manage their money, even if, like Buffet, it means 'outsourcing' their philanthropy to someone more capable—in his case, the Gates Foundation.

The 'new' philanthropy is said to be more technocratic and less people oriented, to exercise more control, and to be less flexible and directed away from a social justice agenda. The decisions regarding allocation of resources are primarily driven by the donors 'who focus resources, assemble professional teams, set measurable targets and develop clear plans to achieve them.[14] In this way of doing things, the donors are said to be more data- and report-driven, rather than compassionate and instinctive. There is also said to be a greater tendency, among the new philanthropists and corporate foundations, to set up their own implementing organizations rather than to make grants.

A final change is that many donors like Warren Buffet, Bill Gates, and Mark Zuckerberg want to make a difference here and now, and therefore want to spend their philanthropic dollars in their own lifetime. They are therefore giving away the bulk of their money while alive, rather than after death. Also, some of them want to give away money directly without endowing a foundation which may perpetuate their name but which may not spend the money according to the way they would have wished.[15] Social investment using a mix of for-profit and non-profit models is also gaining favour.

[14] Olivier Kayser, 'A New Architecture Needed', *Alliance Magazine*, 1 September 2008.

[15] The study by Beth Breeze and Theresa Lloyd, *Richer Lives: Why Rich People Give, Directory of Social Change* (London: Directory of Social Change, 2013), is an in-depth study of what drives rich people to give to charity in the UK. It is based on new research with over eighty wealthy UK donors and others, reported in 2013.

New Trends in India

All these changes are being reflected in India as well. The typical traditional approach of Indian donors in general conformed more to reactive giving—simple ad hoc giving of donations on request by an individual or an organization, and without monitoring either end use or expecting any impact.

An alternate approach adopted by most traditional Indian foundations was to undertake their own philanthropic projects such as schools, hospitals, themselves, rather than giving of grants, proactive or responsive.

While the bulk of Indian donors continue with one of these traditional approaches, five major trends are discernible. One, the emergence of more grant-making foundations than before; two, the adoption of more business like practices in the management of foundations; three, more collaborations between foundations and other social actors; four, collective giving or pooling of donations of small donors for a particular purpose; and five, the emergence of investment in social start-ups as an alternative to, or in addition to, operating own projects or grant making.

More Grant-making Foundations

Today many new foundations are thinking of turning grant-makers, spurred by the demand of NGOs for funds and the realization that good grant making can play a central role in the pursuit of social change. Good grant making means devolving power and putting resources in the hands of people and institutions to make their own decisions and to shape their own futures.

The Tata Trusts, the country's leading philanthropic organizations, have passed through different phases through their long history, going from being operating trusts to grant making and now once again combining the two approaches. (See case study in Annexure II to Chapter 9.)

The Azim Premji Foundation and the Bharti Foundation too have had different approaches at different times. The Premji Foundation started as a grant-making foundation, making grants to some NGOs. However, the Foundation's unfortunate experiences with some of them, most particularly a lack of integrity on the part of the recipient organizations, led it to give up grant making and to operate its own programmes and projects. Now, once again, it has done some rethinking. Though it has recently decided not to convert itself into a grant-making foundation, it has decided to add grant making to its philanthropic portfolio by having a separate organization for the purpose, to be called the Azim Premji Philanthropic Initiatives. One reason given for this change was that while their work on the ground is a long-term venture, slow to show results, some quicker outcomes are required to keep everyone enthused. Some initiatives, carefully picked, have a good potential for this, and therefore add value to the portfolio.

The Bharti Foundation, too, started out by giving grants to organizations in the area of education for underprivileged children, before deciding to build and run schools themselves (the Satya Bharti schools from 2006), presumably for the same reason of being able to ensure quality of outcomes.

The lack of integrity and accountability among organizations is an unfortunate but an existential reality which is the main cause of donors giving less than they can and also of choosing to operate and control their own projects.

The Indian preference for operating own philanthropic projects corresponds with a broader Asian bias of retaining operational control over family philanthropic initiatives, rather than working collaboratively or as grant-making entities.[16] The UBS-INSEAD study on family philanthropy in Asia found that in 2010, two-thirds of private foundation funding in India went to their own operational activities and one-third as grants to other organizations.[17]

Certainly, NGOs who look to foundations for non-governmental funds would like to see much more grant making.

After the Companies Act of 2013, the number of corporate foundations which give funds to outside agencies has increased, since they have been established specifically to carry out the company's CSR activities and as yet do not have the experience or expertise to run social development projects themselves. They find it easier, for the present, to give grants to NGOs to achieve their chosen social objectives.

Some foundations are a combination of both operating and grant-making styles. They undertake some projects themselves, but also

---

[16]   *UBS-INSEAD Study on Family Philanthropy in Asia*, p. 42.

[17]   *UBS-INSEAD Study on Family Philanthropy in Asia*, p. 50.

give money to others for their work. The National Foundation for India, for instance, operates as a funding agency giving grants to NGOs, but also undertakes its own programmes such as running campaigns on various issues. The Avantha Foundation too directly operates some projects, but under its Governance programme gives funds to elected representatives, and also works with NGOs to help elected representatives gain expertise.

In short, no clear trend is discernible as far as the operating versus grant-making debate is concerned. Each style has some merit, as well as drawbacks. The owners' involvement and control has the advantage of the vision and passion of the founder owner, as well as close monitoring, both of which ensure quality outcomes. Grant-making or arms-length philanthropy, where professional experts in different fields decide on goals and strategies on the basis of scanning of social needs and organizations best suited to meet them, can lack the commitment of an owner, as well as a broader vision, but has several other advantages. One advantage is that it makes non-government, and non-foreign funds available to civil society organizations to allow them independence to undertake activism, or to experiment with processes, methods, and systems which can speed up development.

The other advantage is that grants can be used to make a large impact on a social problem by using them as building blocks. To give an example: a grant-making foundation will first identify a critical issue which needs support. If this issue is preservation and revitalization of the traditional performing arts which are disappearing under the onslaught of modernity, then a first round of grants may go to researching and documenting such arts; the second round may go to giving training in archiving the material so gathered, and to dissemination of the findings to scholars and modern performers. Another round of grants can go to individual artists and theatre companies to produce contemporary theatre, integrating the traditional and modern idiom to create a new genre. This way of using money is unlikely with government grants, which are distributed rigidly according to particular schemes.

Reform of Management Practices

A second noticeable trend is the demand, both within and without foundations, for change and reform in internal foundation practices. This trend is embodied in philanthrocapitalism, described above.

If one looks only at owner control and engagement in a foundation, this new approach is not very different from the traditional Indian style of philanthropy. What is different is the stress on results and impact by insisting on efficient systems, close monitoring of results, and the scale of operation in a philanthropic venture. This may have been there in instances of great institution-building by older philanthropists who set up colleges and hospitals, but was greatly missing in smaller foundations and their initiatives.

In an interview this author did with Ratan Tata in June 1997, soon after he took over as the group chairman of the Tatas, and as chairman of the Tata Trusts, he said that his effort was to streamline the working of the trusts for bigger impact. This would be reflected in giving more meaningful amounts to a smaller number of grantees, and 'simultaneously trying to bring the professional approach of our companies into our Trusts'. Another significant statement in the same interview was his emphasis on self-help. In his words, 'While we will always have a niche for individuals in distress, ... I am keen to channel more meaningful amounts towards programmes which have an element of self help to put people on their feet'. He added that while his own philanthropic preference was education, it was not so much formal and conventional education as vocational education and skills creation which interested him.[18]

Ever since he took over, he has brought in change in the ways the Trusts function. Earlier, partners and projects were chosen mostly on 'instinct' and decisions were based on 'compassion'. Therefore, only four to six officials sufficed to co-ordinate with hundreds of 'partners' or NGOs. Now the team on the ground has increased to twenty-five from just six earlier to co-ordinate with various partners. Present and prospective partners are subject to intense vetting and the emphasis on financial reporting has gone up significantly. Projects now get reviewed every six months. If the milestones are not met by partners, grants are stopped.

The Trusts have adopted other corporate practices such as periodic evaluation of their work by the best professionals, and strategic planning, to keep at the cutting edge. Professionals have been inducted

[18] Pushpa Sundar's Interview with Ratan Tata, 'Philanthropy Must Strengthen Self-help', *Sampradaan* 1 (June 1997): 3–4.

not only at the management but also at the Board level. This has led to support for research in several fields, including science and technology, and collaborations with leading global research institutes like Massachusetts Institute of Technology for research on frugal engineering aimed at serving the underprivileged, an issue close to Tata's heart.

Other donors too, especially newer entrants into philanthropy, are adopting business thinking in their philanthropy, one feature of which is to think big and think of scale, which distinguishes them from NGO operations doing similar work. For instance, the Bharti Foundation, through its Satya Bharti Schools programme, has enrolled over 33,000 children across 250 Satya Bharti Schools, of which 233 are primary schools, twelve elementary, and five senior secondary. These schools are spread over six Indian states: Punjab, Haryana, Uttar Pradesh, Rajasthan, Tamil Nadu, and West Bengal. Further, the Bharti Foundation uses the Standard Operating Procedures (SOP) Manual in all of its schools.

Some have put in strong management information systems (MIS) and automated processes of collecting data which help in decision-making. Metrics have become important in foundations too, and the talk is of measuring outcomes and impact, and tracking plans, so that they can be modified midway, if required.

Dr Reddy's Foundation tracks its trainee programmes through highly elaborate MIS systems and monitors parameters such as placement and retention ratios, average salaries in placements, revenue and recovery ratios, and variances in operational parameters across its 120 centres spread over the country. The Bharti Foundation, too, tracks parameters such as internal and external audits at schools, monthly school reports, school cards, various types of classroom assessments, and teacher subject knowledge tests.

Adoption of corporate culture by foundations is seen in other ways. Starting with adoption and customization of the corporate concept of variable salaries linked to performance, they have introduced review and monitoring mechanisms, and work of individuals and departments is clearly defined through key results areas. Dr Reddy's Foundation was one of the first to adopt an incentive pay structure for its staff, linking incentives to the number of school dropouts that its teams trained in their classrooms, the number of trainees placed in entry level jobs, and the number of retentions out of the placed aspirants. Many other foundations have followed suit.

The newer foundations coming from corporate backgrounds are also using the media and communication technologies more successfully to achieve their objectives.

For instance, the Wildlife Conservation Trust, funded by the Hemendra Kothari Foundation, used mass communications strategies to catalyze change in its target issue, wildlife conservation. In 2009, the Wildlife Conservation Trust partnered with the Indian mass media network NDTV, and one of India's largest mobile telephone operators, Aircel, to launch a major mass media campaign to increase public awareness around wildlife conservation, and particularly on saving the Tiger. The Save Our Tigers campaign, coordinated across multiple media and making heavy use of Bollywood celebrity endorsements, ignited the public's imagination across the country—there were marches, cycle rallies, and signature campaigns demanding action before it was too late. The campaign included a 12-hour telethon that raised a total of $1 million—$0.5 million from the public, matched by $0.5 million by Hemendra Kothari.[19]

How different such methods of operation are from the way Indian foundations have operated in the past will be realized from the next chapter. The methods as well as language found in these newer foundations are different in that they talk of 'value', 'profit', and 'return on investment', though the parent business and the foundation may not always hold the same understanding of these terms. However, it must be noted that the foundations adopting such new corporate practices are but a very small fraction of the total and the bulk of Indian foundations operate as before on shoe-string budgets, and without standard methods and procedures.

There are both pros and cons to the extension of business culture and systems to foundations. The growing emphasis on discipline,

---

[19] Nidhi M. Reddy, Lalitha Vaidyanathan, Katyayani Balasubramaniam, Kavitha Goraopali, Sharad Sharma, 'Catalytic Philanthropy in India: How India's Ultra-high Net Worth Philanthropists are Helping Solve Large-scale Social Problems', Centre for Emerging Market Solutions (CEMS) at the Indian School of Business, Hyderabad and FSG Social Impact Consultants, February 2012.

accountability, planning and results, direct involvement, and entrepreneurial culture is welcome. It has helped streamline foundations and improve results and impact, and one hopes that more foundations will follow suit.

However, success in business and beneficial social change are very different things. Some business foundations give only one-to-five year grants, set annual targets which are monitored monthly, especially to help decide whether to renew a grant or not. This short-term outlook is limiting, because social issues are complex and not amenable to quick solutions in a year or two. Social change is a slow process, and cannot be rushed in the same way as business operations. Results take a long time to come and often it is difficult to quantify impacts where they consist of intangibles such as changes in attitudes.

Many successful business philanthropists like Warren Buffet, Bill Gates, and Azim Premji are on record that it is far more difficult to spend money wisely in doing social good than it is in doing business, and that philanthropic work needs patience, tenacity, and empathy. It is different from business. One has to change one's mindset significantly if one has to make a difference.

A long-time commitment based on a case-by-case basis and a flexible approach alone will result in lasting solutions. Besides, the gain in efficiency and rigid adherence to business norms may not make up for the lack of a social vision, compassion, and passion which ought to underlie philanthropy. Otherwise, it can become only an exercise in spending money.

If G.D. Birla had acted purely as a businessman and strictly calculated the cost benefit ratio of giving a grant to C.V. Raman, India's leading scientist of the early twentieth century, to import the needed research equipment from abroad, India might have lost a Nobel Prize winner. Fortunately, Birla and other wise philanthropists after him recognize that not everything that is applicable to the business sector can or should be applied to the social sector.

Successful philanthropy requires risk-taking on potential social gain, which may not always make good business sense. Company foundations, especially those created for implementing the company's CSR programmes, will not be so forward looking and will be risk-averse. They are likely to fall back on safer and well-known areas of need, rather than to find and target emerging problems. The danger is that they will do only as much as is required to be CSR compliant.

Collaboration

The third emerging trend is towards more collaboration between foundations, and other organizations, especially with government organizations, in order to increase outreach and impact.

Collaborations between foundations, family and corporate, has been more common in the West than in India. A good example of such global collaboration is the very recently formed Breakthrough Energy Coalition, started by twenty-eight world industry leaders including Bill Gates, Ratan Tata, and Mukesh Ambani, to invest in research for technologies that will bring affordable, clean, and reliable carbon-free power.[20]

So far, there have been a few instances of a number of large donors collaborating on a project, one of the few such being the Population Foundation of India, where a number of donors like the Tatas, led by J.R.D. Tata, joined other big business houses like the Bharat Rams and others, in what was a common concern. But there is more of this now.

Today, professionals and new entrepreneurs, especially, are getting together to seed and fund initiatives collaboratively, many of them in partnership with government.

One initiative which illustrates this is that of the Akshaya Patra Foundation, a charitable trust headquartered in Bangalore, which has been created not by an individual philanthropist but a group comprising missionaries of ISKCON Bangalore, corporate professionals, and entrepreneurs, to fight issues like hunger and malnutrition in India. It implements the Mid-Day Meal Scheme in government schools and government aided schools. Its state-of-the-art kitchens cater to over 1.4 million children from 10,661 schools across ten states in India. The initiative addresses two major issues: it boosts school attendance, and tackles malnutrition. It works with eight state governments to implement this school lunch program.

The Dasra Girl Alliance represents another instance of multi stakeholder partnerships. Launched in 2013, it is a partnership between USAID, Kiawah Trust, and the Piramal Foundation, whose aim is

---

[20] Reported in *The Times of India* , 'Led by Gates, 20 Biz Titans Launch Clean Tech Coalition', 1 December 2015.

to build a thriving ecosystem to empower adolescent girls, and to improve the health outcomes for mothers and children.

To tackle domestic violence, identified as an area of concern by Dasra's research, the Azim Premji Philanthropic Initiatives and USAID have brokered and funded partnerships with five non-profits including SNEHA, Swayam, and Vimochana, who deal with the issue on the ground.[21]

Finally the newly established Ashoka University, near Delhi, is the collaborative effort of forty-six philanthropists.

Public–Private Partnerships

Apart from donor collaborations, public–private partnerships (PPP) are also evident. The political culture of Indian philanthropy is reflected by the close ties between politics and business—and thus, by extension, between business philanthropists and government. Indians still hold high expectations from the government, even after the path of economic liberalization that the country has followed. Therefore, the government is still viewed as an essential partner in philanthropic ventures, especially to achieve scale. It has not only more money than private philanthropists ever will, but also laws and policy on its side.

A majority of operational foundations feel that it is their role to pilot models that the government can then replicate, as 'innovation will not come from the government'. Foundations and NGOs both are thus keen on leveraging government schemes, sometimes indirectly, as when foundations help their recipients to draw on government programmes. Otherwise, foundations may have to pursue more modest missions.

Many foundations have entered into partnerships with the government or signed various Memorandum of Understanding (MoUs) to execute the government's own schemes. For instance, the Azim Premji Foundation has been working with various state governments to improve equity and quality of government schools for the past twelve years. The Ministry of Rural Development piloted a training and

---

[21] See Dasra Annual Report 2014–15, *Catalyst for Social Change* (Mumbai: Dasra, 2015).

placement programme for rural youth in conjunction with Dr Reddy's Foundation. A total of approximately 36,000 youth were included in this pilot, spread across all the states of India. Later, the ministry scaled up the programme with more than fifty partners across the country.

The corporate GMR Varalakshmi Foundation employs a PPP model for vocational training programmes.

Although the Indian government has a wide range of welfare schemes, there is a large amount of government money earmarked for social causes that is not spent each year, for reasons ranging from political interference to red tape and corruption. Partnering with the government by philanthropists has the advantage of seeing this money drawn into public use. However, since the Indian government is a large and complex system, a certain level of patience and skill is needed to work with it, including a long-term approach, which does not appeal to everyone.

But some like Kiran Mazumdar-Shaw, Chairman and Managing Director, Biocon, is one who favours co-investing with the government on good government schemes because, bringing in a good PPP model, which has checks and balances for the private sector to assess governance and see how money is being managed, will ensure more philanthropy coming into the system. She also argues for collaboration between philanthropists for scaling up good projects and learning from each other. Not everyone can give at the scale of the Tatas, the Birlas, and Gates, she says, but by joining resources together, the giving can have as much impact, and unless we make a bigger impact, we will not see social change.[22]

Ajay Piramal, Chairman, Piramal Group, also believes that in India, if you want to make a significant change, you have to partner with the government because the problems are so large that no amount of money any foundation or individual puts in will be enough. On the other hand, private foundations can experiment with new models and take risks to develop workable models, which the government can then boost up.[23]

---

[22] Ahona Ghosh, 'New Intent and Bold Innovation in Corporate Philanthropy'. *The Economic Times Bureau*, 19 June 2012.

[23] Ahona Ghosh, 'New Intent and Bold Innovation in Corporate Philanthropy'. *The Economic Times Bureau*, 19 June 2012.

Another philanthropist working with the government is Vineet Nayar, whose Sampark Foundation has signed an MoU with the government of Punjab to retrain its teachers from class I to V. Seven months after quitting as CEO of HCL Technologies, Nayar, 52, plans to wean away the teachers of Punjab's government schools from the dreariness of chalk, board, and books, and nudge them to use computers and other new devices to teach kids.

In sum, there appears to be a growing acknowledgement that greater cooperation between philanthropists and the government is essential for development.

Collective Giving

The fourth and one of the most gratifying trends of recent times is the emergence of collective giving, including online donations.

Online donations through portals such as that of the Give India Foundation, which screen and evaluate the potential beneficiaries for would-be donors, and then channel the donations forward to organizations working on the ground, offer either total freedom to NGOs to decide what to do with donated funds, or compliance with donor wishes.

Whereas online giving represents one way of collectivizing giving, with a number of small donors unknown to each other, giving either to a particular NGO or to a particular cause, another form is high-impact collective giving, where the combined energies of many donors known to each other are directed towards a particular cause.

Nimesh Sumati and Rajesh Kacholia, Mumbai-based business-men, have strung together an informal network—Caring Friends—of over 400 HNWIs who fraternize occasionally, exchange notes, and give to select high-impact NGOs across eighteen states, for whom they have raised over rupees 250 million each year. The power of a collective towards a common goal can lead to phenomenal outcomes. It is an informal operation very different from the grant-making foundation models of yester year or the individual or family-led model at the other end. No proposals are sought, no MOUs are signed. Caring Friends does not even have a bank account but givers and the NGOs work in a close relationship. Initiatives such as these find the services of infrastructure organizations like GiveIndia and its

First Givers Club, invaluable for the support services they provide, like audits, reporting, and releasing of funds. It frees them to scale up and measure the impact of their philanthropy.

Social Investment and Social Entrepreneurship

The final major trend is investing in the equity of social ventures rather than giving grants. Philanthropy is a powerful tool for change, particularly when it is used with markets in collaboration. In a market-driven ethos, the lines between the economic and social sectors are blurring, with each borrowing terminology and method-ologies, and learning lessons from the other. As a result, two new ideas have entered the lexicon connected with altruism, which have further broadened the concept of philanthropy. These are venture philan-thropy and social investment, also called social entrepreneurship.

Venture philanthropy is the social parallel to venture capitalism. It implies an investor's backing, with funds, towards ideas which have social rather than commercial potential, nurturing them to fruition, and later monitoring and evaluating results in business terms of impact and value added. It implies due diligence of the social worthi-ness of the proposed venture, building portfolios of socially useful projects, and backing them with resources. The quantum of profit is a secondary consideration. It offers a way to invest in charities that are testing new approaches to solving old problems.

Many new entrepreneurs-turned-philanthropists are choosing to promote social entrepreneurship as a way of bringing transformative change in society, rather than using the traditional grant-giving or operating foundation model.

For instance, Vinod Khosla, an NRI venture capitalist, believes that rather than traditional philanthropy, 'There need to be more experiments in building sustainable businesses going after the market for the poor, because there is not enough money to be given away in the world to make the poor well off'. Mr Khosla's advocacy of the bootstrap powers of capitalism is part of an increasingly popular school of thought: businesses, not governments or non-profit groups, should lead the effort to eradicate global poverty. By backing busi-nesses that provide education loans or distribute solar panels in vil-lages, they believe, commercial entities can help people in poverty better than most non-profit charitable organizations. Khosla says, 'I am relatively negative on most N.G.O.'s [*sic*] and their effectiveness', 'I am not negative on their intentions'.[24]

People are discovering that doing good in the world and doing well for yourself are not mutually exclusive. By creating *shared value*, one is focussed on finding synergy between an entrepreneur's business goals and the possibility of simultaneously doing good to society. One instance may be the Chotukool fridge, developed by the Godrej group for rural areas. A low-cost product which runs without electricity, because typically many rural areas in India are without electricity, it is a business model which brings profits to the business and also meets a felt social need.

The social entrepreneur uses tools of business to tackle social problems. In a market-led world, investment of capital or wealth in profit making ventures is decided solely on the basis of the quantum of profit it brings the individual investor or company, though it may incidentally have benefits for society, such as creating more jobs and incomes. However, an investor may be prepared to accept below market-rate return on his investment, because the end goal is social impact for the benefit of society, in needed but underserved areas such as energy, health, or water, which would otherwise not get served if the quantum of profit is the sole motive.

Accordingly, today's philanthropists engage in social action not only through outright donations but by participating in the equity of social businesses. The profits they realize are then again ploughed back into other philanthropic ventures. The philanthropists are no longer giving money with no expectation of any return, as in classic philanthropy. Instead, the philanthropists are looking for impact from their monies.

People like Pierre Omidyar, creator of the eBay online auction site, are creating structural shifts in the way people think about charitable giving for the public good. In March 2004 he announced that the Omidyar Network would house both a foundation and

---

[24] Vinod Khosla, in a telephone interview from his office in Menlo Park, California, to Vikas Bajaj, 5 October 2010. Downloaded from http://www.nytimes.com/2010/10/06/business/global/06khosla.html?_r= 1&pagewanted=all#h[].

an arm that would also invest in for-profit companies. Omidyar and other social venture capitalists like him argue that it is not true that business is only about making money and non-profits are about helping people. The profits from investing in for-profit social ventures are ploughed into philanthropy through the foundation, which gives grants to individuals, creating social change through their non-profits. Omidyar's hybrid philanthropy lets the people decide how they would like to spend his philanthropic money, through the internet contact network.[25] Similarly with the Google Foundation. Instead of grants, the trend to invest in equity of social enterprises is likely to strengthen, as NGOs reinvent themselves as social enterprises.

The new approach is strategic, market conscious, knowledge based, and high-engagement, as donors seek to concentrate their own money on select problems and seek to attract other donors and government to join in the effort. Prepared to take risks with their resources, they are seeking innovative solutions which can then be adopted on a larger scale by governments.[26]

For instance, Ronnie Screwvala, who promoted the film and TV production company UTV and later sold it to Disney, intends to guide philanthropy towards an entrepreneurship model, for which he has started the Swades Foundation as a vehicle. He devotes 35–40 per cent of his time, and his wife Zarina works fulltime with it. The Foundation has worked on sanitation and water in Raigad district of Maharashtra for a decade. But today his aim is higher, namely to help around 10,000 rural entrepreneurs to set up their own businesses. One of these projects is to help rural women in Maharashtra's Raigad district to start a small factory to produce sanitary napkins and sell them in the villages. Other projects include cashew processing, mushroom farming, desi (indigenous) chicken rearing, and so on. Once these ventures take off and reach a revenue stream of around rupees 1.65 billion, he hopes to exit, leaving behind a self-sustaining model, and move to a new area. This exit plan is unique to his model of philanthropy. His model

[25] Michelle Conlin and Rob Hof, 'The eBay Way', *Business Week, e.biz* (15 December 2004): 104–5.

[26] Conlin and Hof, 'The eBay Way'.

of philanthropy is influenced by C.K. Prahlad's seminal concept of fortune at the bottom of the pyramid.[27]

Anand Mahindra, Ajay Piramal, Narayana Murthy, Kris Gopalkrishnan, and Shibulal are, apart from investing in purely philanthropic work, also investing in for-profit incubators of early start-ups. They see it as a way of addressing the problem of poverty through enterprise rather than handouts.

Ratan Tata, though from a tradition of old-style philanthropy, too has added funding social ventures to his philanthropic portfolio. He has invested rupees 20 million in his personal capacity in a start-up—Swasth India—started by two IIT Bombay graduates for low-cost healthcare services for low-income people.

As a result of the trend to fund social ventures, the definition of philanthropy is set to change. Till now the emphasis was always on non-profit activity to bring about change. But today's philanthropists see the end outcomes as more important than whether the activity is for-profit or non-profit. Instead of the earlier stipulation that philanthropy is giving money without expectation of any return, the emphasis now is on the words, 'without expectation of *personal* profit'.

It is a development which links philanthropy even more closely with capitalism, but assures that social enterprises, wary of commercial capital, still thrive. Social entrepreneurs seek both equity and grants because seed capital for social ventures, where returns are uncertain and take longer to come, is considered high-risk by venture capitalists. Grants lower this risk, and leave entrepreneurs free to focus on their product development without worrying about money. The choice before the New Age philanthropists now is not only whether to give and how much, but also whether to spend it in grant support or early stage equity?

By 2014, grants to social ventures have seen a rise of 100 per cent since the turn of the century. Social ventures in healthcare, water, education, and energy have received money from Gates, Dell Family Foundation, eBay's Omidyar Network, and others. Can such individuals legitimately be called philanthropists, or do they continue to be businessmen? Many more such questions are likely to arise as

[27] Suman Layak, 'Startups at the bottom of the Pyramid', *The Economic Times Magazine*, 12–18 April 2015.

the lines between philanthropy and its new variations get blurred, especially since the angel investors also do capacity building or mentoring, that is, donating their time along with money.[28]

India's start-up ecosystem is seeing the emergence of a culture of giving and sharing in kind as well as money. Corporates are offering free workspaces to start-ups, successful professionals are giving their time generously to mentor young entrepreneurs. Experienced practitioners are offering mentorship and running training classes and workshops—all generally for no, or low fees. Such helping hands are a huge support for fledgling ventures.

It is mostly done selflessly, with no expectation of immediate return, and many do so because they themselves have been beneficiaries of the system and of similar gestures by others in their formative years.

Anand Deshpande, Chairman of the Pune-based Persistent Systems, dedicates three to four hours every Saturday to mentor early stage start-ups. 'I'm a sounding board for them. I meet at least half-a-dozen startups every week. And I don't do it with any self interest. I don't intend to pick up a stake in them', he says.[29]

Not surprisingly, the culture of 'paying it forward' is strongest in Bengaluru, with Yahoo, Microsoft, Intel, and Thought Works leading the way. In Pune, Persistent, Symantec, and BMC Software have also launched unique initiatives to help others. But it is happening elsewhere too.

To sum up, today's philanthropy is a mix of old approaches superimposed by new ideas and practices, with grant making as well as a direct connection between the owner of the wealth and the ultimate recipient unmediated by grant-making professionals; an emphasis on small projects, giving where it is really needed, or alternatively, very large projects involving several partners; a mix of profit and non-profit mechanisms; and wider use of internet technology to connect and transfer resources so that the donor directly monitors where his money goes and who receives it.

---

[28] See Interview with Vineet Rai, 'Electrifying Bihar—the Role of Philanthropy and Social Investment', *Alliance Magazine*, 1 June 2011.

[29] Quoted in Sujit John and Shilpa Phadnis, 'How Indian Startups are Seeing a Culture of Giving And Sharing', *Times News Network*, 30 January 2015. http://economictimes.indiatimes.com/articleshow/46064550.cms?utm_source=contentofinterest&utm_medium=text&utm_campaign=cppst.

9

The World of Indian Foundations

What distinguishes a Trust is not its ability to give or the extent or range of its giving but the character of its giving. It is important for a Trust to maintain its 'pioneering' character and this can only be done adequately where from time to time a Trust initiates and fosters new institutions and new types of service to society. For a great Trust the large project, carefully designed and executed, must always be a major objective. Even in the routine giving of grants and donations the Trust must constantly bear in mind the 'pioneering' factor.[1]

In 1888, the American writer-cum-philosopher Oliver Wendell Holmes advised those with means to 'Put not your trust in money but your money in trust'. It is an advice which has been followed by many wealthy individuals, families, and companies all over the world, judging by the numerous religious and charitable trusts in existence everywhere. Such trusts are a tangible manifestation of the instinct of piety and benevolence inherent in the human race, as well as one of the most popular mechanisms for using wealth to meet societal needs and to bring about social change.

[1] Professor R.D. Choksi, quoted in R.M. Lala, *Heartbeat of a Trust* (New Delhi: Tata McGraw-Hill, 1984), p. 25.

A charitable trust refers to the creation of an endowment or the vesting of income or property in perpetuity for charitable purposes. Abroad, the term more commonly used for such charitable endowments is 'foundation'. The Foundation Directory, USA, defines a foundation as 'a non-governmental, non-profit organization having a principal fund of its own, managed by its own trustees or directors, and established to maintain or aid social, educational, charitable, religious or other activities serving the common welfare'.

In India the terms 'trust' and 'foundation' are used interchangeably, the object of both being the furtherance of some public purpose with the use of private funds. The term 'foundation' is often used to denote even those organizations without an endowment, who seek funds for their charitable work. But here the term is used in the limited sense of an organization with an independent endowment, using its own funds for charitable purposes.

The value of charitable funds lies in the fact that they represent an addition to and an alternative to government funding of welfare and development, and that they can, if properly utilized, have a significant catalytic impact on social change. By catering to the socio-economic, cultural, educational, and religious needs of society, charitable trusts have played a noteworthy role in supplementing government provision. Without them, society would have been worse off, and the government would have had to make greater provision for the same.

Because foundations represent an endowment in perpetuity, they are financially secure, and can make long-term commitments and take risks in supporting innovative but difficult and unproven ventures, which a government cannot or will not, under usual circumstances. Foundations, unlike the government, can support tiny or big organizations according to their own judgement of what is good for society, can take a long-term view, and be creative without being subject to political pulls from vote-bank politics.

While many have heard of big American foundations like the Rockefeller, Ford, and Carnegie, and now the Bill and Melinda Gates Foundation, few know much about India's own foundation world or the role that foundations have played and can play in India's development. If asked to name some Indian foundations, few can go beyond the Tata or Birla Trusts, though now a few newer foundations such as the Azim Premji and the Shiv Nadar Foundations have gained a high profile and greater recall value. But the fact is that India has had a large number of trusts since the late nineteenth and early twentieth centuries.

A Brief History

Historically, Hindu trusts were endowments created for religious and/or secular purposes, such as carrying out of Vedic sacrifices or other religious objectives, when they were referred to as *ishta* charity. When charitable funds were used for other pious or socially useful acts such as construction of water tanks, feeding of the poor, relief of the suffering, education, and so on, they were categorized as *purta*. The creation of a trust required *sankalpa* or the resolve to give and also *utsarga* or *renunciation of ownership* of the gift by the founder. This condition of renunciation was an important condition which, however, was and is often flouted, with trusts being used for personal benefit as well as public purposes.

As described in Chapters 3 and 5, *wakfs* were created under Islamic law for charitable purposes by vesting the property in God, but are now managed by state-nominated trustees.

Modern trusts and foundations are a legal form inherited from the British, and are largely a twentieth-century phenomena. During British rule, the government became concerned at the misuse of religious and charitable funds in India and applied the British legal form and criteria to the organization of charitable funds. A distinction came to be made between private and public trusts. The essence of a charitable trust became, under British law, public benefit, as against private benefit. A second requirement of a public trust was that the funds were to be utilized irrespective of caste, religion, sex, community, or colour. In reality, neither of these conditions have always been fulfilled by public trusts.

The Pioneers

One of the earliest modern foundations to be set up was the N.M. Wadia Foundation. Nowrojee Wadia (1837–1909) was one of the first Parsis, indeed the first Indian, to set up a full-fledged foundation on the lines of those in the West, predating not only the Tata Trusts but also the great foundations set up by Mrs Russel Sage, Carnegie, and others in America. The N.M. Wadia Foundation, set up in 1909 by Nowrojee Maneckji Wadia, marked the culmination of the beneficence of the Wadias. Maneckji bequeathed it rupees 8.9 million (nearly a million sterling) for the alleviation of distress and promotion of happiness of people, irrespective of caste, creed, community, or country.[2] This last was a radical and pioneering concept at a time when all charity was directed to people of one's own religion or caste.

More specifically, the Trust was for maintenance and education of orphans, building and maintenance of hospitals, relief of the poor and distressed, protection of animals, and relief during natural calamities, as well as for traditional charitable objects such as the marriage of poor women, and meeting expenses on the Navjot ceremony of poor Parsi children.

The secular, non-sectarian object of the Trust caused a furore among the Parsis who, though public-spirited and charitably disposed towards fellow Parsis, were still, with some exceptions, communal minded. Jamsetji Tata (who faced the wrath of the Parsi community for his decision to locate the Institute of Science at Bangalore), Sir Phirozshah Mehta, and Sir Dinsha Wacha welcomed the new trust and condemned the growth of sectarian tendencies in the social and political life of India. Defending his decision, Wadia said, 'By the term charity I understand that it should be of a cosmopolitan character and that sectional charity is no charity at all'.[3]

The first fifty years of the twentieth century can legitimately be called the Golden Years of Indian philanthropy. Whereas in the earlier period only two or three large and modern trusts had been set up, this period witnessed a proliferation of trusts and foundations. What is significant is that though the wealth came from the business of the founder, they were not 'corporate' foundations as understood

---

[2] Pushpa Sundar, *Beyond Business: From Merchant Charity to Corporate Citizenship* (New Delhi: Tata McGraw-Hill, 1999).

[3] Quoted in R.P. Masani, *N.M. Wadia and His Foundation* (Bombay: Popular Book Depot, 1961), p. 104.

today, but were the outcome of the personal decision and charity of the founder; many were bequests out of personal fortunes. The foundations either established prestigious institutions themselves or gave money to others to create them. Earlier, money had been dispensed through foundations to meet immediate social needs, but the new foundations began to view giving as an instrument of social change.

Two of the most important foundations of the time which have continued to be leaders in the field of philanthropy were the Sir Ratan Tata Trust and the Sir Dorab Tata Trust. If the name Tata is synonymous with philanthropy in India, it is because of the foundation laid by these two trusts. They are among the best known not only in India but in the world for their cosmopolitan and progressive outlook, and have been profiled in some detail in Annexure 2 of this chapter.

Other trusts established in the years leading up to Independence and in the decade thereafter were the AMM Foundation Chennai, the Shri Ram Foundation Delhi, the Jamnalal Bajaj Foundation, the Pirojsha Godrej Foundation, the K.K. Birla Foundation, and the Lupin, Dhirubhai Ambani, Hinduja, and Bhoruka Trusts. Some were set up to memorialize loved ones or an important personage, as in the case of the Dayawati Modi Foundation, the C.P. Ramaswamy Aiyar Foundation, and the Rajiv Gandhi Foundation. Others were created by business corporations such as the Mahindra Foundation.

Mostly, these foundations preferred to initiate and operate their own philanthropic projects like schools and hospitals, and the bulk of the funds were utilized by them for the purpose, only smaller amounts being given to outside projects. They largely focused on in-house projects in the fields of health, education, or community development.

Foundations Today

Size of Sector

Though the numbers of trusts in India are believed to be substantial, there is an almost total absence of reliable information about them in the public domain, because there is no single all-India enactment for registering or regulating public charitable trusts, in spite of representations and recommendations by civil society representatives and the government's own panels on the subject. As mentioned in Chapter 4, there is a plethora of laws, different for different states and religions. There is also a dichotomy in the operation of state and central laws.

Government departments concerned with charitable activities, namely the Registrar of Societies, Offices of the Charities Commissioners, and the Income Tax department, do not keep information disaggregated according to whether the non-profit organizations are fund-seeking or fund-giving organizations, both being called trusts. Moreover, such information as is kept by charitable authorities is either not in the public domain or is not in a form that is useful for the purposes of analysis.

One factor which inhibits compilation of data on trusts or foundations by non-governmental agencies is that most donors are uncomfortable about providing financial details such as total assets, amount of total annual contributions made, or average size of donations/grants, and prefer to keep a low profile. When Sampradaan Indian Centre for Philanthropy (SICP) compiled the first directory of donor organizations in 1997, many of those approached for information indicated that they did not want to be listed. Some did not want the publicity because they felt they could not cope with the requests for donations that would ensue. Though not stated explicitly, others feared unnecessary problems with Income Tax or other authorities. Sampradaan updated its directory a few times since, and a few other sources of information, such as the web portal http://www.charitabletrustinindia.com/index.html have now come up, but the data gap still remains acute.

According to the *Final Report on Non Profit Institutions in India*, only 29 per cent of all legal philanthropic entities in India were established before 1990. Following economic liberalization, the number doubled in the decade 1990–2000. A more dramatic increase followed between 2001 and 2011, when 42 per cent of all trusts and foundations were established.[4]

---

[4] Formal legal entity to manage family philanthropic activities: 1930s: 4 per cent; 1960s: 13 per cent; 1970s: 8 per cent; 1980s: 4 per cent; 1990s: 29 per cent; 2000–11: 42 per cent; in 'Philanthropic Unit: Decade of Establishment—India', *UBS-INSEAD Study on Family Philanthropy in Asia*, 2011, p. 42.

The boom in foundation formation witnessed during the last two decades in particular is due to a variety of reasons noticed earlier, namely new wealth creation on an unprecedented scale; growing dissatisfaction with the government's ability to meet the social challenges; the enactment of the Companies Act of 2013, which has compelled many companies to set their own foundations to carry out CSR programmes; and the example set up by Warren Buffet, Bill Gates, and Mark Zuckerberg of pledging between 50 and 99 per cent of their wealth for social benefit during their lifetime.

In consequence of the growth, the foundation world has become more visible and dynamic than before. While a majority of foundations in India continue to be small and limited both in their vision and in their outreach, a small but growing number of trusts are forward-looking and pioneering social change.

Types of Foundations

Though all foundations are registered as public trusts or societies, the foundation space includes a wide variety of origin, scope, and style of functioning. Existing foundations fall into one of several categories: older foundations, family and corporate; new foundations set up by new entrepreneurs and companies; autonomous foundations set up by groups of public-spirited people; those set up by NRIs; trusts set up by religious organizations but for development purposes; and community foundations.

Older Foundations

Among these are the Tata Trusts of course, but also the Birla Trusts, Mahindra Foundation, the AMM Foundation, the Singhania Foundation, and many others, too numerous to name. Most of these foundations are operating foundations in the sense that they implement their own projects, which are mostly institutions such as schools, colleges, and hospitals. But some of them have moved with the times and are taking up new issues and new approaches. The most notable of these are the Tata Trusts, which are described in Annexure II.

New Foundations

The new foundations have been started by HNWIs or families, or by companies owned/promoted by those families or managed professionally. Many of the new entrepreneurs are from the middle class, with middle-class values, and appreciate that wealth creation has to go hand-in-hand with redistribution of wealth via philanthropy in order to nurture future economic growth. They have established modern mega foundations, named either after themselves or the company, to translate their vision into reality.

As mentioned earlier, the line between family and corporate foundations in India is blurred since the Indian corporate sector is dominated by family businesses. Generally, family businesses and even companies set up a separate organization for philanthropy in the form of a foundation or trust, funded by the business but run under the leadership of the business family, though they also recruit non-family professionals to implement the programmes. Not infrequently, the foundations are started with donations of corporate shares that obscure distinctions between family and corporate foundations. In 2012, the top ten Indian philanthropists gave over two billion dollars, mainly by transferring business shares to set up foundations.[5]

Some of these foundations are funded by donations or endowments made by corporate heads in their personal capacity, while others are set up directly by companies and draw their income from the parent company. While the Infosys Foundation draws support from the parent company, the Shiv Nadar Foundation is funded by Shiv Nadar and his family's personal wealth, as is the Azim Premji Foundation, These last two foundations are now among the biggest and most dynamic of the new Indian Foundations.

Other instances of company-cum-personal foundations are the Bharti Foundation, established by its promoter Sunil Mittal, the Varalakshmi Foundation of the GMR Group's promoter G.M. Rao, and Dr Reddy's Foundation. G.M. Rao, who started as a jute trader three decades ago and went on to create a rupees 50 billion

---

[5] Arpan Sheth, *Indian Philanthropy Report* (Mumbai: Bain and Company, 19 March 2012).

enterprise spread across energy, airports, and roads, has committed rupees 15.4 billion ($340 million) towards the CSR arm of the GMR Infrastructure Group, called the Varalakshmi Foundation. This endowment is equivalent to the entire portion of G.M. Rao's personal share of the whole business. With a presence in twenty-two locations in India and abroad, its focus is on spreading education and vocational training to provide sustainable livelihood to the people, especially the youth.

Others which are part of this new phase are the Jindal South West Foundation, the J.M. Morgan Stanley Foundation, Eicher Foundation, Bharti Foundation, Nandi Foundation, Byrraju Foundation, the ABB India Foundation, and the Ambuja Cement Foundation, to name but a few.

Among company foundations are those set up by banks and include the ICICI Foundation and the Axis Bank Foundation, and the Rashtriya GraminVikas Nidhi (RGVN) established by the National Bank for Agriculture and Rural Development (NABARD).

Autonomous Foundations

Autonomous foundations are those which are independent of families, individuals, or companies and have been set up by a group of civic leaders to address special social concerns. They have their own endowments and independent governing boards. Among these are the National Foundation for India, the Give India Foundation, Indian Foundation for the Arts, the Population Foundation of India, and the Dalit Foundation. In this category can be included foundations set up by industry associations such as the Federation of Indian Chambers of Commerce and Industry (FICCI), called the FICCI-SEDF (FICCI Social and Economic Development Foundation).

A variation is the hybrid foundation arising from the growth of collective philanthropy, that is, aggregation of small donations given by the public to non-profit organizations to achieve a special public purpose. Child Rights and You (CRY), Concern India, and HelpAge illustrate this new hybrid type of foundation which both raises funds from the public at large and then gives them out to other non-profit organizations serving the same cause.

Another variation of the autonomous foundation is the community foundation established by and for the benefit of a geographical community, described in Chapter 6. The earliest of these in India, the Bombay Community Public Trust, and the United Way of Baroda, set up towards the end of the twentieth century, have been joined by the Valley Dew Community Forum in Coorg, and a few others. However, the community foundation, one of the fastest growing philanthropic models in the world, has not caught public imagination in India and remains a rare instance.

Religious Foundations

The uncertainties of the times have increased an interest in religious and spiritual matters, and giving to religious organizations is at an all time high. Some of the more progressive religious leaders and organizations, like Mata Amritanandamayee, Sri Sri Ravi Shankar, and Gurumayee are using some of this money for social development, and have formed foundations for the purpose which go beyond the religious remit to work on secular lines and undertake projects for wider social benefit.

Foundations Established by Non-Resident Indians (NRIs)

Many of the Indian diaspora, among whom are several NRIs, are actively engaged in doing philanthropic work in India, for which they have established foundations. Among them are the Sehgal Foundation, the Gururaj Deshpande Foundation, the Loomba Foundation, the Hans Foundation of Manoj Bhargava, and several others.

The foundation space in India also includes several foreign foundations, set up either by multinational companies like Dell and Microsoft, or by individual philanthropists like Bill Gates. They have joined the older foreign foundations such as the Ford Foundation. Though active in India and contributing to Indian philanthropy, they are not being noticed here as Indian foundations.

Scope

Foundations have been established for a wide range of purposes—from education to protection of cows, feeding of the poor to

promotion of arts and culture. Some are single issue foundations focusing on children (CRY) or old people (HelpAge), while
others focus on education (Azim Premji Foundation) or the arts
(The India Foundation for the Arts).

Others are multi-focus (Sir Ratan Tata Trust, Godrej Foundation,
Hyundai Motor India Foundation), working on several issues such as
livelihoods, health care, education, vocational training, environment,
road safety, and the arts as their thrust areas.

Still others are geography-specific, such as the Rashtriya Gramin
Vikas Nidhi (RGVN), which works specifically in and for the North
East. Many foundations, especially those established to fulfil the
social responsibility requirements under the Companies Act, generally work round their company's operations on broad development
issues such as livelihoods, health, or women's literacy. The Ambuja
Foundation, for instance, works in over 928 villages in twelve states
where the Ambuja Cement Company has its plants, on development
projects for local benefit.

Some choose issues about which the founders feel passionate but
which do not necessarily synergize with their company's business.
Women's empowerment is the focus of several foundations, such
as the Mahindra Foundation, established by the Mahindra Group.
Another example is the Hemendra Kothari Foundation, started by
the chairman of DSP BlackRock Investment Managers, which works
on environment and especially wildlife, which is a passion with its
founder. It has adopted twenty-five national parks and works with
forty NGOs to influence people living in and around forests against
poaching, and helps them by providing some of life's essentials:
healthcare, job training, and educational facilities.

Education continues to remain a favoured focus for a majority
of foundations. Thus, leading foundations such as the Azim Premji
Foundation, the Infosys Foundation, the Bharti Foundation, and the
Shiv Nadar Foundation, as well as many others, focus on primary
education, though the main business which created the wealth for
the founders is information or communication technology. The
Bharti Foundation, set up in 2000, helps underprivileged children
gain access to quality school education across rural India.

Some of those working in the broad field of education, like
the Reliance Foundation, the Jindal Foundation, the Shiv Nadar

Foundation, and the WIPRO Foundation, are focussing on both primary and higher education. They have either established universities themselves or have given donations to institutions of higher learning.

Healthcare is perhaps the next most favoured focus area. Many foundations use their funds to set up hospitals or some allied activity. For instance, the Reddy Foundation, established by the pharmaceutical company Dr Reddy's Lab, has chosen healthcare as one of its prime focus areas. The Infosys Foundation, which also has healthcare as one of its focus areas, constructed the Infosys Super-specialty Hospital on the Sassoon Hospital premises in Pune. This hospital caters to poor patients. Apart from constructing hospital wards, donating hi-tech equipment, and organizing health camps, the Foundation also distributes medicines to economically weaker sections in remote areas.

The environment, arts, and empowerment of women are some of the other more popular areas for which foundations have been set up.

The Infosys Foundation, for instance, has helped revive the art of the weavers of Pochampalli village in Andhra Pradesh, and helps to organize cultural programmes to promote artists in rural areas of Karnataka and Andhra Pradesh. It honours artistes from different parts of India. Today, the scope of the Foundation's activities has widened to identifying under-privileged artists from different walks of life, be it writers, painters, poets, or musicians who do not have access to contacts or help. It assists them on a 'need' basis, offering financial assistance, and promoting their art.

Research, in pure science or the social sciences, is supported by few, though this is emerging as a niche area for some. In one of the biggest philanthropic contributions to the pure sciences, Kris Gopalkrishnan, one of the founders of Infosys—the IT company which pioneered the IT revolution in India—has committed through his foundation, the Prateeksha Trust, rupees 2.25 billion over a ten year period, to develop a Centre for Brain Research at the Indian Institute of Science in Bangalore. It is one of the single largest donations the 105-year-old institute has received from an individual. The Prateeksha Trust funds education, research, innovation, and entrepreneurship.

Similarly, Nandan Nilekeni, another Infosys co-founder, has established the India Foundation to fund research in the social sciences, while the Infosys Science Foundation annually gives what has been referred to as India's Nobel Prize, to outstanding individual researchers in five different science fields.

While the scope has certainly broadened to include non-traditional fields, very few foundations are as yet supporting work in areas such as political and administrative reform, human rights, and social justice, or addressing issues such as caste or religious discrimination, gender parity, and so on. There is very little funding too for research or action on minority issues, either by Muslim foundations or by secular ones.

Annexure 1 at the end of this chapter gives a snapshot of some of the leading Indian foundations and their work.

Whither Indian Foundations? A Critique

Achievements

Undoubtedly, Indian foundations have several achievements to their credit, especially the larger, better known ones. Without them India would be poorer in many ways. As already noticed, some have built up India's social infrastructure of schools, colleges, hospitals, and welfare organizations such as orphanages and old age homes. Others have pioneered in new fields such as social work, scientific research, teaching pedagogy and curriculum development, cancer research, management education, and vocational training. Still others have helped revive dying arts or crafts, or encouraged new creative work in literature, art, and performing arts, taking up the slack left by vanished royal patrons.

There are those like Bharatiya Agro Industries Foundation (BAIF), who have experimented with and improved agricultural and veterinary practices, while others have supported work on wild life and conservation of the environment.

While they may not have done pathbreaking work, there are several who have provided the necessary funds for scholarships and awards, for dissemination of ideas through lecture series, and donations to the needy for distress relief of various kinds.

What Ails Indian Foundations

Though it would take many pages to describe the good work done by many of India's foundations, by and large, the Indian foundation world is still very much in the charity mode, and its impact as a whole is limited due to the following reasons.

Skewed Composition

Though large, the composition of the donor sector is skewed in terms of the size and income of trusts and the scope of activity. At one end are a minority of very large, multi-focus secular organizations for the benefit of all, regardless of caste or creed, with incomes running into millions, and whose goal is transformative change rather than charity. Their number, though small at present, is growing. At the other end are numerous small trusts with low incomes and staff. They work mainly in the charity mode, giving small donations on request. Sometimes an annual lecture or an award is the sum total of their activity.

Almost 85 per cent of the trusts are religious trusts who have to use their funds strictly for achieving their religious objectives. Some of the religious trusts like the Tirupati Devasthanam Trust have income running into several hundreds of millions, but most others have incomes just sufficient to achieve their religious objectives. Even where income is substantial, little is available or spent on developmental purposes. Apart from legal requirements about spending on religious objectives, trustees lack vision or desire to interpret religious objectives broadly enough to serve secular charitable causes. There are of course some exceptions, such as the Gajanan Maharaj Trust, the Kalyanji Anandji Trust in Gujarat, the Satya Sai Baba Trust in Karnataka, and so on.[6]

Of the non-religious trusts, many are defunct and exist only on paper. A vast majority have very low incomes amounting to only a few thousand rupees, barely enough to meet administrative expenses. According to the Comptroller and Auditor General (CAG)'s Report

---

[6] See, Pushpa Sundar, ed., *For God's Sake* (New Delhi: Sampradaan Indian Centre for Philanthropy, 2001).

No. 5 (1991–5), as of March 1992, of the 72,129 trusts in India then, approximately half, that is, 39,485, had incomes below the taxable limit. An equally large number, that is, 31,775, had income between the taxable limit and rupees 5 hundred thousand. Only 869 had incomes above rupees 5 hundred thousand per annum. Unfortunately, later figures are either not in the public domain or not readily available.

Under/Non-utilization of Funds

It is not only that the income of most trusts is small. Income is also non-utilized or underutilized. A 1991 study by the Consumer Education and Research Centre of Ahmedabad found that of the approximately 8,000 trusts in Ahmedabad registered with the Charities Commissioner, only 144 had incomes of over rupees 1 hundred thousand, amounting in the aggregate to rupees 44.2 million. Of this, almost 16 per cent, or rupees 7.292 million was being unused. Another 16 per cent was set aside as 'reserve funds', bringing the total of unutilized income to 32 per cent of an already small amount. Though later data is not available, the situation is unlikely to have changed much since then and the Gujarat story is probably typical of the rest of India, though the incomes of big trusts have increased several times since that date, due to the booming stock market.

Proliferation of Trusts

One reason for a number of small, rather than a few big trusts is the preference of individuals to set up a separate trust in the name of a loved one or for a particular purpose, instead of giving the money to already established organizations for charitable use. This tendency exists even in the case of large business houses.

Typically, each large business house has several small trusts, each for a particular purpose such as setting up a college, a hospital, a research institution, or for sports and so on, instead of a single large foundation with several programmes of giving in different fields of interest. Partly, this is because of the preference, mentioned earlier, for controlling and operating charitable projects. Partly, it is because such trusts are meant to memorialize somebody or to perpetuate a family or company name; but mainly it is to avail of tax benefits.

The preference for creating one's own trusts or foundations, whether on the part of individuals or companies, is also due to non-existence of, or a lack of knowledge of, or lack of confidence in other organizations working for the same purpose. One consequence of this is that charitable/developmental organizations depend more on government and foreign foundations which are better known, rather than on Indian foundations. It also prevents cross-sector cooperation.

Since Ratan Tata took over as Chairman of the Tata Trusts, he has begun a process of consolidation and coordination of the objectives and work of all the Tata Trusts, though the different trusts still retain their legal identities. Other trusts set up by a single family or company can benefit by emulating this example.

Lack of Impact

Though the newer wave of foundations described have begun well, it will take several years to see their impact on India's intractable problems of poverty, illiteracy, deprivation, and social injustice. Large, well managed, visionary foundations are such a small fraction of the total that even if each had a big impact, their overall contribution to changing Indian society would still be miniscule. This is not only due to the smallness of foundation funds, but to the way they function and other systemic reasons, as elaborated below.

Ad Hocism

Beyond the small progressive fringe, most Indian foundations do not have a long-term vision, a defined, articulated, and publicized policy for giving, or strategy planning to guide the functioning of the foundations beyond specific social projects. For many, giving is in the nature of a one-time donation, rather than long-term grants according to a planned strategy. Giving is in response to requests, rather than as a result of understanding the social situation and where the gaps are, since there is no systematic scanning of the field of choice. Active seeking-out of good projects, ideas, or people/organizations to fund is uncommon. Though this kind of reactive giving has the advantage of being a bottom-up approach and meeting real felt need, even this can benefit by having an overall perspective and definition of a field of operation.

Lack of Professional Staff

A big part of the problem, of course, is the low income of a large number of trusts, which also means that the foundation world is extremely thinly staffed. In such cases, the trust is generally entrusted to an accountant who merely looks after financial transactions and has little knowledge of the social scene. In a corporate foundation, the work is looked after by some department in a company. Small foundations in particular fear that they will get more requests for assistance than they can cope with, even though it is a fact that charitable money does not get fully utilized.

But even in medium sized and big trusts, professionalization of philanthropy is yet to take place. Of course there are exceptions, but by and large, organizational development and capacity-building issues which would lead to more effective giving are not given importance.

In the West, the foundation sector is looking seriously at staffing and human resource (HR) development, with discussion focusing on the kind of people foundations need—whether generalists or specialists, permanent staff or consultants, people from outside the sector or from within, and so on. The role of philanthropic support organizations in promoting foundation staff development is also being debated. In India, there is no debate at all on development of foundations, let alone issues of HR.

One reason why US foundations are conscious of the need to have professional staff is that foundations have to pay out at least 5 per cent of their total assets in charitable grants. Currently, the relatively high rate of foundation formation, combined with a rapid growth in investment income, has led to a situation in which foundation assets are growing more rapidly than grants to non-profit organizations. Consequently, there is pressure on the foundations by both government and civil society to increase their rate of pay-out to at least 6 per cent of assets. In India there is no such requirement to pay out a defined portion of the assets every year, only a requirement to spend

85 per cent of the current year's income in that year. There is also no pressure on trusts by NGOs and charitable organizations, because of lack of knowledge about local trusts.

Ineffective Grant Making

There are fewer grant-making foundations in India than those who want to spend their own money for specific projects. But even where foundations use the grant-making route to make a difference, the idea and possibility of using grants as tools or building blocks to change or develop a particular field, say nutrition, or to achieve certain long-term objectives such as social justice or human rights, has not yet taken root, partly due to a limited understanding of social processes, partly due to a lack of vision, and partly due to an understanding of what good grant making implies.

The decisions to give or not, and for what purpose, are made either by the donor or trustees who, frequently, also do not have either the knowledge of the charitable or development world, nor time to devote towards acquiring such knowledge. There is also a shortage of experts who are specialists in philanthropy and social development, though with compulsory CSR now required of companies, the number of these 'experts' is mushrooming very fast. The result is unimaginative, rather than creative, giving. The focus of a majority of foundations is on quick, visible, tangible results, and therefore foundations are seldom in the vanguard of activism on social issues, or of advocacy for special policies. This role, if played well, can be as important a contribution by foundations as monetary support.

Very few foundations have attempted to train their professional staff for effective grant making, simply because it is not a perceived need in India, in contrast to the situation abroad, where several training courses are available to enhance the effectiveness of professionals working in donor organizations.

Though foundations, Indian and foreign, have insisted on and even funded some training programmes for building the competence of *NGO personnel,* there are few training programmes *for professionals of donor organisations.* When SICP Delhi undertook training workshops for professional grant making, very few foundations sent staff, though the fees were kept very low.

The lack of awareness of what professional philanthropy can accomplish results in a heavy emphasis on a few fields of interest or social sectors such as health, education, and rural development. Many emerging needs are not met, for example, rehabilitation of bonded labour and child labour; museums for education; monument conservation; experimental theatre; public interest litigation; consumer protection; libraries; and social justice issues such as social and political empowerment of oppressed people or minorities.

The benefits of grant support, especially in terms of physical and institutional infrastructure go, by and large, to people from the same class as that of the donors. For example, many of the big colleges, hospitals, auditoria, art galleries, and so on, endowed through private charity, cater to the urban middle class, though some provision is made in educational and medical institutions for the poor. This is not unique to India but, as has been documented by Teresa Odendahl in her *Charity Begins at Home* (1990), is a flaw in Western philanthropic practice as well. It needs conscious effort to make grant making more inclusive and directed towards social justice issues such as caste, gender, and religious discrimination.

While some may give donations for buildings and equipment, very rare is the offer of core support to an institution or organization for a period of years to enable it to establish itself, and meet its running costs. Support for untested, experimental, but potentially promising work is even rarer. In short, foundation-giving is still very much in its infancy.

Ratan Tata is one of the few who has recognized that professional philanthropy requires a well qualified staff commensurate with the amounts to be spent. In a 2005 interview to Synergos, Ratan Tata said 'Philanthropic institutions in India still believe they're charitable and, therefore, must operate on shoe string budgets, that creating an organisation is almost a luxury. This needs to change—they have to recognise that a non-profit has as much responsibility for being professionally run as a corporate body.'[7]

[7] Thomas, Prince Mathews. 'Ratan Tata's Audacious Philanthropic Retirement Plans'. Forbes India Magazine, 13 August 2012, http://forbesindia. com/article/boardroom/ratan-tatas-audacious-philanthropic-retirement-pla ns/33526/3#ixzz2dSBDeMpcying.

A second change he introduced was to insist the trusts start training not only their own staff but also some of their partners to build scale, because most non-profit organizations in India are unable to absorb large amounts of money and scale up their work due to limited capabilities.

Lack of Interaction

The tunnel vision shown by a majority of donors is also a consequence of the fact that with the exception of the few initiatives at collaboration mentioned, most prefer to work in isolation, without much dialogue with their peers, the government, or the grantee community, about expectations, rights, and duties vis-a-vis the other.

Foundation heads, especially of corporate foundations, often feel they know all the solutions to problems, since they have been successful in business, and consequently are less ready to look to or learn from other models.

The SICP had attempted to hold annual conferences to bring Foundation CEOs and professionals together to discuss common problems and issues and to learn from each other. But the attempt was not successful.

Fortunately, there is a small change for the better and Dasra's annual Philanthropy Forum is receiving a better response. A second change is that several of the new foundations believe that they should seek the best partners wherever, and not only in India. Ratan Tata believes that Indian foundations must also work abroad. Having seen the operations of international foundations from close quarters as a Trustee and Board member of foundations like the Ford, he is open to collaborations with other foundations like the Bill & Melinda Gates Foundation or the Ford Foundation.

There are others too who think like him. Among them is the founder of the Biocon Foundation, Kiran Mazumdar-Shaw. She believes that excellence should be the only criteria and if work can be done better by partnering with a foreign organization, so be it.

Lack of Supporting Infrastructure

The lack of knowledge of the social sector, and lack of training for professionalizing philanthropy is in many ways related to the lack of infrastructure for promoting philanthropy. In the Indian foundation world, there are no formal networks like Donors Forums, or Grantmaker's Associations like abroad, and individual foundations operate as separate entities. Thus, one cannot talk of an autonomous foundation or philanthropic sector working towards common goals and interests in the same way as one can of the voluntary or NGO sector. One reason for such an absence is that till recently, and even now, charitable foundations are looked upon merely as an adjunct of the parent organization and there are very few foundations, such as the Ford or Rockefeller, which are totally independent of the companies which brought them into existence. Second, no common threat or goal has brought them together for common action, as happened in the USA when the foundation world was at one time under attack from congressional investigations.

Finally, the leadership which could make such a network or association happen is also missing. The Business for the Arts, in USA, which brought together companies or HNWIs interested in the arts, had David Rockfeller take the lead to bring others to the table. Similarly, the Council on Foundations or Foundation Centre, two national organizations to serve the foundation sector, were established by top business leaders.

One positive outcome of the Gates and Buffet visit to India is that it has brought home to Indian philanthropists the need to network for bigger impact.

Whereas in the USA and other developed countries big foundations have had major impacts on society and influenced social policy, in India the foundations have had hardly any impact beyond the benefits of certain projects. The strong debate that exists in the USA about the role that foundations should play in society, and especially their advocacy role on controversial issues, is absent in India. One particularly relevant issue today is who holds the government to account. As funds become tighter and government becomes the main paymaster for many voluntary organizations, the voluntary sector is less able to challenge governments. And perhaps it is time for foundations to step into the breach.

Indian foundations have never played an advocacy role, and have tried to steer clear of controversy, especially in such matters as social justice, community conflicts, and so on, and it is unlikely that given the present pro-market environment they will begin now. But it is a role that foundations should keep in mind, since foundations can be leaders on societal values just as much as, or even more than, civil society organizations, given their money power.

Lack of Transparency and Accountability

Finally, philanthropy as a noble instinct should be above unethical dealings. But though a few foundations are well-organized and managed, there is lack of accountability and a regrettable lack of transparency in the operations of a high proportion of trusts, especially those formed in the education and health sector. Many have been formed for the purpose of tax evasion and to launder black money. Misappropriation of funds for private benefit by trustees, lack of transparency in operations, and absence of annual reports available in the public domain or on demand characterize many trusts. Though they expect their grantees/beneficiaries to be accountable, they do not themselves follow the same rules

Many trusts prefer to keep a low profile because they do not want scrutiny of their dealings. Some clearly are not above board, but even when they have nothing to hide, not many publish annual reports highlighting their activities; or if they publish reports, as progressive trusts like the Biocon and the Azim Premji Foundations do, they do not include the financials. It is simply not part of the organizational culture in the country, though encouragingly, some of the newer and bigger foundations have now begun to publish their financials as well as achievements.

In India, philanthropy is intrinsically personal and may only become more transparent and professional over time in response to external pressure.

To conclude, to meet its self-declared goal of transformative change, the foundation world would be well advised to take several measures such as consolidation of several small trusts, training of professional staff, and making common cause to set up a 'Chamber' for foundations on the lines of the US Council of Foundations.

Annexure I A Snapshot of Indian Foundations

Sl. No.	Name of Public Trust/Foundation	Company/ Collaboration	Managing Trustee/ Chairperson	Areas of Contribution	Flagship Programme
1	Adani Foundation	Adani Group	Priti G. Adani	Religious, educational (Adani Vidya Mandir), Medical (MHVs), other Charitable objects	Adani Vidya Mandir
2	Akshaya Patra Foundation	Jamsetji Tata Trust (550 million over five yrs), Infosys, Kelloggs and many other corporates	Madhu Pandit Dasa	Nutrition, education & Mid-day meal (primary & Upper primary)	Akshaya Patra Meal to school children (10 states, 22 locations, 10,912 govt. schools covered)
3	Bharti Foundation (2000)	Bharti Enterprises/ Bharti Group of Companies	Sunil Bharti Mittal	Elementary, Pri. & Sec. school & Higher Education Programmes (on partnership)	Satya Bharti School Program (6 states, 7 schools, villages covered)

(Cont'd)

Annexure I *(Cont'd)*

Sl. No.	Name of Public Trust/Foundation	Company/ Collaboration	Managing Trustee/ Chairperson	Areas of Contribution	Flagship Programme
4	Axis Bank Foundation 2006	Axis Bank		Emergency medical care for highway accident victims, education to underprivileged, Livelihoods	
5	Reliance Foundation (2010)	Reliance Industries Limited	Nita M. Ambani	Rural Transformation, Education, Healthcare, Urban Renewal, waste land management and Arts, Culture & Heritage	Sir HN Reliance Foundation Hospital & Research Centre will be a world class tertiary health care facility
6	Shiv Nadar Foundation (1994)	HCL	Shiv Nadar (Wife Kiran Nadar is also actively engaged in creative philanthropy)	Rural and Urban transformation, School and Higher education as inclusive centres of learing, Art & Culture	Vidya Gyan (poor rural children); pan India Shiv Nadar Schools, K-12 Schools; Shiv Nadar University (2011), Kiran Nadar Museum of Art

7	Sir Ratan Tata Trust & Allied Trusts (Navajbai Ratan Tata Trust, Bai Hirabai J.N. Tata Navsari Charitable Institution, Sarvajanik Seva Trust) (Started in 1919)	TATAs	Mr Ratan N. Tata (for all the trusts he is the chairperson)	Rural Livelihoods, Education, Rural Health, Art, craft and culture, Small grant Programme (170 districts in 17 states of the country)	Small Grants Programme (SGP): classified under a 'special' category; Major funding is directed to operating agencies (e.g. For Livelihood-Pradan and Cini)
8	Sir Dorab Tata Trust and Allied Trusts (J.N. Tata Endowment for Higher Education of Indians; Lady Tata Memorial	TATAs	Mr Ratan N. Tata (for all the allied trusts)	Grants collectively made by the trusts to institutions, non-governmental organizations and individuals; Conservation of Indian folklore and cultural heritage; maternal & child healthcare issues; developmental projects in natural resource	Trusts collectively have made 3 large grants (in 2013–14): to Akshayapatra Foundation to implement midday meal programme; Establishment of the Tata Centre for Technology & Design (in partnership with MIT, USA and IIT Mumbai); to Indian

(Cont'd)

Annexure I (*Cont'd*)

Sl. No.	Name of Public Trust/Foundation	Company/ Collaboration	Managing Trustee/ Chairperson	Areas of Contribution	Flagship Programme
	Trust; J R D Tata Trust; Jamsetji Tata Trust; R D Tata Trust; Tata Education Trust; Tata Social Welfare Trust; and J R D and Thelma J Tata Trust)			management, rural livelihoods, health and education, in Jharkhand, Chhattisgarh & others; Urban Poverty & Livelihoods; Media, Art and Culture; Projects on Civil Society Governance and Human Rights, Individual grants, scholarships	Institute of Science, Bengaluru to pursue rigorous research in Alzheimer's disease. Support to expand Executive Education Programme to Harvard Business School, USA; Intervention for poor households with 21 partner NGOs.
9	Dr Reddy's Foundation	Dr Reddy's Laboratories	Mr Satish Reddy	Economic Empowerment of women; Sustainable Livelihoods & Nutrition for rural households; Promoting theatre art & Culture among children; Quality Education & School Improvement	SIP for 25 government English and Telgu Medium Schools; Pudami Schools for street/slum children; Kallam Anji Reddy Vigyalaya (KARV) and KARV-Junior College; Tie up with

| 10 | Infosys Foundation (1996) | Infosys Ltd. | Sudha Murthy | Support for five focused areas: Healthcare: Education: IT education; Teacher's Training. Programs; Destitute Care (NGO partnership); Rural Development; Culture: Promoting & sponsoring art forms and artists/artisans, | Infosys Prize; SPARK-IT programmes to boost IT skills; Raichur Devdasi Project; Shalegondu Granthalaya—rural libraries; InFLUENCE); Estab. of chairs & courses at IISc & IIIT in Bengaluru and TIFR, Mumbai); Healthcare programme for tribal girls in partnership with SEARCH, Restoration of ancient Raja Raja Dinkar Kelkar Museum, Bengaluru. |
| | | | | Programmes (SIP); School-Community Partnership in Education (SCOPE) programme (School drop-outs/street children) vocational trainings to youths (with special ability and from marginalized sections | Business to Youths (B2Y) and CISCO networks for job placement; Livelihood Advancement Business Schools-LABS |

(Cont'd)

Annexure I *(Cont'd)*

Sl. No.	Name of Public Trust/Foundation	Company/ collaboration	Managing Trustee/ Chairperson	Areas of contribution	Flagship Programme
11	Tech Mahindra Foundation	Mahindra Group	Dr.Loveleen Kacker (CEO)	Model vocational Trg. to underprivileged youths, currently 25 centres and expecting to expand to 50 SMART centres by 2014–15	Tech Mahindra SMART Programme SKILLS-FOR-MARKET TRAINING
12	Azim Premji Foundation	Wipro & subsidiaries (IT sector)	Azim Premji	education and related development areas	Azim Premji University, Demonstration Schools (4 states), Field Institutions, State and district Institutions developed as resource centres working on the three areas of sanitation—Public Toilets,
13	GMR Varalakshmi Foundation (GMRVF)	GMR Group (energy & infrastructure conglomerate)	G.M. Rao	charitable activities in areas of education (primary, secondary and tertiary education), Healthcare, Running Technical & learning institutions, Hygiene and	Individual Sanitary Lavatories and creating sanitation awareness, across 7 states with

No.	Organization	Source/Endowment	Promoter	Focus/Activities	Thrust Areas	Initiatives
14	Soonabai Pirojsha Godrej Foundation in 1974	Godrej & Boyce Manufacturing Co. Ltd	Adi Godrej	Immunization for children, family welfare and nature conservation, through four main trusts. Mumbai's second largest nature reserve of mangroves spread across 1,000 acres at Vikroli has been maintained. Culture and fine arts through the Godrej Dance Theatre at the National Centre for the Performing Arts in Mumbai. Ad hoc grants.	Sanitation, Livelihood & empowerment, Urban & Rural community development	government; 8 state-of-the-art vocational training institutes; GMR Chinmaya Vidyalaya; Udayachal Schools: Providing Quality Care and Education; Teach for India (TFI)-a nationwide movement which places outstanding college graduates and young professionals, who commit two years to teach full-time in under resourced schools. Godrej Memorial Hospital
15	Arghyam (2001) (public charitable foundation)	personal endowment from Rohini Nilekani to realize vision of safe, sustainable water for all	Rohini Nilekani	WatSan focussed grants-making organization. Focus on Rural/urban Groundwater & Sanitation (provision also for Non-Programmatic grants.		supporting India Water Portal (a Digital Commons initiative of Arghyam, credible source of knowledge on water and related issues in India); Scaling and advocacy

(Cont'd)

Annexure I *(Cont'd)*

Sl. No.	Name of Public Trust/Foundation	Company/ Collaboration	Managing Trustee/ Chairperson	Areas of Contribution	Flagship Programme
16	The Hans Foundation (2009)	US-based entrepreneur Manoj Bhargava	Ms. Sweta Rawat	Disease prevention, children's education and forest regeneration in the State of Uttarakhand; Custom designed Healthcare solutions (Mobile Health Clinics and boats) for rural communities; Livelihood promotion (women entrepreneurs in Rajathan); healthcare support and infrastructure for special children	Hans Foundation Hospitals (THFHs) in Uttarakhand; Mobile Health Clinics; Satya Special Schools for special children;, Mental health Kiosks, vocational training to children with Autism; Supporting Mental and Newborn Survival Initiative (MANSI); VEER programme to provide Job to persons with disability
17	National Foundation For India (1992)	Independent Grant making cum fund raising Organization Jointly founded	Ms Syeda Saiyidain Hameed	Supporting 200 grassroot organizations across 14 states; grants made under seven portfolios- Elementary Education, Health, livelihood	Social Justice Philanthropy Initiative (SJPI); Media Fellowships; youth internships for exposure to development

18	Aditya Birla Centre for Community Initiatives and Rural Development	by a group of distinguished individuals led by Late C. Subramaniam	security (rural/urban), Citizen and Society, Peace and Justice, Local Governance, Development Journalism; annual fellowships and awards to individuals/ community leaders	challenges. Awards of various kinds; Focus on North East India
		Aditya Birla Group	Ms Rajashree Birla	Healthcare & Family Welfare; education; the girl child; sustainable livelihood; women empowerment; infrastructure development, Global interventions.	Aditya Birla/FICCI CSR Centre for Excellence; Rural Technology Parks; BITS (Pilani, Goa, Dubai, Hyderabad) & BIMTECH at Greater Noida & Bhubaneswar)

Annexure II

Profiles of Two Major Foundations

Two of India's major foundations are profiled below, chosen to represent an Old Economy foundation, and the other a New Economy one. They are also two of the largest foundations in India, and illustrate two different approaches to philanthropy—arms-length philanthropy and the direct hands-on approach.

The Tata Trusts

The Trusts are a conglomeration of two big trusts, the Sir Dorab Tata Trust (SDTT), and the Sir Ratan Tata Trust (SRTT), and many smaller units. They are the leading grant-making trusts in India, and stand out in a scenario of mostly operating foundations, though that is not their main claim to fame.

When Sir Jamsetji Tata established Tata Sons in 1887, he founded not only an industrial empire but also a philanthropic tradition which was carried forward by his illustrious sons, Sir Ratan, the younger, and Sir Dorab, the elder. It was continued by J.R.D. Tata, and the torch was then passed on to Ratan Tata, who recently stepped down as the chairman of the business conglomerate, but continues to head the Tata Trusts. The Tata trusts have been unique in pioneering the art of giving in India.

When charitable giving by the wealthy was mainly restricted to giving money to those in dire need or distress, the Tata Trusts began the practice of 'constructive philanthropy'. In Jamsetji Tata's words, 'What advances a nation or community is not to prop up its weakest and most helpless members as to lift up the best and most gifted so as to make them of the greatest service to the country'. He wanted his philanthropy to educate and develop the faculties of the young men of India. Accordingly, he set up the Jamsetji Tata Endowment Fund to enable the brightest individuals to go abroad for higher education. One of the many who drew on this particular benefaction in contemporary times was the late President of India, K.R. Narayanan, a Tata scholar, who hailed from a poor Dalit family. Jamsetji also provided funding for the

Tata Institute of Science (now the Indian Institute of Science) at Bangalore.[8]

His son Sir Ratan, before his untimely death at the age of 47, had willed a large portion of his fortune for the charitable trust which was set up in his name in 1919, with an initial endowment of rupees 7.5 million, largely in the form of shares in Tata Sons.

It was the first major Indian foundation in the modern sense of the word, and the first of six major trusts established by the Tata family between 1918 and 1947.

According to the terms of Sir Ratan's will, the Trust Fund was to be utilized towards 'the advancement of Education, Learning and Industry in all its branches including education in the economy, sanitary science and art or for the relief of human suffering or for other works of public utility without any distinction of place, nationality or creed'.

Sir Dorab Tata followed suit with endowments in the name of his wife. Lady Dorab Tata was known for her active interest in social welfare and the women's movement, so when she died of leukaemia, Sir Dorab established two trusts in her name—The Lady Tata Memorial Fund, created in 1932, one-fifth of whose income was to be spent on an annual award to an Indian scientist working anywhere in the world, for solutions to alleviate human suffering, and the remainder for research on leukaemia and other blood diseases. The second, the Lady Meherbai D. Tata Trust, was specifically devoted to women's emancipation and has disbursed money to enable women graduates to go abroad to study social work. Two things worth noting from this early history is that the Tata Trusts very emphatically wanted the benefaction to be available to all, irrespective of caste or creed, at a time when the trend was to give only to one's own community.

---

[8] The story of the Tata Trusts has been chronicled very ably by R.M. Lala in *The Heartbeat of a Trust* (New Delhi: Tata McGraw-Hill, 1984); and *The Art of Effective Giving* (Delhi: HarperCollins, 2011). Also see *Sir Ratan Tata Trust* (New Delhi: Samapradaan Indian Centre for Philanthropy, 1997); and Pushpa Sundar, *Beyond Business: From Merchant Charity to Corporate Citizenship* (New Delhi: Tata McGraw-Hill, 2000), pp. 179, 187–91, 307–8. This profile has drawn on these extensively.

Second, the Tata Trusts have, from their early days onward, had a cosmopolitan outlook, and have sought out excellence wherever it is found, whether in India or abroad.

Just before his death, Sir Dorab Tata created the SDTT for relief of distress from natural disasters, and for education and research, especially medical, scientific, and industrial research. The wealth he turned over to the Trust included substantial shares in Tata Sons and allied companies, his landed properties, and twenty-one pieces of his late wife's jewellery, among them the famous Jubilee Diamond. The total benefaction was valued at rupees 10 million.

The two flagship Trusts—the SRTT and the SDTT—worked together, complementing and supplementing each other's work. Though ad hoc giving to comfort the poor and sick has continued to be a part of their work since they receive a large number of requests for help, they were, and continue to be, among the few foundations and trusts in India who understand the distinction between giving to meet social need, and giving as a tool to engineer social and economic change.

In the 1920s, the Ratan Tata Trust invited F.S. Markham of the Museum Association, London, to advise on how best to proceed to meet its objectives. He advised both the SDTT and the SRTT to concentrate on one or two directions for a period of two to five years in order to secure the greatest possible advance. Accordingly, the Trustees decided that the Trust should undertake such projects as are too major to be undertaken by individuals and as bear a genuine relevance to national welfare, apart from extending support to individuals in need. Keeping this advice in mind, priority was given to education and research institutions.

The last of the Tata Trusts before Independence was set up by J.R.D. Tata. Born in France in 1904 and educated in Paris and Bombay, Jehamgir Ratanji Dadabhoy Tata (or J.R.D., as he was popularly known), epitomised in himself the best of the East and the West—the scientific temper and liberal outlook of the West, combined with the humanistic tradition of the East, as represented by his forefathers. In 1944 JRD donated his own share of Tata Sons and other companies to start the JRD Tata Trust, a multipurpose trust for the advancement of learning and relief of human suffering. To it he transferred more shares from time to time. It has since given out over rupees 10 million to causes dear to him, like family planning, and to institutions engaged in literacy and the uplift of women.

Between 1941 and 1966, the Trusts established four great institutions in four very diverse fields—medicine, science, education, and arts, namely, The Tata Memorial Hospital for Cancer Treatment and Research, the Tata Institute of Fundamental Research, the Tata Institute of Social Sciences, and the National Centre for the Performing Arts respectively, each of which has pioneered new ideas, research, or training, and set high standards for others to emulate. The Trusts themselves contributed substantial sums (rupees 40 million) to the projects, and leveraged funds from government and other business houses as well.

In order to achieve their objectives effectively, experts have always been invited to advise them. One of the best articulations of the role a foundation could play in making social impact was that by Dr Clifford Manshardt, a noted expert on social work who had established the Nagpada Neighbourhood House to help mill workers. In 1932, the Sir Dorab Tata Trust requested him to suggest how the Trusts funds could be utilized to make the maximum difference, and he outlined the philosophy quoted at the beginning of the chapter, as one which ought to guide a foundation. This was a novel philosophy for an Indian foundation in those days, and its adoption by the Tata trusts set an example for others to follow.[9]

Influenced by international trends, in 2000 the Tata Trusts began to undertake strategic philanthropy on the basis of a review by an external expert. There was a shift from funding major prestigious projects to supporting 'innovative' projects in the programme areas, and to more grassroots work.

Now the Trusts work in six major areas including education, health, media and art, and civil society, giving grants to institutions (25 per cent of total), to individuals, (6–7 per cent), to relief (2–3 per cent), and the rest to NGO partners who number around 800.

---

[9] Till 1998, SDTT's history and style of giving is recorded in R.M. Lala's *Heartbeat of a Trust*. It comprised, literally, of 'institution building'—identifying a niche area with the help of experts and then devoting the major part of Trust resources to establishing and nurturing a prestigious institution till it was handed over to the government or became autonomous.

In Financial year 2013–14, the SRTT and SDTT and allied trusts disbursed approximately $86.71 million (approximately rupees 5.64 billion).[10] This figure is estimated to have gone up to $100 million (rupees 6.5 billion) in 2015.

After Ratan Tata became Chairman of the Tata Trusts in 1991, he introduced several changes in the functioning of the trust, some of which have been mentioned earlier in the volume. One of the other changes is a greater thrust on funding social enterprises to help people at the bottom of the pyramid.

Another important change is a transition to becoming an operating-cum-grant-making foundation. While the Trusts will not run their own projects as such henceforth, they will work in close partnerships with a few identified civil society organizations like PRADAN, AKRSP, and BAIF on a new Transform Rural India initiative. In every case the aim is to make a difference to the community they work with and to make the work sustainable.

While introducing professional practices, Ratan Tata wants to ensure that the trusts do not lose out on compassion and flexibility, and more importantly, the ability to innovate and scale up projects. A Small Grant Scheme was started in 2004 that gave grants of rupees 1 hundred thousand to innovative projects, including one to doctors from All India Institute of Medical Sciences (AIIMS) who set up a successful and replicable low-cost rural healthcare model in Chhattisgarh.

Importantly for philanthropy in India, the Tata Trusts have influenced a new-generation of philanthropists to follow in spirit and practice, and if Tata is successful in bringing other emerging philanthropists together to build a stronger community of philanthropists, the Tata Trusts will have remained faithful to their founders' vision.[11]

---

[10] From Annual Reports of the Sir Ratan Tata and allied Trusts and the Sir Dorab Tata and allied trusts, both for FY 2013–14. Conversion rate Rs. 65: $1.

[11] Prince Mathews Thomas, 'Ratan Tata's Audacious Philanthropic Retirement Plans', Forbes India Magazine, 13 August 2012, downloaded from http://forbesindia.com/article/boardroom/ratan-tatas-audacious-phil-anthropic-retirement-plans/33526/5#ixzz2WYLNMuh7.

The Azim Premji Foundation

What distinguishes the Azim Premji Foundation is neither its years of experience nor its field of work—education—nor any exceptional achievement as yet, but that it represents the largest philanthropic contribution by an Indian individual in contemporary times.

In 2001, Azim Premji, promoter and Chairman of the WIPRO group, established the eponymous foundation as a non-profit organization out of his personal wealth, and not as a company foundation. In December 2010, he allotted 213 million of his personal shares in Wipro, about 5 per cent of his shares in the company, then worth about rupees 80 billion (approximately $2 billion) to the Foundation so that it would get roughly rupees 1.4 billion a year from the dividends that the shares earn.

By 2015, Premji had donated over 21 per cent of his WIPRO stake (worth around rupees 275.14 billion) to the foundation, to further his vision of contributing significantly to quality primary education for every child in order to build a just, equitable, humane, and sustainable society. He chose to devote a large portion of his personal wealth to education because according to him, education is a powerful vehicle for social change.[12]

The Foundation works both independently and in partnership with the government to create an institutional 'social infrastructure' to improve the quality of education across the country. Its aim is to make deep, large-scale, and institutionalized impact on the quality and equity of education in India, along with related development areas such as health, ecology, governance, and others because of their complex inter-relation, and because they also have a critical bearing on education. The target group for the Foundation's work is primarily India's large underprivileged and marginalized population.

Since the Foundation seeks systemic change through large-scale impact either directly or indirectly, and since such a large impact is possible only by working in close partnership with the government, a large part of its work in primary education is with state agencies, though it also works independently of the government where required.

---

[12] ET Awards 2013: 'Azim Premji Makes Plea for the Less Privileged', ET Bureau, 10 December, 2013.

The main thrust areas of the Azim Premji Foundation are talent development to create committed and competent people who can be change agents; knowledge creation through promoting high quality research and domain knowledge; integration of theory and practice; institutionalized impact through decentralized, autonomous entities which can implement programmes that are locally relevant and build deep relationships with proximate communities and collaborate with local government structures; and building social pressure and extending the reach through strong networking, advocacy, and communications.

The Foundation today works in eight states with more than 350,000 schools. It works at the grassroots level with its own State and District Institutes, located in several states and districts for capacity building of teachers and other functionaries for curriculum development, assessment, educational leadership, and management; and works at the state level for policy issues and advocacy. It has 800 people working for it, and plans to engage 5,000 people in the next five years as it scales up its activities, making it the biggest foundation in India. The Foundation has also set up the Azim Premji University with the aim of producing leaders with a social conscience and an awareness of development issues.

Clearly, it is still too early to see a countrywide impact from the Premji Foundation. A rigorous and independent analysis of its impact is yet to be made, but the large spread of their work shows that they are doing something that has value. That it is valued can be seen from the fact that they work in some of the most disadvantaged districts of the country, with 50–70 of their own staff in each of these districts. The voluntary learning forums they run for government school teachers are reported to have motivated the teachers so much that they spend their own money for transportation and food and to give up their Sunday holidays.

Now, Premji wants to expand the scope of his philanthropic activities by remaking the foundation on the lines of grant-making foundations like the Ford, Bill Gates, or the Tata Trusts. Because the Premji Foundation does not want to dilute its work in education, a parallel venture called The Azim Premji Philanthropic Initiatives was set up in 2014. The reason for the switch is that the education work takes a long time to show results, and some immediate achievements are needed to keep all those involved motivated.

The Initiative is to be focused on the same purpose of building a just, equitable, humane, and sustainable society. It will give grants to other implementing organizations, and expand their field of interest beyond education, into health and nutrition, to improve lives of the marginalized poor. As yet, it is finding its feet.

10

The Gift of Knowledge
Educating India*

The wealth that cannot be stolen,
neither abducted by state,
nor can be divided amongst brothers,
Neither it is burdensome to carry,
The wealth that increases by giving,
That wealth is knowledge
and is supreme of all possessions.[1]

An investment in knowledge pays the best interest.

—Benjamin Franklin[2]

Private philanthropy has played a significant role in educating India. Indians have always had a high reverence for education, especially higher education because, in American historian Stanley Wolpert's evocative words, education is 'the swiftest elevator to the pinnacles of modern Indian power and opportunity'. It is this reverence for

---

* This chapter was originally published as an article, 'Education at the Crossroads' in *IIC Quarterly*, Winter 2015–Spring 2016.
[1] From a Sanskrit Sloka, https://in.answers.yahoo.com/question/index?qid=20100731054136AAb4vQ.
[2] http://www.brainyquote.com/quotes/topics/topic_education.html#ET7Oe6ybFeSRSV7u.99.

education which has attracted philanthropy to it. Education has ever been a favoured field for Indian philanthropy. It was so in ancient times and it is so now.

But as in everything else, there have been changes, both positive and negative, in the way philanthropists have reacted to the opportunities. What follows focuses only on higher education since philanthropy for school education has been noted elsewhere, and on five issues in particular: one, privatization of education masquerading as philanthropy. Two, a preference for establishment of new institutions, especially universities, over giving to existing institutions. Three, among institutions of higher education, a preference for giving to institutions of technology and management, new or otherwise. Four, the internationalization of philanthropy, with wealthy Indians contributing substantial amounts to educational institutions abroad rather than in India, and foreign educational institutions establishing their extension projects in India with a view to tap into indigenous resources. And five, the constraints to increasing philanthropy for education and the measures needed to stimulate it.

Brief History

Epigraphical records indicate that supporting education was a favoured form of charity even in ancient times, and took the form of free feeding houses for poor students, construction of college buildings, endowment of chairs, or grant of land to meet the recurring expenses of educational institutions.

After the establishment of British rule in India, education on Western lines was a ladder to official favour as well as a way to optimize opportunities offered by the new industrialization and contact with Western civilization. The Indian intelligentsia and the new rich, partly from personal inclination and partly aided by government policy, directed their philanthropy to establishing Western educational institutions.

In Bombay, leading merchants Jaggannath Shankarshet, Framji Kavasji Banaji, and Jamsetji Jijibhai gave considerable amounts to the fund for the Elphinstone professorships and for the Grant Medical College; Kavasji Jehangir Readymoney gave large donations for Bombay University and hospitals, totalling in all rupees 1.4 million. The JJ School of Art owes its existence to the endowment given by

Jamsetji Jijibhai. Numerous other philanthropically minded merchants and others came forward in Bombay and elsewhere to fund colleges.[3]

Education, especially for girls, was one of the favourite causes supported everywhere. Millowner Bechardas Ambaidas of Ahmedabad, who endowed the Mahalakshmi Female Training College, was one such donor.

In Madras, one of the greatest of the early philanthropists was Pacchaiyappa, who, inspired by his English friend Norton, established an educational trust which set up the first private college in Madras—Pacchaiyappa's College. In Bengal, Motilal Sheel endowed the Free College.

A catalogue of philanthropy for education before Independence would be incomplete without a mention of one of India's greatest philanthropists, Jamsetji Tata. As mentioned earlier, he launched the J.N. Tata Endowment Scheme in 1892, much before the first major foundation in America. Though it gave scholarships to deserving students for higher studies abroad, since Tata did not believe in encouraging dependence through free charity, the scholarships were loans at a nominal rate of interest, to be paid back in easy instalments. By this means the fund was also conserved for future generations.

But his biggest contribution was the establishment of the Indian Institute of Science, for which he set aside fourteen of his buildings and four landed properties in Bombay in 1898, to create an endowment for an institute of science at Bangalore. The aim was to give India the technological personnel that would enable her to step into the industrial age. It is noteworthy that in order to attract more funds to the Institute, Tata insisted that his own name should not be attached to the Institute, something which is rare in today's philanthropy.

In the rest of India too, the wealthy were giving large donations for education, fired by the nationalist ideals of a free and progressive India. Inspired by Mahatma Gandhi's struggle for freedom, many of the new rich gave for the new Nationalist education, contributing generously to causes such as the setting up of the Benaras Hindu University by Pandit Madan Mohan Malviya.

---

[3] See Pushpa Sundar, *Beyond Business: From Merchant Charity to Corporate Citizenship* (New Delhi: Tata McGraw-Hill, 2000), for more details, esp. pp. 72–3.

In Delhi, Sri Krishna Dass Gurwale, one of the promoters of the Delhi Cloth Mills, established the Hindu College in 1899. It was set up for such Hindu students as would not be sent by orthodox parents to the St. Stephens Mission College, the only other institution of higher learning at the time.

The years immediately following Independence also resulted in the establishment of several well-known educational institutions, such as the Shri Ram College of Commerce, Lady Shri Ram College for Women, medical institutions such as Sulochana Devi Singhania School, Bombay, J.K. Institute of Applied Physics and Technology, Allahabad, and the J.K. Institute of Sociology and Human Relations, among other institutions. Almost every city in India has at least one or two colleges endowed by a private donor.

Philanthropy thus played an important role in building up the higher educational infrastructure in pre- and immediate post-Independence India.[4]

Of the sixteen largest, 'non-religious' trusts set up during this period, fourteen were major patrons of higher education. The net result was that at the time of Independence the net share of private philanthropy in shouldering the burden of public institutions was as high as 17 per cent in 1950. Now it is down to less than 2 per cent.[5]

Interestingly, a major proportion of their grants went to 'public institutions' such as universities that were either directly under state control or some form of public authority, in contrast to philanthropy today, where the trend is to build new institutions. Moreover, grants, although emanating from family trusts were, once made, not under the control of family trusts and were deployed for specific purposes by the terms set by the receiving institutions and not the trust itself. A very different ethic than that followed today.[6]

---

[4] I have covered this period more extensively in Sundar, *Beyond Business*, ch. 4.

[5] Devesh Kapur and Pratap Bhanu Mehta, 'Indian Higher Education Reform: From Half-baked Socialism to Half-baked Capitalism' (Working Papers, Center for International Development at Harvard University, September 2004), p. 26.

[6] Kapur and Mehta, 'Indian Higher Education Reform'.

In this brief summary, four things stand out. One, the motives for starting such institutions were perhaps more purely altruistic than in later times. It was clear to the pioneers of the first wave of wealth creation that for sustained development massive social investment in education, especially in scientific, vocational, and technical education, was necessary. And just as they had initiated a number of new industrial projects irrespective of tariff protection or without expectation of government aid, so they began to make good the gaps in the social field themselves. The result was a proliferation of colleges, universities, technical and research institutes, which were later taken over or supported by government.

Two, many of the pioneers were self-made men with little education, with the exception of the Tatas and the later technocrat entrepreneurs. In spite of, or perhaps because of that, they placed a great deal of importance on education as the golden key which would unlock the doors to prosperity and progress, and therefore gave freely to move India from a backward, agricultural, and tradition-bound society to a strong, modern one.

Three, most of the educational initiatives were confined to urban areas, and to the major towns.

Four, the government played a very positive role in moving the wealthy towards philanthropy, offering tax concessions and titles and awards.

After Independence, with a socialistic pattern of society as the avowed goal of state policy, the state became the predominant actor in development. Higher education became a government preserve. Since a deficit in technology was identified as the reason for India's backwardness, priority was given in higher education to the creation of the prestigious institutes of technology (IITs) which, though predominantly funded by government, also received research funding from private business.

A second fact of note is that apart from the government's role, the development of higher education between the sixties and seventies owes as much to funding by foreign as Indian donors. There was a large influx of foreign funds from the sixties onwards in response to the social and economic troubles faced by India. Foreign aid helped India either to establish many of the higher educational institutions such as the agricultural universities, or to build their capacity in various ways: by providing equipment, or providing funds to send faculty for training abroad; for scholarships to students for higher studies abroad, and paying for visiting faculty from foreign universities through programmes such as the Fulbright programme. A generation of some of the most gifted Indians became inspired by American ideals and commitment to excellence. Many of those who benefited by this Western philanthropy, and by the opportunities offered in America, are among those who are giving philanthropically to Indian development, and especially to education, now. The genesis of the present trend of large philanthropic donations to alma mater institutions abroad can also be traced to this development.

To quote just one instance, John P. Kapoor graduated from Bombay University in 1960 and wanted to study further in India but could not afford it. The State University of New York at Buffalo (SUNY) offered him a graduate fellowship, and he completed his doctorate in medicinal chemistry in 1972. Kapoor went on to become a great entrepreneur in the pharmaceutical industry. In 2000, he gave SUNY $5 million, increasing it to $11 million in 2010.

The most significant indigenous philanthropic contribution of the Sixties and Seventies was the setting up of the Birla Institute of Technology and Science (BITS) Pilani by G.D. Birla's Birla Education Trust, in 1964. Later it was converted into a deemed university.

The three premier Indian Institutes of Management (IIMs) at Ahmedabad, Calcutta, and Bangalore followed, between 1961 and 1973. In the creation of IIM Ahmedabad (estb. 1961), the rich business leaders of the city, like Vikram Sarabhai and Kasturbahai Lalbhai, made valuable contributions in money, time, and expertise. IIM Calcutta too benefited from the contributions of the West Bengal Government as well as foreign donors like the Ford Foundation, and Indian industrialists.

But after the Seventies, genuine philanthropic contributions became rarer as the government raised the tax rates to high levels in deference to the socialistic ideal and to finance development plans. There was a disinclination to invest in big-ticket institutions without government aid.

Philanthropy, if any, became an outlet for the huge amount of black money generated by the high tax rates and the license-permit raj. It encouraged the establishment of numerous charitable trusts as tax saving devices. This was the beginning of what can be called the privatization of higher education in the name of philanthropy, much of which owed little to a genuine philanthropic instinct.

Moreover, since the government offered tax incentives for giving to rural development, the focus of philanthropy also shifted somewhat from benefactions for education, medical facilities, and scientific research, to grassroots community development around company locations. There was also some shift from education to concerns like population control, agricultural improvement, and employment skills for women.

Education and Philanthropy Today

State of Higher Education

The higher education system in India has today become a large and complex system, thanks to public investments, foreign aid, and private contributions. It is the third largest in the world after China and United States in terms of enrolment, comprising a three-tiered structure of selective elite universities and research institutions at the top, second tier public and private institutions in the middle, and finally an array of private institutions providing mass education.

One of the plus points of the system is the widespread access to low-cost university education for students at all levels. The expansion of the system with pockets of excellence has also enabled Indians to innovate and become leaders in many fields. This is the good news.

The bad news is that there are still many challenges. One of these is a well-documented supply–demand gap. India has a low rate of enrolment in higher education, at only 12–15 per cent, compared to 26 per cent in China and 36 per cent in Brazil. There is an enormous unmet demand, a large proportion of which is being met by private, often for-profit, 'unaided' colleges and universities, at which standards are often questionable.

By and large, the quality of teaching and learning in both public and private institutions is low. India has fewer than twenty-five universities in the top 200, and only four Indian institutes feature in the top 400 universities in the world, though some more are entering the lists. The system churns out ill-prepared and unemployable graduates due to a chronic shortage of faculty, poor quality teaching, outdated and rigid curricula and pedagogy, and lack of accountability and quality assurance. Only 10 per cent of general graduates and 25 per cent of engineers and MBAs are estimated to be employable. The state of academic research is lamentable. India spends less than the other fast growing economies on research and development.

Other challenges include uneven growth, with lack of access for lower castes and backward regions; and lack of autonomy even for prestigious institutions, with much intervention and interference by the Human Resources Development (HRD) ministry. In short, 'Indian higher education faces a crisis of identity, resources and governance'.[7]

A major reason for this state of affairs is lack of funds. Public expenditure on all education has increased tremendously since Independence, from rupees 644.6 million or 0.64 per cent of GDP in 1951–2 to 3.2 per cent of GDP in 2010–11, and then to 4.29 in 2012–13. Of the total, public spending on higher education was only rupees 267.5 billion in 2013–14, a mere 1.33 per cent of India's GDP for the year.[8] This clearly is insufficient to ensure both expansion of seats and improve quality of education, especially since it is estimated that by 2030 India will be among the youngest nations in the world, with nearly 140 million people in the college-going age group looking for enrolment. More than 250 million additional skilled manpower will be required across the industry and services segments by 2030.[9] What is needed is more private investment to supplement public expenditure.

Privatization of Education, Not Philanthropy

In fact, the share of the unaided private sector has already increased significantly since 2001 in terms of the number of institutions and

---

[7] Ved Prakash, Chairman of the University Grants Commission, quoted in 'Philanthropy in Higher Education Must', *The New Indian Express*, Bangalore, 25 March 2013.

[8] World Bank data: http://data.worldbank.org/indicator/SE.XPD> TOTL>GD>ZS.

[9] FICCI–Ernst & Young, *Higher Education in India: Vision 2030*, Report for FICCI Higher Education Summit 2013 (New Delhi: FICCI-Ernst & Young, 2013).

enrolment. As of 2012, the share of unaided private institutions was 64 per cent of the total number of educational institutions, and 59 per cent of enrolment, an increase of 48 per cent and 79 per cent respectively from just a decade ago.[10] Today, about 60 per cent of higher education is provided by the private sector. Private investment has been particularly steep in professional education, especially medical, technological, and management education.

According to Kapur and Mehta (2004), in the case of engineering colleges, the private sector, which accounted for just 15 per cent of the seats in 1960, now accounts for over 86.4 per cent of seats (and 84 per cent of all engineering colleges). In the case of medical colleges, the private sector dominance is less but the trend is unambiguous: the proportion of private seats has risen from 6.8 per cent in 1960 to 40.9 per cent in 2003. The situation in the 1,000 odd business schools suggests that 90 per cent are from the private sector.[11] The professional institutions have largely come up in response to the hunger for professional qualifications on the part of students to improve employability and the need for a skilled workforce on the part of industry.

India's higher education sector is considered by many as a 'sunrise sector' for investment. In financial year 2014, the size of this market has been estimated well above rupees 3.83 trillion (US$ 62.34 billion), with over 38,000 formal degree/diploma granting higher education institutes.[12] But all of this does not add up to philanthropy.

Increased private investment in education is made up of two parts: the greater part represents a privatization of education in the name of philanthropy, and a smaller part representing genuine philanthropy. Much of the increase in private investment is interested only in the profits to be harvested from providing education and not in improving standards. Even in what is called philanthropy, there is a cynical use of the institution of charitable trusts for the sake of profit and personal gain.

[10] Ernst & Young, FICCI, and Planning Commission of India, 'Higher Education in India: Twelfth Five Year Plan (2012–2017) and Beyond' (November 2012).

[11] Kapur and Mehta, 'Indian Higher Education Reform'.

[12] Deloitte report, *Annual Status of Higher Education 2014* (Deloitte India, 2014).

Most universities and colleges are set up as not-for-profit, tax exempt ventures under section 25 of the Companies Act, but only a small number are philanthropic in intent or practice. The larger number operate as for-profit entities, charging high capitation and tuition fees without giving corresponding value added services. Their income comes from fees rather than endowments and investments, and they make large profits, especially professional colleges, without having to pay taxes on them. The evil of gross capitation fees is growing like a hydra-headed monster, feeding on political patronage and unsatisfied demand, because of which, virtually any institution has a market. Of the 422 medical colleges in India, about half, or 224, are private, thanks to a massive expansion in private medical education from 1996 to 2000. Nearly 60 per cent of the private medical seats were added during this period. Many have been set up as business ventures, and have little or no facilities, no patients, and fake faculty.

According to a recent newspaper report, the going price for an M.B.B.S. seat could range from Rupees 10 million in colleges in Bangalore to Rupees 2.5 to 3.5 million in some colleges in Uttar Pradesh. About 25,000 M.B.B.S. and post graduate seats are said to go for Rupees 120 billion a year.[13]

This is an indication that tax exemptions have attracted huge amounts of black money into the higher education sector. The result is that though there are some private institutions of a high standard, on the whole there is a mushrooming of private, often for-profit, 'unaided', academically mediocre schools and colleges, in which standards are often questionable. These colleges and institutes are little more than teaching shops, whose growth has been aided by the tax incentives offered by the government. Apart from being able to evade taxes, registering as a non-profit charitable trust also allows for easier land acquisition without inviting public interest litigations.

Because of this, the contribution of the private sector to quality education has, by and large, lagged considerably behind that of the public sector.

A majority of these 'teaching shops', where there is no pedagogical innovation or excellence, have thrived only due to the connivance and

[13] *The Times of India* Report, 'Black Money Quota: MBBS, PG Seats Go for Rs. 12,000cr/yr', *The Times of India*, 30 January 2016.

active involvement of politicians and officials. The Special Investigative Team (SIT) on black money, recently appointed by the government to check black money, has in its reports mentioned several studies which have highlighted how the higher and technical education sector, as well as the health sector, are major sources of generation of black money. The studies mention that entities engaged in education through trusts accept large unaccounted amounts as donations which, in a number of cases, are used for personal benefit and tax evasion.[14]

New Philanthropy

However, there is good news too. Though smaller in size than private investment in education for profit, genuine philanthropy also exists alongside the crass commercialization of education. Encouragingly, it is growing. With the revival of the philanthropic spirit towards the end of the twentieth century, many of the new rich have sought to fulfil their philanthropic goals by funding institutions of higher education.

Three distinct trends are visible: one, the establishment of several large, well funded universities in preference to donating to existing public institutions; two, alumni funding of existing institutions of excellence; and three, internationalization of Indian philanthropy.

Establishment of New Universities

Several new universities have been and are being set up by the new philanthropists who have made humungous amounts of money in recent years. These are named either after the donor himself, or the donor company, or in memory of a family member. Creating new institutions finds greater favour with the new wealthy, than giving to existing public institutions, as was the case with earlier philanthropy. Beginning with 2000, several new private universities have been set up by business tycoons. As is the case with non-philanthropic private investment in education, many of the newly endowed philanthropic institutions are for professional education rather than for a liberal arts education, as was the case in an earlier era.

---

[14] Reported in *The Times of India*, 'Panel Wants Capitation Fees under Anti-graft Law', Delhi, 25 July 2015.

The following are some randomly mentioned new universities established between 1990 and the present:

- The Nirma Institute of Technology, established in 1995 by Karsanbhai Patel, the founder of the rupees 25 billion Nirma group, which was followed by the Nirma Institue of Management, and finally the Nirma University in 2003.
- The Dhirubhai Ambani Institute of Communication & Technology in Gandhinagar, Gujarat, established in 2001 by the richest man in India, Mukesh Ambani, in memory of his father.
- NIIT University, to provide education in computer technology, founded by Rajendra Pawar and Vijay Thadani.
- OP Jindal Global University, founded in 2009 by Naveen Jindal, Chairman of Jindal Steel & Power, in memory of his father.
- The Ashoka University, in Sonepat near Delhi, as a collective effort by forty-six philanthropists, led by Ashish Dhawan and Sanjeev Bikhchandani.
- The Shiv Nadar University, set up by Shiv Nadar of HCL.
- The Azim Premji University by the promoter of Wipro, and
- The Adani Institute of Infrastructure Management, created by Gautam Adani, chairman of the $5 billion Adani Group.

A few more are coming up, namely the BML Munjal University from the promoters of the Hero group; a university in Khed district of Pune, to be promoted by Baba Kalyani, promoter of Bharat Forge; and what could be the big daddy of all, Mukesh Ambani's multidisciplinary Reliance University in Maharashtra.

Giving to Existing Institutions

Though the donations to existing Indian institutions by Indian philanthropists pale by comparison to the amounts spent in setting up own universities and colleges, and big-ticket donations given to institutions abroad, they are not non-existent either. Most of these come from alumni of Indian public institutions, and are beginning to grow, though they are most noticeable in the case of IITs and IIMs, which have been able to tap into a large base of professionalized alumni among the Indian diaspora.

One of the biggest donations to an Indian alma mater by an NRI is that of Frank Islam, an Indian American entrepreneur, who gave $2 million to his alma mater Aligarh Muslim University to build the Frank and Debbie Islam School of Management, with an emphasis on entrepreneurship.

Apart from this donation to a public university, most alumni donations go to the IITs, now fifteen in all, and the IIMs. These have received disproportionately high government grants compared to other engineering colleges, or any other higher educational institution. The undergraduates are subsidized nearly 80 per cent by the government while master of technology students receive full scholarships. A majority of them, however, go to the US after being educated at the tax-payers' expense. The donations to their alma mater institutions now represent a pay back.

When the alumni donation trend became visible, the Indian government's HRD Ministry formed the Bharat Shiksha Kosh (India Education Fund) in 2003, to pool the resources for onward granting. The Kosh was officially launched on 9 January 2003.

But by centralizing all overseas donations for education in the Fund, it effectively denied would-be donors any say on the purposes for which the money could be used, or which institutions would receive it. Consequently, it attracted very little money, as most major donors stayed away. Finally, the United Progressive Alliance government reversed the decision, allowing alumni to contribute directly to their alma maters. Since then, direct alumni philanthropy has been growing, and the Bharat Shiksha Kosh is as good as defunct.

However, the government has not given up on being a philanthropist with private funds. In the financial year 2016–17 budget, it announced that a rupees 10 billion Higher Education Financing Agency (HEFA) would be set up to provide greater financial autonomy to higher educational institutions with joint participation from the government and philanthropists. Of the total corpus of rupees 20 billion, rupees 10 billion will come from the government and rupees 2 billion each from five other corporate donors.

HEFA will finance capital expenditure for building quality infrastructure in IITs, NITs, IIITs, and central universities. It would also fund state-of-the-art research labs and other infrastructure.[15] The emphasis is again on elite institutions, but that is inevitable if the goal is to encourage excellence. Whether the government will succeed in attracting philanthropists this time, only time will tell, but it is likely to be more successful than the last time because of the compulsions for corporates to spend CSR money.

Meanwhile, many alumni and non-alumni are interested in funding transformational research, and are funding IITs for the same. Some of the notable donations are by Nandan Nilekani, N.R. Narayana Murthy, and Kris Gopalakrishnan, given mainly for research to professional institutes and research institutions, rather than to the public liberal arts or science institutions. What is heartening is that many of these donations are for supporting non-traditional scientific research and development, which augurs well for breakthroughs in different fields.

Some examples of alumni donations:

- At IIT Bombay, the class of 1975 funded a rupees 20 million tinker lab, where students can go and build whatever they want, free from restrictions of the class curriculum.
- Alumni and Syntel founder Bharat Desai gave rupees 50 million to set up a centre for entrepreneurship.
- Entrepreneur Romesh Wadhwani has committed to give rupees 30 million every year over five years for a centre for bio-engineering in the IIT.
- At IIT Madras, alumni have made contributions to its Healthcare Technology Innovation Centre. Its Silicon Valley alumni have set up a $1 million incubation fund for start-ups. Its 1981 batch set up a rupees 8 million fund for faculty and students to start companies, and the 1984 batch has given a similar amount for a centre for social innovation and entrepreneurship.

Apart from giving money to the institutions, IIT alumni are paying back in other ways. IIT Kharagpur's alumnus, Harish Hande of Selco-India, motivated Kollur Dhananjay to coordinate funds for a rural electrification project named Light for Education. Dhananjay

[15] *The Economic Times* report, 'Higher Education Gets Budget High Five', 2 March 2016.

took Hande's idea on rural education through electrification to another senior IITian, Arjun Menda, whose corporate real-estate industry, RMZ, has been funding education through the Menda Foundation for the past fifteen years. Menda, who disburses 220 higher-education scholarships every year, says he will match all grants the alumni association garners for the Light for Education programme, which provides impoverished tribal children in Karnataka with solar lamps for studying at home. Other alumni have supported the start-ups of other social ventures.

Non-alumni Donations

Non-alumni are also giving to prestigious educational institutions.

• Many of the pioneering IT entrepreneurs have given large grants to Indian institutions as well as to those abroad.
• The Infosys Foundation recently committed rupees 300 million to the Chennai Mathematical Institute to support the faculty and students.
• The Sir Dorabji Tata Trust has given rupees 950 million to IIT Mumbai to work on technologies for the bottom of the pyramid.
• Non-alumni philanthropists Bhupat and Jyoti Mehta have given to IIT Madras, to kick start and run the department of biotechnology there.
• Kishore Chivukula, founder of the Bangalore firm Indo-US MIM, gave rupees 15 million for the IIT Madras satellite project.

Such contributions help IITs do things which would not be possible with solely government grants.

Bharat Ratna awardee and eminent scientist C.N.R. Rao, who is the chairman of the Prime Minister's scientific advisory council, has been very critical of Indian business for not giving more to scientific research. According to him, starting next year, China will top the world with 16.5 per cent of world research publications, overtaking even the US, whereas the quantity of publication of research papers from India has remained at 2–3 per cent.

Some big givers like Infosys co-founder Kris Gopalakrishnan are, therefore, stepping in to fund areas of science and technology conspicuous by their absence in India so far, such as brain research and renewable energy. In 2014, he gave the Indian Institute of Science (IISc) at Bangalore rupees 2.26 billion to set up a brain research institute and has pledged IIT Madras rupees 450 million to set up three chairs on brain research.

Giving for New vs Established Institutions

The preference for establishing new universities over donating to existing ones shows that in the philanthropic sector, there is an increasing withdrawal from public institutions. The reasons are not far to seek.

The setting up of mega projects serves the double purpose of giving back to society and perpetuating the donor's name. The fact that most universities are set up as not-for-profit ventures which give the donor tax concessions also helps.

Where the intention is not genuinely philanthropic, setting up your own institution is an outlet for black money and also offers scope for charging capitation fees to make enormous profits. Neither of such unethical practices would be possible if the donors were to donate to existing public institutions.

The mandatory contribution of 2 per cent of profit before tax for CSR programmes under the Companies Act 2013 is also giving companies a push in the direction of setting up mega projects like universities. For many companies, the amounts to be spent under the CSR requirement are so large that only a big project can absorb such amounts.

Moreover, many of the leading business houses already run schools and colleges and have gained enough expertise to make a university the next logical step. For instance, the Shiv Nadar Foundation had earlier started the SSN College in Chennai. The success of SSN in south India inspired the family to create an institution in north India. Similarly, the Reliance Foundation, along with its associate institutions, runs a network of thirteen schools, and the Azim Premji Foundation was developing and providing free pedagogy to government schools before its university came up. The Jindals and the Munjals run schools close to their plants and elsewhere, and had already set up medical colleges.

Then, there is the huge demand. The gross enrolment ratio (GER), or the ratio of young people who are signing up for courses to the total number of people of that age, is increasing rapidly. By 2030 the number of students in colleges is estimated to go up to 70 million.[16] Building new projects adds more to the existing stock of institutions.

The reason for the distinct preference for endowing professional and technical institutions, rather than institutions for social sciences and humanities, is obvious. The greatest demand from students is for technical and management education of all kinds, since it commands the highest salaries. There is also the huge demand for such skills from employers who face a shortage of the required technical and managerial skills.

For companies, starting new institutions in the company name serves corporate self-interest by strengthening brand recall and has the added advantage of being able to set the agenda and curriculum to provide them with the numbers and type of skills they need, which they cannot do in existing institutions.

The Kalyani International University, for instance, is meant to be a comprehensive offering with a sharp technical focus. Since an industry–academia relationship is important for any technical university, the fact that it will be located in the Khed City Special Economic Zone (SEZ), which is 60 per cent reserved for manufacturing units, is a big advantage. Similarly, the BML Munjal University is planning a model factory with Siemens in the campus, and the courses designed from the ground up.

The fact that in many cases the Chancellors of these universities are the donors themselves also offers them a big advantage in moulding the education to their own vision.

However, not all donors think only of corporate interest. Azim Premji Foundation's CEO Dileep Ranjekar avers that the Premji University has been established with a clear social purpose of developing outstanding professionals in the domains of education and development for the entire country. They would like their students to go to the field and contribute to social change.

The new donors claim that whereas their vision is to create world-class universities offering students the same kind of academic freedom they enjoy in prestigious universities abroad, in existing institutions there is no flexibility, no autonomy, and too much government

---

[16] FICCI-Ernst & Young Report, *Higher Education in India: Vision 2030.*

interference. They cite the example of the IIMs, which had developed as centres of excellence and whose autonomy is now being seriously eroded by creeping government interference. The proposed Indian Institutes of Management Bill will further offer the government greater scope for control over the management of the institutions, though hopefully the proposed HEFA, described above, will help to reverse this.

The new universities can secure higher academic standards by offering better facilities to students and better pay to faculty members, unhampered by existing government standards. They are also able to introduce teaching methods not possible for cash-strapped public institutions. For instance, the Adani Institute of Infrastructure Management, which started a one-year master's programme in September 2014, sent students on a two-week trip to China, Indonesia, and Malaysia to study a variety of infrastructure projects. At the LNM Institute of Information Technology, which opened six years ago, students are given one year to explore different engineering subjects before they choose their major, a practice unheard of in public institutions so far. NIIT freshmen study from a syllabus fashioned by industrialists and academics, and interact with industry professionals in their first year.

The new universities and colleges also hope to offer an alternative to what they see as a misguided public higher-education system, in which students are encouraged to think narrowly and learn passively. Most plan to scale up to become multidisciplinary universities.

But these brave new education warriors may be unable to solve the many problems facing India's education system. One of the reasons why more genuine Indian philanthropists have not turned to funding higher education institutions is the difficulty of getting the several government permissions and acquiring the large amount of land required for a large university. This state of affairs makes many Indian HNWIs prefer to give to foreign universities.

One particularly challenging problem facing all universities in India, public and private, is a nationwide shortage of well-qualified faculty members. Though the philanthropic institutions may be better than colleges started by politicians and others wanting to make or launder money, most of them are, and will continue to be, only teaching rather than research institutions, because of the faculty hurdle.

A second drawback of the new institutions is that they are far costlier than the public sector colleges and universities, and only the most well-off may be able to afford them, thus attracting charges of elitism in education. For instance, undergraduate students at NIIT University pay annual tuition fees of about $8,000, including housing. Graduate students pay about double that, whereas undergraduates at India's premier higher-education institutions—the Indian Institutes of Technology—pay only $1,600 to $2,000, including housing (though this is to be raised shortly).

Even with higher fees, but without any of the underhand dealings noticed in some of the private institutions, the big philanthropic institutions may yet falter on the ground of lack of funds. The first phase of NIIT's development is estimated to cost $21.7 million and by the time it is complete, in about a decade, the total cost will be close to $44 million.

Though NIIT University founders Rajendra S. Pawar and Vijay K. Thadani aim to absorb nearly all expenses during the first few years, after that they will need to look for contributions from other sources like wealthy individuals, and of course, the government. It is a plan common to all the big new start-ups. It is also expected that the institutions will become self-sustaining over the long run, from student fees and consultancies for the government and the industry in computer science and engineering, educational technology, and bio-informatics and biotechnology. This is the way most prestigious universities like Harvard and others sustain themselves. But for the liberal arts and social sciences in India, there is less hope of such succour, since they will not be able to charge high fees, nor secure many consultancies.

Internationalization of Indian Philanthropy

Donations to Foreign Universities

Till now India has been a net receiver of international philanthropy, much of it going to higher education in an earlier era. It is a telling statement on India's growth story that rich Indians are now reversing the flow of philanthropic funds, and giving to educational institutions abroad. It is really these big-ticket donations by leading Indian philanthropists to institutions of higher learning abroad which have brought Indian philanthropy world attention.

Among those who have given to foreign universities are:

- Naveen Jindal, who from his personal fortune gave $200,000, and from his company Jindal Steel and Power Ltd. (JSPL), $2.3 million to the University of Texas at Dallas, after which the university renamed its school of management after him. In return, employees of JSPL and associate firms would be eligible for executive programmes at the university.[17]
- Shiv Nadar has given to create the Shiv Nadar Professor of Engineering Chair at Carnegie Mellon University.[18]
- Ratan Tata, who earned a degree in architecture from Cornell University in 1962, gave $50 million to Cornell in 2008 for agriculture and nutrition programmes and for the education of Indian students at Cornell. In 2010 the Tata Trusts gave $50 million to Harvard Business School to fund a new academic and residential building on its campus, the largest gift received by the institute from an international donor in its 102-year-old history. The building is named Tata Hall.
- Anand Mahindra, Vice Chairman and Managing Director of Mahindra and Mahindra Group, has given $10 million to the Humanities Centre at Harvard. A Harvard alumnus, Mahindra gave the gift, the 'largest' in the Centre's history, in honour of his mother Indira Mahindra. Mahindra's rationale for supporting an already well-off foreign university when Indian universities lack funds so sorely, is that 'to address complex problems in an interdependent world, it is vital to encourage the cross-cultural and inter-disciplinary exchange of ideas in an international setting'.
- N.R. Narayana Murthy gifted $5.2 million, to be managed by his son Rohan Murthy, to Harvard University Press to publish translations of Indian classics.
- Nandan Nilekani donated $5 million to Yale University to underwrite the Yale India initiative.

---

[17] Reported in *The Indian Express*, 'Jindal, his firm gift $2.5m to US varsity', 17 October 2011.

[18] From http://www.shivnadarfoundation.org/press-releases/Philanthropy-on-a-wing-with-Shiv-Nadar.pdf.

- Smaller, less well known groups and their leaders, like Xander Group founder Siddharth Yog, have also donated to universities abroad. Yog gave $11 million to Harvard.
- Kiran Mazumdar-Shaw has instituted two post-doctoral fellowships for Indian students for studies in Oncology at MIT Boston.
- The latest to join the ranks of philanthropists giving to educational institutions abroad is Indra Nooyi, Pepsico's India-born CEO, who in January 2016 gifted an undisclosed amount to her alma mater, the Yale School of Management, becoming its biggest alumni donor and the first woman to endow a deanship at a top business school.

Foreign Educational Institutions in India

A second aspect of the internationalization of Indian philanthropy for education is that many Western universities are opening their centres here. Thus, the Chicago University has set up a centre here to support the work of its faculty, to provide a platform for inter-disciplinary collaboration, and to create an intellectual hub where students from the US and India can meet for exchange of ideas. It offers programmes in India to undergraduate, graduate, and professional students. The Brookings Institute too has set up a unit here for research-related exchanges. Similarly, the Sommerville College in Oxford has also recently taken the decision to establish a charitable entity in India in the form of a non-profit company. The funds are to be used within India for research, seminars, and conferences, and to fund students to pay their fees at Oxford.

An underlying, though unspoken motive behind such initiatives appears to be that they will attract Indian philanthropic capital as well as donations from foreign donors in India and help swell the students, and thence the coffers in the parent bodies, in a tax-effective way. There is no data so far to indicate whether it has, in fact, attracted Indian philanthropic capital.

A Critique

The donations to institutions abroad, in particular, has caused much heart burning in Indian institutions and raised questions as to why Indian philanthropists should give to already well-funded institutions like Harvard University and think tanks like Brookings Institution, when there is a crying need to improve standards in Indian universities and research institutions hamstrung for resources.

There are, of course, pros and cons to the internationalization of Indian philanthropy. Taking the cons first, critics point out that Indian think tanks in particular are hamstrung by lack of funding, in contrast to US think tanks and research institutions which have huge budgets. For instance, the Washington-based Brookings Institution has a budget of $160,000, the Rand Corporation of around $250 million (in 2009). Similarly, for the other big think tanks like the Heritage Foundation and others.

In India, one would be hard put to think of any think tank or research institution with comparable resources, though lately some new organizations such as the Observer Research Foundation (ORF), funded by the Reliance group of companies, and the Centre for Public Affairs and Critical Theory at Shiv Nadar University, funded by the Shiv Nadar-led HCL, have emerged. But apart from a few older ones such as the Centre for Policy Research, NCAER, and ICRIER, to mention a few with budgets round rupees 50–100 million and staff ranging from 20 to 100 or so, they are a small blip on the national scene.

By and large, Indian research bodies are small-time operations, and have inadequate funds and facilities. Quite a few of the larger ones have been helped by the generosity of foreign donors like the Ford Foundation, rather than by indigenous philanthropy. Not surprisingly, they always take a second place in global ranking even though there are first-class minds in these institutions. The result is that independent input into India's policy matters is woefully small, and a credible, non-partisan alternative to government thinking does not emerge on several controversial matters such as nuclear power, large dams, genetic engineering, and so on. Ironically, as captains of Indian business liberally fund Ivy league US universities, India's think tanks are struggling to survive.

To quote the late George Verghese, veteran journalist, 'The ability of the think tanks to speak the unspeakable and think the unthinkable without fear of political, diplomatic or market consequences is invaluable in injecting new ideas and concepts into policy debate'.[19] But for this they need independent and arms-length funding from enlightened philanthropists who recognize the need for research for progress in society.

Critics also mention the business argument against giving to international institutions. Pratap Bhanu Mehta, for instance, points out that investment in Indian institutions would give a higher rate of return. Typically, endowing a single chair at a top American university costs between $7–15 million. The intellectual return on that money, properly invested in India, will still be considerably higher. The total annual budget of India's leading institutions in the realm of culture, whether it is the Sahitya Akademi, or Lalit Kala Akademi, or Sangeet Natak Akademi, is close to what it takes to endow a single chair in the humanities in the US.[20]

Others claim that the philanthropic gestures of Jindal, Tata, and other donors have as much to do with the giver's ego as to their sense of altruism.[21] To have globally prestigious universities name research centres and other buildings after them announces to the world, as few other things can, that they have arrived!

Some others are troubled by the possibility of potential philanthropic capital being drawn away from Indian institutions towards outreach centres of foreign universities in India, especially since Indians are very brand conscious as far as foreign degrees are concerned. They point out that while a free flow of ideas is to be welcomed, the programmes offered in India may not be the best suited to India or may be ones where Indians may have as much knowledge or more. The Sommerville College is said to be interested in developing a programme on sustainable development, though it may be questioned whether a Western view of what is sustainable is superior to what insiders feel is best for India.

It is also argued that, funding foreign educational institutions, whether in India or abroad, is likely to reinforce and perpetuate an

---

[19] Quoted in 'THINK YOU' feature article in *The Economic Times*, 5 September 2010.

[20] Pratap Bhanu Mehta, 'Charity at Home?', *The Indian Express*, 19 October 2010.

[21] Chidanand Rajghatta, 'Alumnus faces ire for $400m gift to Harvard', *The Times of India*, 5 June 2015.

intellectual hegemony so that only the Western viewpoint prevails and is accepted as authoritative, even over the views of those from within the culture itself.

The decision by the Murthys to base the project to translate and publish Indian classics in the classical and vernacular languages in the Harvard university has, in particular, sparked a debate round this issue. The grant has been criticized on the basis of economics (it could be done much cheaper in India), on the ground that it avoids capacity building of Indian institutions, and that it prevents an intellectual diversity. It is argued that India must stop being a mere consumer of knowledge produced elsewhere and become a producer of knowledge itself. And its self-image needs confident assertion through an acceptance of its ideas globally. But with the premium on Western universities and Western intellectual dominance aided by Indian philanthropic donations, India's sense of itself, its own history and past, its own problems, is more likely to be shaped by biased knowledge produced elsewhere, if India's own intellectual traditions do not receive support and encouragement from philanthropists.

In defence of the grant, Rohan Murthy and others have pointed out that the classics belong to the world, that Indian education policy has itself neglected the study of classical languages and so scholars of the calibre required are not coming up, that the project will bring together scholars of repute from all over the world, and that the Murthy family has equally philanthropically supported leading Indian research institutions such as the Bhandarkar Institute and the Bharatiya Vidya Bhawan.[22]

In support of international grants in general, it is also pointed out that given the state of higher education institutions in India, many may not be able to absorb money of the kind that was offered to Harvard and others. It is further pointed out that many of these same donors have also given substantially for other causes and organizations in India.

The Indian outcry is not surprising when similar feelings have been voiced in America itself over large donations to Harvard at the

---

[22] For the debate, see Makarand Paranjape, 'The Problem with Pollack' *The Indian Express,* 21 March 2016; Rohan Murthy, 'The Classics Belong to the World', *The Times of India,* 6 March 2016; and Swapan Dasgupta, 'If We Won't Save Sanskrit, Why Stop Foreigners', *The Times of India,* 3 April 2016.

expense of smaller universities there, who typically educate lower-income students and themselves are cash-strapped. John Paulson, who made his fortune betting on the housing market collapse and who was an alumnus of the Harvard Business School in 1980, gave a $400 million donation to Harvard. The gesture brought criticism both for the donor and for Harvard, already the richest university in the world with a $36 billion endowment, greater than the GDP of a hundred countries.

To my mind, that major philanthropists have chosen to give to foreign institutions rather than Indian is unfortunate but understandable. International philanthropy no doubt deprives Indian institutions, but philanthropy, as a purely voluntary act, must allow the donor to exercise choice. It is also an acknowledgement of the donors' gratitude for the quality education received from their alma maters which has enabled them to succeed in their careers. Indra Nooyi, for instance, credits her experience at the Yale School of Management for 'forever altering the course of my life', and said her gift 'pales in comparison with the gift Yale gave me—the fundamental understanding that leadership requires an expansive world view and a deep appreciation of the many points of intersection between business and society'.[23] If one appreciates the alumni donations to Indian institutions, then one must understand these international donations in the same spirit.

There is also the simple fact that the top echelons of Indian capital are becoming increasingly global, jockeying for access and influence. Giving large amounts to highly visible institutions boosts the brand image of their companies and adds to their market value. Moreover, such donations have personal benefits for the donors in terms of name and fame abroad. Many of the foreign institutions name buildings and Chairs after the donors or give honorary doctorates to them.

If the highly sophisticated fund raising campaigns of premier institutions like Harvard, University of Chicago, and Cambridge are juxtaposed with the total absence of any fund raising efforts by Indian public institutions for higher education, then again the donations are understandable.

[23] *The Times of India*, 'Nooyi Becomes Yale's Biggest Alumni Donor', 14 January 2016.

Finally, several donors like Kiran Mazumdar-Shaw believe that since good philanthropy flows out of a donor's passion for a cause, where and whom to give should be a purely personal decision based on a donor's judgement as to who or what cause will best use their money. Certainly in today's global world, there should be no xenophobia about philanthropy. If excellence resides in foreign institutions, rather than Indian, then work there should be funded for the good of humanity at large.

I believe that internationalization of philanthropy is inevitable and that the identification of India's elites with institutions abroad will only deepen in the coming years, especially with the next generation of HNWI families already heading abroad for further studies.

Moreover, it also has a positive side. One, it encourages excellence wherever it is found, and adds to global progress, which is bound to benefit India too. Two, it creates a good image of Indian business abroad. Three, the new donors are but following the example set by India's own merchant communities like the Chettiars who, when they entered new markets, built temples and other charitable institutions in the new markets first, thus sending out a signal of being trustworthy businessmen. Philanthropy has been used as a sweetener since olden times.

The better knowledge, values, and business practices learned in world renowned universities will also raise the bar in Indian business and in Indian educational institutions, since most of the donations have linked the grants in some way to Indian students, researchers, and organizations. Many of the Indian donors are seeking to leverage their donations to ensure collaboration for Indian universities and institutions in India. For instance, a donor to Ashoka University, who is also a donor to Wellesley College, a leading liberal arts college in the US, is looking to bring the best practices on women leadership to Ashoka through a collaboration.

Lastly, one must realize that international philanthropy plays a political role, improving international relations between the countries. At a national level, it is in some way a paying-back for the American investment, financial and intellectual, in Indian education. The donations make a powerful statement, recognizing the extraordinary role played by the American education system in not just transforming individual Indian lives, but in building arguably the strongest bond between the people of the two countries.

Thousands of Indians went to the USA to study, helped by grants and tuition support and the like. A generation of some of the most gifted Indians became inspired by the American commitment to academic excellence. They are now sending philanthropic contributions to Indian organizations. It is payback time.

Finally, as Indian philanthropy matures, donations to Indian institutions are bound to increase in number and volume, while the international grants may remain the exceptions.

Constraints

Before this can happen, the constraints to philanthropic investment in higher education must be removed. So far, the government has allowed private players to expand higher educational facilities only because of its own fiscal deficits; its need to meet the increased reservation requirements by expanding supply; and because education offered a convenient source of patronage.[24] But while increased state funding of public institutions is essential and must increase, there is a strong case for more philanthropy in education. Its leverage value and catalytic nature make it invaluable for transforming education.

The remedy for the ills in private higher education is not to stop or restrict private investment but to ensure that more genuinely philanthropic capital enters the space by putting in proper policies and checks and balances in place.

It is possible to attract more philanthropic capital to education because education has always had an appeal to HNWIs, because it is non-controversial, and the impact can be easily measured. This needs to be put to good account. But more than investment in brick and mortar, the philanthropic capital must focus on systemic change and quality standards.

Though there are several bucket shop ventures without honesty of purpose, and the profit is siphoned off without giving value to students in return, all bona fide institutions should not be tarred with the same brush. A bona fide institution, according to Asish Dhawan, the co-founder of Ashoka University, can make money only if capital expenditure and the real estate costs are not factored

---

[24] Kapur and Mehta, 'Indian Higher Education Reform'.

in, and only an operating profit is possible. But even that may take 7–10 years or even longer, if there is a research thrust. Therefore, even these non-profit institutions have to find ways to become financially independent, and just the fact that they charge high fees should not be held against them, provided, they offer scholarships liberally to meritorious students of limited means, and offer truly quality education. Great universities around the world also charge high fees and have, alongside other diverse ways of funding themselves—research grants, donations, and other philanthropic contributions.

The new crop of philanthropists who have set up new universities and colleges expect to provide the capital expenditure for some years and operational expenses for a few more, and then expect either the government to chip in or other philanthropic sources to kick in. This is not very different from the way the older philanthropic institutions had operated. Institutions like the Indian Institute of Science, Tata Institute of Social Sciences, were all endowed by private philanthropy and from recurring grants by the promoters, but as they expanded, they had to meet the cost from sources other than interest from the endowments.

There is some truth in the argument that good students from the better-off classes and schools will leave poorly funded and equipped public institutions in favour of the newer, well-funded entities, leaving the older public institutions intellectually deprived. But just as water finds its own level, the intellectual elite will go where their potential is fully realized, including foreign universities. This is not necessarily bad so long as merit is recognized through liberal use of scholarships. Then, older public institutions which were centres of excellence will be replaced by newer ones, private or public, until the exodus leads to a reappraisal on the part of the government, which in turn could lead to reforms in the educational structure and polices.

It has also been argued by some like Pratap Bhanu Mehta that contemporary Indian philanthropy in Indian higher education does not come up to the standards set up by philanthropists in the past, and that though the new wealthy have the resources to set up universities and research centres on a scale comparable to the renowned institutions in the West, or even in places like Singapore, they have not done so.[25]

[25] Mehta, 'Charity at Home?'.

But this is to show undue pessimism. Our older philanthropic institutions, when they first started, would also have faltered till they matured. It is only on hindsight that all appears to be rosy. Most of the new universities set up by the new breed of entrepreneurs have come up since 2000. For a university to come up to world standards, requires more than a decade, and sometimes even a century. Given time, it is likely that some of these brave new initiatives will match the standards of the older Indian institutions and even those of some of the global universities, like the National University of Singapore. If they are on a modest scale now, one of the factors is also the difficulty of acquiring land, given India's extreme land scarcity.

So, instead of decrying what genuine philanthropy exists, ways must be found to remove the several constraints which hold donors back, as well as to improve its impact by removing the abuses.

One of these constraints is the lack of autonomy in public or publicly aided educational institutions. Donors of scale, whether NRIs or Indians, hesitate to commit large resources unless they also have a say in its use, and an institutionalized mechanism to have their voice heard. However, the governance structures of most higher education institutions are so poor that such mechanisms are non-existent and government interference with institutional autonomy rampant. One reason why the IISc has attracted such a large donation from Kris Gopalkrishnan is that it has set up the new Brain Research Centre as an autonomous society, which gives it full freedom to operate, free from government rules and regulations, while also drawing on the intellectual and physical facilities of the institute campus.

While the corporate sector and India's elite can be criticized for not paying sufficient attention to India's public universities, where many of them studied, universities must also shoulder blame. Apart from a few exceptions like the IITs and the Indian Institute of Science, Bangalore, higher education institutions have not attempted to tap the huge alumni resource.

'The best public universities in India such as Delhi, Bombay, Banaras Hindu University, Calcutta and Madras have had some of the finest scholars from India. But none of them has attempted to reach out to their alumni', according to P.C. Jain, Principal of Sri Ram College of Commerce (SRCC), Delhi. If the SRCC now looks unlike any other government college with rundown build-ings and poor facilities but like a corporate office, it is thanks to the generous contributions from well-placed alumni who responded with 60 million rupees (US$ 1.3 million) towards state-of-the-art equipment and pledged more to renovate the college library and construct a centrally air-conditioned block.

But change is coming in slowly. Surprisingly, a major publicly funded institution like the All India Institute of Medical Sciences (AIIMS), which till now would not have looked outside the gov-ernment for funding to improve its education facilities, has raised money from philanthropic sources. Two chairs, one each in the department of Obstetrics and Gynaecology and the Cancer Centre, are to be funded by private philanthropy. The Infosys Foundation too will give the Institute rupees 100 million to fund travel fellowships to young doctors, scientists, and faculty. Plans are also said to be afoot to set up an AIIMS endowment fund.

But the above institutions are exceptions rather than the rule, and only show what can be achieved with indigenous philanthropy, if it is tapped properly.

More aggressive fundraising will, however, not help unless the reg-ulatory regime changes. It is difficult, if not downright counterpro-ductive, for public colleges and universities to tap private resources or seek to leverage old school ties with alumni to raise funds, because of the University Grants Commission's practice of deducting such philanthropic contributions from a university's grant-in-aid. It leaves little incentive for these institutes to conduct aggressive fundraising campaigns. A more enabling regulatory regime would surely help.[26]

A major difficulty in putting private investment to good use is the difficulty in distinguishing real philanthropic activity from masked profit-making, since by definition, all Indian universities and private colleges are 'non-profit' organizations. Unless there is some clarity on this, the abuses may continue. A recent Supreme Court judgement has, in fact, come down in favour of continuing profit making in private educational institutions. In a recent (March 2015) judgement favourable to educational institutions, the Supreme Court has ruled that surplus income earned by educational institutions cannot be

[26] See *Indian Express*, editorial, 1 February 2014.

taxed, and that imparting education should not be termed a for-profit activity merely because it yielded high returns. Where an educational institution carries on the activity of education primarily for educating persons, the fact that it makes a surplus should not lead to the conclusion that it becomes an institution for the purpose of making a profit. However, the Court recommends that the government should examine the activities of such organizations more closely.

What this really boils down to is that all philanthropic activities, or non-profit organizations claiming tax benefits, must operate primarily for a public purpose. Even if they make a profit, there should be a substantial public benefit, rather than private gain. Second, such organizations should be debarred from distributing their net earnings, if any, to individuals who exercise control over them, such as members, officers, directors, or trustees.[27]

In addition, the SIT on black money, mentioned earlier, has recommended banning of cash contributions to educational and religious bodies and charities, as also amendments to the Prevention of Corruption Act to treat personnel of schools and colleges accepting donations as public servants.

In addition, the government must tighten licensing standards, improve quality assurance without impinging on autonomy of institutions, put in place a rating framework which emphasizes student learning outcomes and research—not facilities and infrastructure—and finally, there should be a regulatory mechanism that can oversee all educational institutions—public and private.[28]

Select private participants can also be invited to establish high-quality institutions through a public private partnership model.

To conclude, every effort should be made to nurture the nascent shoots already visible, and to channel them in the right direction.

---

[27] Kapur and Mehta, 'Indian Higher Education Reform'.

[28] Ashis Dhawan, 'Time to Recognise Private Universities' Role in Putting India on the Global Education Map', *The Economic Times*, 13 July 2014.

PART IV

FUTURE VISION

We have to work towards making philanthropy unnecessary. It has to focus on removing inequality: not just wealth disparities, but injustices in politics, culture and society that compound inequality and limit opportunity.

—Darren Walker (2015).

11

The Unfinished Agenda

It is not enough to give, responsible giving must be done with thought. It must be marked by reflection, respect for the other party, and enhanced humility on the part of the donor.

—Jacob Neusner

In the space of three decades, there have been slow but sure changes in Indian philanthropy. The very concept of what is considered philanthropy has broadened beyond traditional giving by individuals and foundations, to giving as part of CSR, and investing in for-profit ventures for social benefit.

The background and characteristics of the new philanthropists are significantly different, as are the outcomes they themselves and society expect from their giving. The state–philanthropy relationship has become more complex, with greater demands by the state on the resources of the rich, and more collaboration between the two for achieving common social goals. The philanthropic agenda has diversified, with new approaches being tried out.

In size, the amounts donated have steadily increased to $5–6 billion or 0.3 per cent of India's GDP. Though still far below the levels of the West, they are better than neighbour China's figures, amounting to 0.1 per cent of GDP. Donations by some individual donors run into millions of dollars or crores of rupees, and giving by the younger generation, of both HNWIs) and the middle class, is on the rise.

The earlier chapters have documented these changes in some detail. It now remains to draw up a balance sheet of the achievements and shortfalls, and to look ahead.

The Good News

The foregoing has already given details of all that is new and praiseworthy today, so this short section only summarizes the highlights.

To begin with, there is a greater awareness of the need for and the potential of philanthropy for bringing about social transformation, and of the fact that the government cannot be the sole actor in development. After a long interregnum of several decades between 1960 and 1990, there is once again some enthusiasm for contributing more to the public good, even though it is still thinly spread.

Spatially, the reach of philanthropy has widened from one's own immediate locality, caste, kin, and religion, to a national and even international level, though not surprisingly, the immediate takes precedence over the distant.

Western philanthropy is acknowledged to be largely elitist—by the rich, for the rich—in spite of much talk of social justice. The beneficiaries of philanthropic initiatives such as libraries, art galleries, theatre, prestigious universities, and leadership programmes continue to be largely the upper or middle class, and the facilities they represent are mostly accessed by the social and intellectual elites, though social justice issues such as equal opportunities for migrants, and gender and racial discrimination are coming to the forefront.

In India, on the other hand, the trend has been to make philanthropy more non-elitist. While earlier the focus was largely on urban communities, now rural, interior areas and communities have come onto philanthropy's radar. There has been a welcome shift from largely building prestigious institutions and civic infrastructure, to supporting rural grassroot causes such as water harvesting, rural energy, rural education, and most of all, to providing livelihoods to curb poverty. Environmental issues like sanitation and air and water pollution, which affect society as a whole, are being tackled. And the conscious effort to bring education, health, and nutrition to women and girl children to reduce the gender gap is another step in a non-elitist direction. However, the elitist bias has not been completely eliminated and is visible in the establishment of new elite universities, and in support for intangible objectives such as building leadership, capacity, and efficiency of institutions, and women's empowerment, where there is still an upper caste, upper/middle class, and male bias in use of scarce resources.

In common with other countries in Asia, a more strategic approach has resulted in an emphasis on innovation, scale, and more efficient execution for a deeper, wider, and more long-term impact on social issues. The possibility of collaboration to achieve both scale and impact has also entered the calculations of those who want a bigger bang for their buck. One danger of the trend towards more government–philanthropy collaboration, of course, is that it can undermine the independence of philanthropy to test and follow its own strategies, and the freedom to criticize government policies and concepts. But for the present, the evidence on this, either pro or con, is too thin to make any judgement.

The Flip Side

The flip side is that in spite of the gains, Indian philanthropy is yet to become a potent force for change. Though many seeds have sprouted, cumulatively they are yet to bring about fundamental changes in the social structure.

Prime Minister Narendra Modi, in a recent speech to captains of business and industry, reminded them that risk-taking was in their DNA, implying that they were not being true to their dharma. If the creators of wealth have been risk-averse even in their business role, it is not surprising that their philanthropy has been even more timid. A few schools and hospitals here and there, some scholarships, and vocational training courses do not add up to philanthropy which causes disruptive change. They are more in the nature of charity.

Very few philanthropists can be said to be unique trend setters, or their work path-breaking. To be fair, it takes time for long-term changes to become evident. It is too early to say whether the Shiv Nadar Foundation's investment in rural children's education will produce the unique leadership change which is its aim. Similarly with other efforts. It is difficult at this stage to judge whether the many initiatives afoot can create the wave which will erode the rocks of stultifying habits, thoughts, and practice of long years of stagnation.

But it appears that only a few of today's givers have a vision of the society they would like to create with their money, which their predecessors in the First Golden Age had. They had pursued a vision of an independent, progressive India, free from colonial rule and aroused from the slumber of centuries of superstition, ignorance, and poverty, and had devoted their money to making that vision a reality.

Today, except perhaps for Azim Premji and Ratan Tata, not many have articulated their vision of what they would like their money to do for India. Mostly, they have identified some niches in the social infrastructure and put their money to fill the gap. Compared to the resources the present philanthropists possess, the amounts being devoted by them to building new institutions, to controversial issues such as social justice and communal harmony, or to pioneering new products and processes to benefit humanity at large, are miniscule.

One role of philanthropy is to support and encourage excellence. In 1885, Leland Stanford, who gave an endowment of $5 million to create Stanford University, in a letter to one of the trustees, wrote 'To make our institution all that I want it to be it must turn out students who shall be able to influence and direct thought in the way of elevating the masses. It seems to me that the great question for statesmen and for humanity is how shall the great body of the people be lifted up, made intelligent, able to avail itself of the advantages of its labour.'[1]

This is very similar to Jamsetji Tata's ideal of constructive philanthropy, which, though quoted earlier, bears quoting again. He said, 'What advances a nation or community is not to prop up its weakest and most helpless members as to lift up the best and most gifted so as to make them of the greatest service to the country. I prefer this constructive philanthropy which seeks to educate and develop the faculties of the young men.' The greater effort today, and rightly so, is to lift up the weakest of the masses, but by means of charity, rather than by giving them tools to help themselves. And the emphasis on promoting excellence, wherever found, is missing.

---

[1]   Quoted in Brian O'Connell, *Philanthropy in Action* (Washington: The Foundation Center, 1987), p. 32.

How many of our foundations or philanthropists today are helping to build excellence in disciplines crucial to the nation, such as medical ethics, judicial and electoral reforms, scientific research to end perennial droughts and the drinking water problem, or to grow crops which can improve nutrition, or to deal with plastics or toxic waste? Several new universities have been started by the new philanthropists, but how many have helped existing universities to become better?

In the quest to meet mass needs, few have devoted money to this pursuit of excellence in individuals or institutions, bar a few such as the Infosys Awards, which award excellence not at the end of a career for lifetime achievement, but early on, when it needs support and encouragement. Too few of today's philanthropists are putting money on ideas and on individual talent to enable people to realize their potential. We need today's rich to back a potential Ambedkar, a C.V. Raman, or a Ramanujam. One of America's leading foundations is said to have allowed exceptionally promising individuals to just put their feet on the desk and think! The story may be apocryphal, but the idea is clear.

Philanthropy can help to heal wounds left by conflict as well as prevent it. In the USA, millionaire Vanderbilt, after whom the University is named, located it in Nashville in the deep south of America, not only to bring the benefits of excellence in education to the more backward South, but also to rebuild the nation's unity after the American Civil War. When making the gift of half a million dollars, Vanderbilt said, 'If the School, through its influence contributes even in the smallest degree to the strengthening of ties which should exist between all geographic sections of our common country, I shall feel it has accomplished one of the objects that has led me to take an interest in it'.

Too little money has been devoted in India to causes and solutions for communal conflicts, a major source of loss of lives and resources.

Private American foundations have been key factors in the extraordinary uplift in the status of the United States as a leader in scientific and engineering progress during the last forty years.[2] Of how many Indian foundations can one say that?

Bangalore has come to be a big hub for technology-generated new wealth. It has also come to be a leader in the new philanthropy, along with Mumbai. And yet social consciousness is visible only in

[2] Weaver, quoted by O'Connell, *Philanthropy in Action*, p. 37.

a few top names, such as Azim Premji, Nandan Nilekani, Narayana Murthy, some of the other Infosys founders, and Kiran Mazumdar-Shah. When asked to name some mid-range philanthropists, some of those in the social sector were stumped for names. In fact, one of them groused that many CEOs draw top dollar salaries, but do not contribute much to social causes.

While there has been a welcome shift from a focus on giving for education and health, by and large, there is still a lack of imagination in choosing one's charitable preferences.

At the 103rd Indian Science Congress in Mysuru during 3–7 January 2016, several eminent speakers pointed out how India is lagging behind in research of various kinds. For instance, healthcare research gets only 0.6 per cent of GDP, so that less than $1 is spent on each Indian for health care research.

Nobel Laureate David Grosse has warned that India will never be able to invent anything if science and scientific research are not given their due. He pointed out that in 2000 India and China were both investing 0.8 per cent of their GDP on research and development. By 2010 China's outlay doubled to 1.8 per cent, while India remained at 0.8 per cent; in 2014, India still invests only around 0.9 per cent.[3]

The McKinsey and Co.'s October 2013 survey, *Designing Philanthropy for Impact*, confirms the narrow vision of today's givers. It observes that ninety per cent of donor contribution in India is concentrated in only ten out of fifty possible sub-sectors. The sub-sectors favoured are: housing; healthcare (maternal care, neo-natal care, primary healthcare, medical care for differently abled, elderly care, and AIDS and infectious disease); and disaster relief (but not prevention).[4]

In particular, not enough charitable resources flow to social justice issues, that is, causes which would benefit the most marginalized sections of society such as dalits or tribals, or to those organizations with least access to government or foreign funds. This is what the McKinsey

---

[3] David J. Grosse, speaking at the 103rd Indian Science Congress in Mysuru, 3-7 January 2016, reported in *The The Times of India*, 'Change or India Cannot Invent', 6 January 2016.

[4] Ramesh Mangaleswaran and Ramya Venkataraman, *Designing Philanthropy for Impact: Giving in the Biggest Gaps in India* (Mumbai: Social Sector Practices Team, McKinsey & Company, October 2013).

study, quoted above, calls a niche gap—causes which are important in themselves but which are not perceived to be so by a large section of the population, or where the urgency of need is not recognized.

What is needed to advance the weakest sections is not merely some education and income earning opportunities, but more fundamental changes in social structure and power equations.

The quantum and pattern of giving by the new rich in fact indicates a basic development illiteracy. Even educated people do not know what is socially important, what an organization engaged in a public cause expects to achieve, how it plans to do so, which are good organizations, and so on. Social development goals are not well articulated either by the government or by NGOs or others in the social sector, with the result that no synergy is built up and people play their own little game in their own little corner. Apart from a lack of understanding of the structural causes of poverty and illiteracy and social inequality, those with money to give have neither the time nor the desire to learn about them, or expose themselves to the issues first hand. Consequently, they tackle surface symptoms rather than the underlying structural issues, for some of which the rich themselves are to blame, not poor governance alone. Spending a few millions of rupees on scratching the surface is not likely to make much difference beyond salving their own conscience. This is why the trend towards investment in encouraging social entrepreneurship is more valuable than a few grants to a few NGOs.

Finally, better quality philanthropy does not happen in India because the humanities and social sciences are comparatively neglected in favour of an emphasis on technical and professional education, and business management training is divorced from social development education.

A Caveat

To be fair, most of the new philanthropists have come into big money recently and it takes at least two generations both to want to give it away to society and to understand how to give it wisely. Besides, it needs the existence of a basic culture of giving to give more and give it well, and the fact that for many decades the culture of giving was dormant, as well as the absence of a good infrastructure for promoting wise giving, has constrained even those with good intentions.

Finally, it will take time for many of the major initiatives such as new universities and funding of scientific research and of social entrepreneurship to show results. Therefore, it may be both premature and discouraging to pass judgement at this stage. In fact, the Azim Premji Foundation started its grant-making initiative along with its direct education initiatives reportedly in order to see some results in the medium term. Since its education initiatives will take a long time to show changes in processes, systems, and attitudes, all those involved in the philanthropy needed to see some more tangible success on the ground in a shorter timespan, so as not to feel discouraged.

Moreover, it is necessary to realize that even with all the resources and best intentions in the world, there are limitations to what philanthropy can accomplish. Despite the large amount of resources devoted by the Indian government and multi-lateral and bilateral agencies to social development, the impact has been modest. It would be naïve, therefore, to think that increased funds from philanthropy will 'solve' India's poverty problem.[5] Though multi-million dollar donations are needed, one must be realistic and see them as only a catalyst triggering change, and use them well by setting priorities.

Moreover, certain of the solutions needed to energize Indian philanthropy lie in the domain of other actors such as the state. Some money which could have come into philanthropy will never make it to the formal philanthropic field because it is ill gotten or tax-evaded wealth. Instead of its legal use for society, donors find it easier to salve their conscience by donating it to temples or other religious organizations. It is for the state to take action here to see that such money is brought into circulation and incentivized to be put to good use.

The Unfinished Agenda

The agenda for future action follows from the lacunae highlighted in previous chapters and the forgoing analysis.

---

[5] Devesh Kapur, Ajay S. Mehta, Moon R. Dutt, 'Indian Diaspora Philanthropy', in *Diaspora Philanthropy and Equitable Development in China and India*, eds, Geithner F. Peter, Johnson D. Paula, and Chen C. Lincoln (England: Global Equity Initiative, Asia Center, Harvard University, 2004), p. 205

Changing Attitudes

The popular perception is that the Indian rich are not charitable, barring a few. But as observed in Chapter 2, Indians are as charitable as any others, but not philanthropic. They give informally, and to known individuals in need, and to religious institutions. The general approach to giving is still that of charity—relief of symptoms, rather than long-term change to tackle root causes.

This is not to disparage the role of charity. Though organized social-change philanthropy is a desired goal, there will always be need for humanitarian distress relieving charity. Fortunately, there is a lot of charity for such purposes in India, but its potential to also contribute to social transformation has been ignored. Philanthropy does not necessarily have to follow the American way, but our own traditions of giving need to be revived and directed to a collective social goal. It is imperative that small charitable resources are pooled and better organized and monitored so that abuse of charity ceases, and their social impact increases.

Though givers' beliefs and attitudes resist change, and therefore replacing or reforming religious giving will be hard to do, efforts need to be made via education and media campaigns to shift people to organized collective charity for social change. For HNWIs, donor education will have to stress the difference between charity and philanthropy in order to encourage them to think big, take risks on their social investment, and show innovation and enterprise in giving. Philanthropic orientation has to change from 'giving back' to 'solving social problems'.

This implies thinking beyond short-term funding of 'projects', and instead make commitments to encourage problem-solving attitudes, strengthen newly created institutions and processes of social change, and to nurture talent.

Better Practices

Both foreign donors and Indian NGOs believe the future lies in Indian donors taking over the funding of Indian NGOs. But many NGO leaders are sceptical about Indian philanthropy making up the deficit left by withdrawal of foreign donors. According to them, the gap between domestic funds available to civil society and international funds is too wide, not only in terms of quantity but also quality. Most recipients of foreign aid have valued it not only for the larger pots of money but also for the consultation and advice that went with it, for allowing flexible use of funds to experiment with according to need, and the importance of networking. They feel that it will take a full generation or more before domestic funding can reach the size or match the quality of foreign funding, and that Indian donors need to learn from their foreign counterparts the art of giving. This is yet to mature in India because in the Indian psyche it is the government which must be the provider. It will take time to overcome this mindset.

Because grant making is not the default condition in India, expertise in grant making has not developed. For grant making to make a real impact on social transformation, there must be a good understanding on the part of the foundations of what is good grant making and how to use grants as building blocks.

While the world of organized philanthropy has gained with more strategic use of resources, one must beware of too tight a control, for now it sometimes looks as if it has lost the passion and spontaneity of charity, which was earlier possible because the large donor himself made the decisions. With the adoption of arms-length philanthropy and a philanthrocapitalism approach, the programme officer mediating between the owner of wealth and the grant seeker, and lacking full authority to dispose of the funds, is cautious, fearing that failure could reflect on his capability and his job.

A recent study by the Centre for Emerging Market Solutions (CEMS) at the Indian School of Business, Hyderabad, and FSG Social Impact Consultants,[6] suggests that the evolution of catalytic philanthropy in India can be accelerated by considering a broader set of critical social issues for primary funding focus; building the capacity and professionalization of the NGO sector; promoting more donor-friendly policies; and creating philanthropy associations to accelerate learning and advance the field.

---

[6] Study by Nidhi M. Reddy, Lalitha Vaidyanathan, Katyayani Balasubramaniam, Kavitha Goraopali, and Sharad Sharma of Centre for Emerging Market Solutions (CEMS) at the Indian School of Business, Hyderabad, and FSG Social Impact Consultants, *Catalytic Philanthropy in India: How India's Ultra-high Net Worth Philanthropists are Helping Solve Large-scale Social problems*, 2012.

While current practice has begun to concentrate on measurement and develop tools for measurement, on selecting the right organizations to support, and on getting together a strong team, donors do not always ensure that the design and strategy are correct to achieve the impact on a societal scale. For this, availability of appropriate information and data on sources, amounts, recipients, and impact of philanthropy is absolutely essential.[7]

More Diversification in Charitable Preferences

As mentioned earlier, there is a need to shift from the set traditional giving patterns to a more diversified portfolio in tune with emerging needs. This again calls for better donor education to change mindsets and policies.

Instances of gap causes which can be funded are promotion of philanthropy itself, art and culture, preservation of traditional handicrafts, rehabilitation of prisoners and jail reform, and so on. Philanthropists must consider some of these issues as equally important to fund.

There are many other important concerns for philanthropy to address in future. A sample agenda could be:

- Supporting the building of new leadership not only in the field of organized philanthropy but also in society generally, based on values, ethics, and notions of responsibility.
- Promoting macro ethics of systems which have impact on the citizens, such as parliament, the judiciary and the bureaucracy, the medical profession, business, and universities.
- Supporting the development of 'soft power' to deal with conflict situations, whether between communities or nations.

More Professionals

More diversified and qualitatively better giving will happen only when there are well qualified and trained philanthropy professionals in foundations and companies. Because of the ad hoc, sporadic, and reactive nature of much of current organized philanthropy,

---

[7] Reddy et al., *Catalytic Philanthropy in India.*

professional expertise in philanthropic giving which would enable the donor or programme officers of foundations to take bold and visionary decisions has not developed. Lately, in a search for quantification and measurement, the spirit of philanthropy, and the role played by intuition and fiscal daring have taken a back seat. The professionals now in charge of philanthropy appear more concerned with the number of grants made, completion of projects within given time periods, and measurement of impact, rather than visionary thinking. In general, in Indian foundations the programme staff are rarely given the latitude to take bold decisions, which are only taken by the owners of the philanthropic resources. In any case, there is an acute deficit of well-trained philanthropy professionals, especially now that CSR has become mandatory and companies are also seeking experts in social development.

The agenda for the future requires intermediary organizations, business schools, schools of social work, and others to run more courses to train professionals in philanthropy, like Sampradaan had done in its 'Give, Give Wisely' workshops on how to make philanthropy effective by choosing the right design and strategy, selecting the right organizations to support, and monitoring and evaluating the outcomes.

Making Good the Knowledge Gap

To enable Indian philanthropy to replace international aid in any major way will need several infrastructural improvements, including more research to provide accurate knowledge about the overall contours of Indian philanthropic giving, and to base donor education on this.

The McKinsey study quoted above lists four important sets of questions in connection with giving, namely what are the gaps in terms of sectors and sub-sectors of societal activity and what causes these gaps? What are the gaps in terms of modes of intervention? How can philanthropists make the right choice of how to give and where to give in order to make their giving more effective? And finally, what good practices or examples exist, which can guide them. To be able to answer them, one needs much more information and data than is available to us today. It is one of the main reasons why donors do not give more or give only to niche areas, or why the impact of the giving is less than commensurate.

Though the contours of Indian philanthropy are better known today, thanks to research by SICP, CAP, PRIA, Bain and Co., Dasra, and others, there is much that we still do not know, and this constitutes the unfinished agenda for research. For instance:

- Except for the few Annual Surveys on philanthropy conducted by Bain and Co. since 2010, we have no other trend data to say whether we are becoming more or less generous; whether, how, and how much of new wealth is being channelled into philanthropy; and what is the likely impact, if any, of an inter-generational transfer of wealth on philanthropic giving. There is also almost no data as to where the charitable rupee goes. Surveys of different kinds, repeated at least every 3–5 years, are essential to enable us to track changes in charity and charitable preferences. It is also important that the surveys use uniform or comparable methodology and parameters to make the data credible.
  - Understandably, most of the research attention so far has been focussed on urban givers and especially the HNWI strata, since it represents the largest value in giving. But there are also rich landlords, farmers, and small industrialists in India's second-tier cities, who mostly route their charity through religious groups, but can also be motivated to give for various local initiatives. Again, minimal attention has been paid to medium- and small-scale enterprise and whether, and if so, to what, they give a portion of their profit. More data is needed on both of these.
  - We need to know more about the rich indigenous traditions and practices of different communities, different size of enterprises, as well as about rural philanthropy, so that ways can be found to bridge the two worlds of charity and philanthropy.
  - The rising middle class is another group to monitor; their individual donations may not be as dramatic as those of India's billionaires, but the numbers add up to substantial amounts.
  - We do not have enough base line data even about the world of organized philanthropy, such as how many charitable foundations there are; how many are grant making and how many operate their own philanthropic projects; what proportion of the total charitable resources come from

foundations; what are the pros and cons of operating versus grant-making foundations; or what impact have our foundations in the total had on the course of social development.

- Some other useful research could be devoted to tracking of giving by trusts and foundations by field, to show which fields are underfunded and why, and by type of donor (NRIs, International donors, Indian foundations, corporations, and so on).

- A study of how many philanthropic dollars come out of each industry sector, compared to that industry sector's contribution to India's GDP, would confirm whether, for example, the IT sector is in fact the most generous. Geographically mapping philanthropic projects (foundation reach) over India's poor districts or conflict-districts may also reveal what areas receive the most attention, which are neglected, and where philanthropy can be directed. We need empirical research on corporate giving programmes, as is being undertaken by the Conference Board and the Foundation Center in the USA, and the Charities Aid Foundation in the UK.

- Case studies of corporate and other giving for training of professionals of donor organizations are missing but necessary.
- Research is also needed on government–philanthropy partnerships and other collaborations to know whether and why they succeed, and whether independence of philanthropy is indeed compromised.
- Finally, there is almost no research on what difference tax incentives make in the decision to give, and whether differential incentives have served to draw charitable resources into selected areas.

Philanthropy must become a field of enquiry in our universities or research institutions. We have hardly any centres specializing in research on civil society and philanthropy, and this is a gap which should be addressed by some philanthropists.

Making Common Cause

Organized Indian donors are individual players and making common cause with other donors in order to make a bigger impact is still alien to our ethos, so that there are few examples of donor partnerships for joint funding of really big ventures. While NGOs have learnt to value collaboration and partnerships, organized Indian donors still do not see themselves as belonging to the larger non-profit sector where they have common concerns and problems and something to learn from each other. Collaboration, though on the rise, is still the exception rather than the rule, because it involves giving up some individual control.[8]

If we are to have a truly 'civil society', one in which a high level of cooperation and mutual support prevails, then the trend towards partnerships needs to be strengthened, with companies and foundations actively seeking out partnerships at various levels—community, district, regional, and national—and with a variety of organizations such as NGOs; other corporations with similar interests and goals; foundations, Indian and foreign; rotary clubs; and government agencies. Such mutually supportive relationships between the various sectors—state, commercial, and non-profit—are essential to guarantee a democratic and economically strong society.

Ethics and Accountability

Philanthropy has ever been used to buy status and a good image in society. At the same time, it has also fronted questionable behaviour, such as evading taxes, buying political patronage, and influencing public policy for personal commercial gain. Many have made wealth through unethical means, but later used it for the benefit of society. The 'robber barons' of the nineteenth and early-twentieth century America made money through exploitation, but to their credit, also endowed huge foundations. Though a desire to save on taxes was a major consideration, as also to burnish their tarnished reputations, they used their money to determine what sort of society America was going to be. The influence of those foundations on American society has been immeasurable.

Carnegie provided poor areas with libraries and schools because he wanted to turn America into a meritocracy where any aspirant could rise. Others founded art galleries and museums because they wanted to ensure that American society was a refined one. But, according to

---

[8] Fulton Katherine, Gabriel Kasper, and Barbara Kibbe, *What's Next for Philanthropy* (Monitor Institute, July 2010), p. 8, http://monitorinstitute. com/what-we-think/.

one critique, of the super millionaires of America today, only George Soros and Ted Turner, and now Buffet and Bill Gates and his wife, have done anything on the same scale or with the same imagination about the kind of society they want.[9]

In India too, the fortunes of many of the first generation of philanthropists of the Parsi and Gujarati merchant communities in the mid-nineteenth century came from the opium trade, which can well be called a trade in human misery. With the exception of Jamsetji Tata and Jamnalal Bajaj, who were well known for their ethical principles, many industrial fortunes made and later spent on philanthropy were made from some sharp practices like hoarding and black marketing. But as in the American case, the end use of the fortunes was of benefit to society.

In contemporary India, Ramalinga Raju, the promoter of Satyam Technologies, which rose rapidly to become a premier IT company till its fall due to the underhand dealings by him, was known for his philanthropy. He had given liberally to several social causes and had set up a foundation to support development.

The popular film star Salman Khan is known to be very charitable and to give liberally to a variety of social causes through his Being Human Foundation. Yet, allegedly, his irresponsible behaviour led to the death of some footpath dwellers in a hit-and-run case in Mumbai. There are other documented cases of the coexistence of philanthropy with lack of ethics.

Donors complain of lack of accountability on the part of those who receive charitable resources, and this is often cited as a major reason why they give less than they can or ought. There is very rightly a demand from philanthropists that there be accountability and transparency on the part of recipients, but often they themselves do not play by the same rules. Very few trusts and foundations themselves publish annual reports containing the details of their assets, activities, or grants. Surprisingly, not even the Azim Premji Foundation, today's leading foundation, publishes its financials in its Annual Report.

One has only to talk to a Director of Income Tax Exemptions to learn of the lack of transparency, accountability, and misuse of tax provisions on the part of those who have endowed charitable trusts for public purposes. There is self-dealing and flouting of the

---

[9] Katherine et al., *What's Next for Philanthropy*.

mandatory pay-out and other conditions which enable a donor to enjoy tax exemptions. Hospitals, schools, and colleges are established as charitable concerns to gain tax and other benefits, rather than as purely altruistic gestures, and are used as commercial concerns.

Anu Aga, currently a Rajya Sabha Member and former chairperson of Thermax, concedes that there is hypocrisy in business, for business sometimes gives for social welfare with one hand and takes away with the other in dishonest or unethical dealings.

The introduction of mandatory CSR contributions by companies has reportedly introduced another element of dishonesty and misuse of the philanthropic trust. Since the mandatory CSR spends disclosed by companies in their annual reports do not have to be vetted by auditors, and since the financials of charitable trusts also come under little scrutiny except in a few states like Maharashtra, some companies are using unscrupulous charitable trusts to fabricate CSR spending and to turn black money into white.[10]

Whether good outcomes justify questionable means is a question which is yet to be resolved. Many would believe that it does, if the social wrongs cannot be prevented in any case. It deserves to be a subject of public debate. Meanwhile, it cannot be gainsaid that greater transparency on the part of donors is needed. Philanthropy of the future must be an ethical philanthropy, and associations of donors or a chamber must take up self-regulation as an important agenda.

A related issue is that failures need to be more frankly acknowledged, so that philanthropists can learn from each other's mistakes. Philanthropists must get used to public scrutiny and criticism.[11]

Leadership

Leadership in the business sector has not necessarily translated into leadership in the Indian philanthropic sector. Very few of India's

[10] Report in *The Economic Times*, 'In CSR Trusts, Black Turns White and Vice Versa', New Delhi, 21 October 2015.

[11] *The Economist*, 'Faith, Hope and Philanthropy: What the New Breed of Donors Can Do—And What It Can't', 23 February 2006, http://www.economist.com/node/5517704.

present philanthropists, except some like Ratan Tata, Azim Premji, and N.R. Narayana Murthy, talk about philanthropy to encourage and inspire others, or to put pressure on the government for legislative changes, the way Bill Gates and Warren Buffet are doing now or as David Rockefeller or J.R.D. Tata did in an earlier period. Fortunately, some of the younger and more socially conscious philanthropists like Rohini Nilekani, Mohan Pai, and Roshni Nadar are more vocal, and are on record as saying that givers must publicize their giving to act as an example and for the sake of peer pressure.

To build philanthropic leadership, more platforms are needed to bring philanthropists together to exchange views and discuss experiences on the lines of the annual conferences of the Council on Foundations, which bring together several hundred business leaders and CEOs of foundations round a theme, or the annual Dasra Indian Philanthropy Forum, which has just started doing the same in India.

Support Organizations

As discussed in the chapter on promoting philanthropy, India needs to develop a more comprehensive and effective infrastructure to encourage a culture of giving, to channel its resources more strategically for impact, and to be the voice of the philanthropic sector. Support organizations are still largely absent. Till now, only foreign foundations like the Ford, the Rockefeller, and the McArthur Foundations, besides the indigenous Tata Trusts, have shown an interest in supporting efforts to promote philanthropy per se. But in future, more philanthropists must see the creation of an infrastructure for promoting philanthropy as one of the essential social needs to be addressed by philanthropy, and devote resources to it accordingly. The creation of an apex national organization to act as a chamber or the voice of philanthropy will require not only substantial funds but also top leadership.

It is not only foundations and philanthropists who need to be concerned about an appropriate infrastructure, but also would-be recipients. Organizations in civil society also need to give a thought to how giving of time, money, and skills can be made easier for business, because in a real world, it is the exceptional, rather than the average businessman who will go out of his way to seek people, causes, and organizations worthy of assistance, or who will initiate catalytic action.

Intermediary organizations in the voluntary sector, such as associations or networks of NGOs, and rating agencies for NGOs, such as Credibility Alliance, GuideStar, and Give Foundation, can facilitate philanthropic giving by collecting and disseminating appropriate information on worthy causes and organizations; developing a credit rating system for charitable organizations; and improving interaction between the corporate and the non-profit world.

Debate, Discourse, and Role of Media

If Indian philanthropy is to become a potent force for progress, there must be more discourse on it, more exact knowledge about it, a more favourable policy environment, and an openness to winds of change blowing in other sectors and in other countries.

Because charity became the subject of a public discourse at the beginning of the twentieth century, traditional modes of giving were creatively transmuted into newer, more efficient, and 'progressive' forms. Charity became more secular, less sectarian, and more oriented to human betterment. Today there is hardly any discourse on philanthropy, other than some showcasing of individual acts of philanthropy.

The challenge before philanthropy is to envision where it fits into our desired vision of society. Would-be philanthropists must be prepared to discuss more openly and more often than they do at present, their vision of society and how they intend to realize that vision through their philanthropy. Only then can the conflicting and sometimes unreasonable expectations society or sections of it have of philanthropy be reconciled.

The media can play an important role in this discourse, bringing lesser-known causes to light, pushing for greater accountability in giving, and encouraging informed debate on theoretical issues. It must ask hard, critical questions that would make HNWIs think about their values in philanthropy, rather than merely report individual acts of generosity.[12]

---

[12] Emily Jansen, 'From Gaining to Giving Wealth: the Shaping of Private Indian Philanthropy', Draft Paper, International Development Research Centre (IDRC), Canada, October 2012.

Making private acts of giving more public will inspire (or shame) others to give more. The *Hurun Annual List* of the top philanthropists is a step in the right direction.[13]

State and Philanthropy

The government continues to be omnipresent, and still the most important actor on the development scene. Since it is large and complex, it requires patience and skill to access its resources or to work with it. Here too, a chamber-like body of donors would be helpful for a dialogue with government.

The state must see stimulating social development as of equal importance as stimulating economic development, and therefore must have more proactive government policies to make giving easy and beneficial for donors.

While a National Policy for the Voluntary Sector was framed and adopted some years ago, it did not have much to say on philanthropy. And Sampradaan's comprehensive Report on Charities Administration for the Planning Commission, unfortunately, remains unimplemented.[14]

Tax subsidies or exemptions are one way of encouraging the flow of resources into desired channels. It would be to the government's advantage to know whether it does lead to more charity or whether the state is losing revenue unnecessarily.

While it is important to allow people the choice of where and how much to give, if a larger impact on social progress is the desired goal, the state will also need to devise policies which will link up philanthropic resources with large and important national goals and programmes, such as was attempted by the Bharat Shiksha Kosh. Even though it was a failure due to improper conceptualization and implementation, the idea is again being tried out in the Swachh Bharat Kosh (Fund for the India Cleanliness Campaign), which seems to be meeting with more success.

---

[13] Pushpa Sundar, *Beyond Business: From Merchant Charity to Corporate Citizenship* (New Delhi: Tata McGraw-Hill, 2000), p.356.

[14] Sampradaan Indian Centre for Philanthropy, *A Review of Charities Administration in India* (New Delhi: Samradaan, September 2004).

Recognition

Finally, the government and society need to recognize and appreciate the role of philanthropy. To restore prestige to philanthropy as an act worthy of honour, and to accord recognition and status to those who contribute to social progress and well-being, the state should consider including philanthropy among the categories considered for the highest national awards.

Leading non-profit organizations, too, could consider establishing awards for philanthropists who in their view have done the most to make a difference to society, as is being done in countries like the UK. There a number of awards, such as the Spears Award for Philanthropy Adviser of the year, and the annual STEP Awards for Philanthropy Team of the Year have been instituted to recognize and celebrate those who contribute to philanthropy as well as its promotion.[15]

Future Vision

While private initiative and assistance is and will continue to be needed to help cope with India's problems, merely running more schools, hospitals, or training centres to add to what the government is doing will not be its *best* role, and the wealthy will need to rethink where their comparative advantage lies in social development. Outlined below are some of the roles which private philanthropy still needs to play:

- Keep the institutions of civil society alive and promote individual freedom, social justice, and civic responsibility by supporting private non-profit groups engaged in such work.
- Push forward the frontiers of knowledge by supporting research and experimentation in areas that the government will not or should not undertake.
- Spot and support the talented maverick, the social activist, and the scientist/artist with a 'bee in his bonnet'.

[15] Theresa Lloyd and Beth Breeze, 'How Has UK Philanthropy Changed Over The Past Decade?', 15 October 2013, www.alliancemagazine.org.

- Create what Robert Putnam calls 'social capital', which refers to features of social organization such as networks, norms, and trust that facilitate coordination and cooperation for mutual benefit. Social capital enhances the benefits of investment in physical and human capital. Philanthropy can promote values of citizenship and civic obligation and activities that strengthen the character and cohesiveness of social life, by funding networks and other kinds of organizational infrastructure.
- Encourage a culture of reciprocity and partnerships by leveraging other funds and bringing the synergy of the other two sectors—government and NGOs—to development.

In the words of Matthew Bishop, keen commentator on global philanthropy, 'Philanthropy of the future will need to be innovative, thoughtful, analytical, driven, collaborative and, brutally honest and self-critical about how they are doing'.[16]

If the agenda outlined above is seriously implemented by HNWIs, business, civil society, and the state, then hopefully we will see an India which is a caring and sharing society; where giving is a way of life; and where equality of income and opportunity is the goal of philanthropy—a society where the philanthropic sector has become influential enough to impact public policy.[17]

In short, the future vision is one of more donors giving more, and giving wisely as well.

[16] Mathew Bishop, 'Philanthrocapitalism Goes Global', *Alliance Magazine*, 1 September 2008, www.alliancemagazine.org/feature/philanthrocapitalism-goes-global/.

[17] Based on Pushpa Singh, Ingrid Srinath, Anmol Vellani, and Priya Vishwanath, 'The Future of Philanthropy in India: Waiting for Take-off', Mimeo, undated.

Bibliography

Books and Reports

Acs, Zoltan J. and Sameeksha Desai. September 2007. 'Democratic Capitalism and Philanthropy in a Global Economy', *Jena Economic Research Papers 2007–056.* Jena, Germany.

Agarwal, Sanjay. 2010. *Daan and Other Giving Traditions in India.* Delhi: AccountAid India.

Alekseeva, Olga. 2007. *History of Trust in Distrustful Times.* Moscow: Ekksmo Publishing.

Baha, Abdu'l. 1971 [1956]. *The Secret of Divine Civilization.* Wilmette, Illinois: Bahai Publishing Trust.

Bharat Ram, Vinay. 2011. *From the Brink of Bankruptcy: The DCM Story.* Delhi: Penguin.

Birla, Krishna Kumar. 2012. *Brushes with History (An Autobiography).* Delhi: Penguin.

Breeze, Beth and Theresa Lloyd. 2013. *Richer Lives: Why Rich People Give.* London: Directory of Social Change.

Bremner, Robert. 1977. 'Private Philanthropy and Public Needs: Historical Perspective.' In *Research Papers* sponsored by The Commission on Private Philanthropy and Public Needs, 1: 89–114, Washington D.C.: Department of the Treasury, pp. 89–90.

Bowen, Howard R. 2013 [1953]. *Social Responsibilities of the Businessman.* USA: University of Iowa Press.

Carrithers, Michael and Caroline Humphrey (eds). 1991. *The Assembly of Listeners: Jains in Society.* Cambridge: Cambridge University Press.

Charities Aid Foundation India. 2012. *India Giving Report 2012.* New Delhi: Charities Aid Foundation India.

Charities Aid Foundation UK. 2015. 'A Global View of Giving Trends', *The World Giving Index 2014.* Charities Aid Foundation, November.

Cherian, Mathew. 2014. *A Million Missions: The Non-Profit Sector in India.* Delhi: Authors UpFront.

Dadrawala, Noshir. 2003. *Merchants of Philanthropy: Profiles in Good Corporate Citizenship.* Mumbai: Centre for Advancement of Philanthropy (CAP).

Dasra Annual Report. 2014–15. *Catalyst for Social Change*. Mumbai: Dasra, 2015.

Deloitte India. 2014. *Annual Status of Higher Education 2014*.

Direct Taxes Committee, The Institute of Chartered Accountants of India. February 2009 [January 1978]. *Taxation of Charitable Trusts and Institutions*. New Delhi.

Ernst & Young, FICCI, and Planning Commission of India. 2012. 'Higher Education in India: Twelfth Five Year Plan (2012–2017) and Beyond'. November.

FICCI-Ernst & Young. 2013. *Higher Education in India: Vision 2030*, Report for FICCI Higher Education Summit 2013. New Delhi.

Gandhi, Mahatma. 1930. *Young India*. Bombay: Pragjee Soorjee and Co., 10 April.

Gordon, A.D.D. 1978. *Businessmen and Politics: Rising Nationalism and a Modernising Economy in Bombay, 1918–1933*. New Delhi: Manohar.

Government of India, Ministry of Finance. 1959. *Report of the Direct Taxes Administration Enquiry Committee, 1958–59*. New Delhi.

———. 1971. *Report of the Direct Taxes Enquiry Committee: Final Report* (Wanchoo Committee Report).

Government of India, Ministry of Statistics and Programme Implementation. 2012. *Final Report on Non Profit Institutions in India*. March. http://mospi.nic.in/Mospi_New/upload/Final_Report_Non-Profit_Instiututions_30may12.pdf.

Ghatalia, S.V. 1973. 'Taxation of Industry', in C.N. Vakil (ed.), *Industrial Development of India: Policy and Problems*. New Delhi: Orient Longman.

Heald, Morrell. 1970. *The Social Responsibilities of Business: Company and Community, 1900–1960*. Cleveland, Ohio: Case Western Reserve University Press.

Hurun Research Institute. *Hurun Global Rich List 2016*. http://www.hurun.net/en/ArticleShow.aspx?nid=15703.

———. 2015. *Hurun India Philanthropy List 2015*. Shanghai.

———. 2015. *Hurun India Rich List*. Shanghai: September.

Jansen, Emily. 2012. 'From Gaining to Giving Wealth: the Shaping of Private Indian Philanthropy'. Draft Paper, International Development Research Centre (IDRC), Canada. October.

Johnson, Paula D., Stephen P. Johnson, and Andrew Kingman. 2004. 'Promoting Philanthropy: Global Challenges and Approaches', The Philanthropic Initiative, *Allavida*, International Network on Strategic Philanthropy, Bertelsmann Stiftung, Gütersloh, Germany.

Kalidas. 6th century AD. *Raghuvamsa*.

Kalra, Jitendara. 2013. 'Building Professional Philanthropic Institutions', in Mathieu Cantegreil, Deep Chanana, and Ruth Kattumuri (eds), *Revealing Indian Philanthropy.* London: Alliance Publishing Trust, pp. 57–62.

Kapur, Devesh, Ajay S. Mehta, and Moon R. Dutt. 2004. 'Indian Diaspora Philanthropy', in *Diaspora Philanthropy and Equitable Development in China and India*, eds, Geithner F. Peter, Johnson D. Paula, and Chen C. Lincoln. England: Global Equity Initiative, Asia Center, Harvard University.

Kapur, Devesh and Pratap Bhanu Mehta. 2004. 'Indian Higher Education Reform: From Half-baked Socialism to Half-baked Capitalism'. Working Papers, Center for International Development at Harvard University, September.

Katherine, Fulton, Gabriel Kasper, and Barbara Kibbe. 2010. *What's Next for Philanthropy: Acting Bigger and Adapting Better in a Networked World.* Monitor Institute, July.

Kudaisya, Medha M. 2003. *The Life and Times of G.D. Birla.* New Delhi: Oxford Univeristy Press.

Lala, R.M. 1984. *Heartbeat of a Trust.* New Delhi: Tata MacGraw-Hill.

———. 2011. *The Art of Effective Giving.* New Delhi: HarperCollins.

Mangaleswaran, Ramesh and Ramya Venkatraman. October 2013. *Designing Philanthropy for Impact: Giving to the Biggest Gaps in India.* Mumbai: Social Sector Practices Team, McKinsey & Company.

Masani, R.P. 1961. *N.M. Wadia and His Foundation.* Bombay: Popular Book Depot.

MacArthur Foundation-Intellecap Report. March 2016. *Strengthening Philanthropic Giving and Impact Investing for Development in India.* Delhi: McArthur Foundation.

McGoey, Linsey. 2015. *No Such Thing as a Free Gift: The Gates Foundation and the Price of Philanthropy.* NewYork: Verso.

Mudaliar, Chandra Y. 1974. *The Secular State and Religious Institutions in India.* Wiesbaden: Franz Steiner Verlag.

Murata, Sachiko and William C. Chittick. 1994. *The Vision Of Islam.* New York: Paragon House.

Murthy, N.R. Narayana. 2003. 'Travails of Philanthropy in India', Azad Memorial Lectures. Indian Council of Cultural Relations, New Delhi.

Nielson, Waldermar A. 2001 [1985]. *Golden Donors: A New Anatomy of the Great Foundations.* New Jersey: Transaction Publishers.

O' Connell, Brian. 1987. *Philanthropy in Action.* Washington: The Foundation Centre.

Ostrower, Francie. 1995/1997. *Why the Wealthy Give.* Princeton, New Jersey: Princeton University Press.

Rabinowitz, Alan. 1990. *Social Change Philanthropy in America*. New York: Quorum Books.

Reddy, Nidhi M., Lalitha Vaidyanathan, Katyayani Balasubramaniam, Kavitha Goraopali, and Sharad Sharma, 2012. *Catalytic Philanthropy in India: How India's Ultra-high Net Worth Philanthropists are Helping Solve Large-scale Social problems*. Centre for Emerging Market Solutions (CEMS) at the Indian School of Business, Hyderabad, and FSG Social Impact Consultants.

Rudner, David West. 1995. *Caste & Capitalism in Colonial India: The Nattukottai Chettiars*. New Delhi: Munshiram Manoharlal.

Sampradaan Indian Centre for Philanthropy. 2004. *A Review of Charities Administration in India*. New Delhi: Sampradaan Indian Centre for Philanthropy.

———. 2001. *Investing in Ourselves: Giving and Fund Raising in India*. Delhi.

Sheth, Arpan. 2012. *India Philanthropy Report 2012*. Mumbai: Bain and Company, 19 March.

Sheth, Arpan, and Anant Bhagwati. 2013. *India Philanthropy Report 2013*. Mumbai: Bain and Company, 5 March.

Singh, Pushpa, Ingrid Srinath, Anmol Vellani, and Priya Vishwanath. undated. Mimeo. 'The Future of Philanthropy in India: Waiting for Take-off'.

Smith, James Allen. 2002. *Foundations and Public Policy Making: A Historical Perspective*. Working Paper, California, USA.

Sundar, Pushpa. 1995. Mimeo. 'National Organizations of Business Donors in the USA: Growth and Development'. Paper prepared for the Johns Hopkins International Fellowship Programme in Philanthropy Baltimore.

———. 1997. *Charity for Social Change and Development: Essays on Indian Philanthropy*. Occasional Papers No. 1, New Delhi: Sampradaan Indian Centre for Philanthropy, April 1997.

———. 1997. 'Women and Philanthropy in India', *Voluntas* 7: no. 4 (1997): 412–25.

———. 1998. 'The World of Indian Foundations'. *Directory of Indian Donor Organisations*, pp. 17–23. New Delhi: Sampradaan Indian Centre for Philanthropy.

———. 1999. 'Business, Society and Philanthropy', in *Footprints of Enterprise: Indian Business Through the Ages*. New Delhi: FICCI/Oxford University Press.

———. 2000. *Beyond Business: From Merchant Charity to Corporate Citizenship*. New Delhi: Tata McGraw-Hill.

———. ed. 2001. *For God's Sake*. New Delhi: Sampradaan Indian Centre for Philanthropy.

———. 2006. Mimeo, 'Whither Indian Philanthropy'.

————. 2006. 'State Philanthropy: A New Paradigm for Financing Social Development?', http://pushpasundar.blogspot.in/2006/05/state-philanthropy-new-paradigm-for.html#more.

————. 2010. *Foreign Aid for Indian NGOs: Problem or Solution?* New Delhi: Routledge.

————. 2013. 'Philanthropy in the Building of Modern India', in *Revealing Indian Philanthropy*: 31–9.

————. 2013. *Business and Community: The Story of Corporate Social Responsibility in India*. New Delhi: Sage.

Thomas, Prince Mathews. 2012. 'Ratan Tata's Audacious Philanthropic Retirement Plans'. Forbes India Magazine, 13 August, http://forbesindia.com/article/boardroom/ratan-tatas-audacious-philanthropic-retirement-plans/33526/3#ixzz2dSBDeMpcying.

UBS-INSEAD. 2011. *Study on Family Philanthropy in Asia*. Singapore: UBS-INSEAD.

Upadhyay, R.B. 1976. *Social Responsibilityof Business and the Trusteeship Theory of Mahatma Gandhi*. New Delhi: Sterling Publishers.

Watt, Carey. 2005. *Serving the Nation: Cultures of Service, Association and Citizenship in Colonial India*. New York and New Delhi: Oxford University Press.

Viswanath, Priya. 2003. *Diaspora Indians, on the Philanthropy Fast-Track*. Mumbai: Centre for Advancement of Philanthropy.

Weaver, Warren. 1967. *US Philanthropic Foundations*. New York: Harper and Row Publishers.

Newspaper and Journal Articles

Alliance Magazine. 2011. Interview with Vineet Rai, 'Electrifying Bihar—the Role of Philanthropy and Social Investment', 1 June.

————. 2015. Caroline Hartnell's Interview with Roshni Nadar, 13 May.

————. 2011. Interview with Vineet Rai, 'Electrifying Bihar—the Role of Philanthropy and Social Investment', 1 June.

Beddoes, Zanny Minton. 2012. 'For Richer, for Poorer: Growing Inequality is One of the Biggest Social, Economic and Political Challenges of Our Time. But it is Not Inevitable'. *The Economist*. 13 October.

Bhattacharya, Saumya. 2014. 'A Giver and His Grudge Against Fellow Givers'. *The Economic Times*, 11 November.

Bishop, Mathew. 2008. 'Philanthrocapitalism Goes Global'. *Alliance Magazine*. 1 September.

Bornstein, Erica. 2009. 'The Impulse of Philanthropy'. *Cultural Anthropology* 24, no. 4 (2009): 622–51.

Buffet, Peter. 2013. 'The Charitable–Industrial Complex'. *The New York Times.*, 26 July.

Bukhari, Alison. 2013. 'Philanthropy in India Today', *Alliance Magazine*, 1 June.

Business India Interview. 2014. 'Creating a Community of Givers'. 3–16 March.

Caldwell, Christopher. 2016. 'Donor Beware', *Wall Street Journal Review*, Saturday–Sunday, 12–13 March.

Chanchani, Madhav, Kala Vijyraghvan, and Hari Pulakkat. 2015. 'Ratan Tata and His Happy Space'. *The Economic Times*, Special Feature, 11 June.

Choudhary, Amit. 2015. 'Educational Institutions' Profits Not Taxable: SC'. *Times of India*, 19 March.

Conlin, Michelle and Rob Hof. 2004. 'The eBay Way', *Business Week, e.biz* (15 December): 104–5.

Dasgupta, Swapan. 2016. 'If We Won't Save Sanskrit, Why Stop Foreigners'. *The Times of India*, 3 April.

Datta, Kanika. 2011. 'Charity Begins in Governance'. *Business Standard*, 31 March.

Dhar, Aarti. 2013. 'An Uphill Task'. *The Hindu*, 7 June.

Dhawan, Ashis. 2014. 'Time to Recognise Private Universities' Role in Putting India on the Global Education Map'. *The Economic Times*, 13 July.

Dutta, Vishal, Anumeha Chaturvedi, and Sreeradha D. Basu. 2015. 'IIMs, Alumni Say Bill Will Lead To Erosion of Institute's Autonomy', *The Economic Times*, 26 June.

ET Bureau. 2013. ET Awards 2013: 'Azim Premji Makes Plea for the Less Privileged'. 10 December.

Ghosh, Ahona. 2011. 'Act of Giving: Giving Across Generations'. Economic Times Bureau, 4 October.

———. 2012. 'New Intent and Bold Innovation in Corporate Philanthropy'. *Economic Times Bureau*, 19 June.

Jain, Bharti. 2015. 'Govt Puts Major NGO Funder Ford Foundation Under Watch'. *The Times of India*, 24 April.

Joglekar, Yogini. 2011. 'Youngest Indian Millionaires Lead Asia, World HNIS'. 14 October, dnaindia.com.

John, Sujit and Shilpa Phadnis. 2015. 'How Indian Startups Are Seeing a Culture of Giving And Sharing'. *Times News Network*, 30 January.

Kayser, Olivier. 2008. 'A New Architecture Needed'. *Alliance Magazine*, 1 September.

Karunakaran, Naren. 2014. 'How India Inc's Top Names Like Azim Premji, Ratan Tata, Others Are Driving Philanthropic Initiatives'. *Economic Times Bureau*, 2 October.

————. 2014. 'Indian Money for Indian Think-Tanks'. *The Economic Times*, 4 November.

————. 2014. 'Why They are Giving to Deepen Democracy and Governance'. *The Economic Times*, Special Feature on Philanthropy, 4 November.

Layak, Suman. 2014. 'Reliance's Better Half'. *The Economic Times Magazine*. 12–18 October.

————. 2015. 'Startups at the Bottom of the Pyramid'. *The Economic Times Magazine*, 12–18 April.

Lloyd, Theresa and Beth Breeze. 2013. 'How Has UK Philanthropy Changed Over The Past Decade?'. *Alliacze Magazine*, 15 October.

Manku, Moyna. 2015. 'The CSR–FCRA Contradiction'. *LiveMint*, 23 December, www.livemint.com.

Mahadevan, Anand. 2013. 'Be Super Rich and Be Premji'. *The Economic Times*, 7 March.

Mehta, Neha. 2015. 'Has UGC Run Its Course?'. *The Times of India*, 10 May.

Mehta, Pratap Bhanu. 2010. 'Charity at Home?' *The Indian Express*, 19 October.

————. 2015. 'Death and Taxes'. *The Indian Express*, 22 January.

Menezes, Rohit, Sonali Madia Patel, and Daniel Pike. 2015. 'Giving Back to India', *Stanford Social Innovation Review*, Stanford, USA, 9 November, 17–23.

Milner, Andrew and Caroline Hartnell. 2013. 'Philanthropy in a Changing World Economy: How is Philanthropy Changing?' *Alliance magazine*, 1 June.

Mody, Ashoka and Michael Walton. 2014. 'Story of a Fraying Capitalism', *The Indian Express*, 14 May.

Mohan, Rohini. 2015. 'Govt V/S NGOs'. *The Economic Times*, 2 July, p. 16.

Morris, Sebastian. 2015. 'The Curious Case of India's Fragile Higher Education System'. *LiveMint*. 13 July. p. 7.

Murthy, Rohan. 2016. 'The Classics Belong to the World'. *The Times of India*, 6 March.

Musafer, Shanaz. 2012. 'Power of Policy-making in the Hands of Philanthropists', BBC News, 2 September.

Nelson, Dean. 2009. 'Where Are India's Great Philanthropists?'. *The Telegraph*, 28 July.

Oxfam. 2016. '62 People Own Same Wealth as Half the World: Oxfam'. *The Economic Times*, 19 January.

Paranjape, Makarand. 2016. 'The Problem with Pollack'. *The Indian Express*, 21 March.

Pingali, Vishwanath and Naman Desai. 2015. 'The Mandatory CSR Law's 2% Solution'. *LiveMint*, 17 August.

Politzer, Malia. 2012. 'Arpan Seth: Organizations Need to Spend More Time Nurturing Givers'. *LiveMint.*, 20 March.

———. 2012. 'Under-30s Take Centre Stage in Indian Philanthropy', *LiveMint*, 20 March.

Rai, Archana. 2013. 'With Rs 164 Crore, Rohini to Open Kitty for Governance'. *The Economic Times*, 8 August.

Rajghatta, Chidanand. 2015. 'Alumnus Faces Ire for $400m Gift to Harvard'. *The Times of India*, 5 June.

———. 2015. 'Entrepreneurs Are Made, *Not* Born'. *The Times of India*, 21 June.

———. 2015. 'In a Record, TCS Gifts $35m to US' Carnegie Mellon'. *The Times of India*, 26 August.

Ramanathan, Arundhati. 2015. 'Firms' CSR Panels See Few Meetings in FY 15'. *LiveMint*, Bengaluru, 23 December.

———. 2015. 'IT firms' CSR spending rose nearly five times in FY 15'. *LiveMint*, 11 July.

Ramanathan, Arundhati. 2015. 'FMCG Firms' CSR Spend Up by 57%, Nestle Misses Target'. *LiveMint*, 20 August.

Reddy, Nidhi M., Lalitha Vaidyanathan, Katyayani Balasubramaniam, Kavitha Goraopali, and Sharad Sharma. February 2012. 'Catalytic Philanthropy in India: How India's Ultra-high Net Worth Philanthropists are Helping Solve Large-scale Social Problems'. Centre for Emerging Market Solutions (CEMS) at the Indian School of Business, Hyderabad, and FSG Social Impact Consultants.

Shah, Mihir. 2014. 'Fairy Tale Capitalism', *The Indian Express*, 24 April.

Sharma, Aman. 2015. 'Tighter Norms for NGOs to Track Foreign Funds'. *The Economic Times*, 19 June.

Smith, James Allen. 2002. *Foundations and Public Policy Making: A Historical Perspective.* Working paper, California, USA.

Subramanya, Rupa. 2012. 'Why Charity Is Different in India'. *Economics Journal*, 11 July.

Sundar, Pushpa. 2012–2013. 'Czarinas or Girl Fridays'. *Interrogating Women's Leadership and Empowerment*, *IIC Quarterly*, Winter 2012–Spring 2013, pp. 69–80.

Sundar, Pushpa. 1997. Interview with Ratan Tata, 'Philanthropy Must Strengthen Self-help', *Sampradaan* 1 (June): 3–4.

———. 2012. 'Putting Bharat on Firm Foundations: Decentralized Financing of Rural Development'. *Financial Express*, 30 July.

———. 2013. 'Philanthropy in the Building of Modern India', in *Revealing Indian Philanthropy*, pp. 31–9.

Sunday Times of India. 2015. 'We May Have To Learn To Live With Cancer Rather Than Die of It'. Delhi edition, 9 August.

The Business Standard. 2011. 'Charitable Trusts Under IT Scanner'. 26 May.

The Economic Times. 2010. 'THINK YOU'. 5 September.

———. 2014. 'NRN Becomes Bellweather for Indian Classics'. New Delhi, 21 February.

———. 2015. 'Angels of a Different Stripe, Flocking to Charity Startup'. Delhi, 11 June.

———. 2015. 'Tighter Norms for NGOs to Track Foreign Funds'. 19 June.

———. 2015. 'Top 75 Companies Spent Rs 4,000 cr on CSR in FY 15'. New Delhi, 3 September.

———. 2015. 'In CSR Trusts, Black Turns White and Vice Versa'. New Delhi, 21 October.

———. 2015. 'Tata Trusts, Khan Academy Plan to Deliver Edu Online'. *The Economic Times*, 7 December.

———. 2016. 'Higher Education Gets Budget High Five'. 2 March.

The Economist. 2006. 'Faith, Hope and Philanthropy: What the New Breed of Donors Can Do—And What It Can't'. 23 February, http://www.economist.com/node/5517704.

———. 2011. 'The Rich and the Rest: What To Do (And Not Do) about Inequality'. 20 January.

The Indian Express. 2012. 'Three Women Behind India's Top IT Tycoons Step Forward to Tell All'. 27 December.

———. 2014. 'Editorial'. 1 February.

———. 2015. 'Premji, Nadar Among 20 Richest Techies: Forbes'. 13 August.

———. 2015. 'Healthcare to Swachh Bharat, How Firms Spent CSR Funds'. 23 November.

———. 2015. 'Mandating CSR Spends Akin to Taxation'. 7 December.

The Times of India. 2013. 'Cook Two Extra Meals, Launch Thousand Smiles'. Chennai, 23 June.

———. 2015. 'Cos Act Amendment Allows Use of CSR Funds in Startups'. 5 May.

———. 2015. 'Use Zakat Money to Promote Modern Education'. 22 June.

———. 2015. 'Panel Wants Capitation Fees under Anti-graft Law'. Delhi, 25 July.

———. 2015. 'No. of New Rich to Grow Fastest in India, Says Study'. New Delhi: 24 September.

———. 2015. 'Mittal Takes Rs. 5 cr Pay Cut for Legal Aid Initiative'. 27 November.

———. 2015. 'Led by Gates, 20 Biz Titans Launch Clean Tech Coalition', 1 December.

———. 2016. 'Change or India Cannot Invent'. 6 January.

———. 2016. 'Nooyi Becomes Yale's Biggest Alumni Donor'. 14 January.

————. 2016. 'Black Money Quota: MBBS, PG Seats Go for Rs. 12,000cr/ yr'. 30 January.

The New Indian Express. 2013. Ved Prakash, Chairman of the University Grants Commission, quoted in 'Philanthropy in Higher Education Must'. Bangalore, 25 March.

Thomas, Prince Mathews. 2012. 'Ratan Tata's Audacious Philanthropic Retirement Plans'. Forbes India Magazine. 13 August, http://forbesindia. com/article/boardroom/ratan-tatas-audacious-philanthropic-retirement-plans/33526/5#ixzz2WYLNMuh7.

Times News Network. 2014. 'Science Needs Corporate Funding, C.N.R. Rao Says'. 13 May.

Tomei, Anthony. 2013. 'Changing Roles in a Changing World', *Alliance Magazine*, 1 June.

Vij-Aurora, Bhavana. 2015. 'Ford Foundation Needs MHA Nod For Giving Grants'. *The Economic Times*, 24 April.

Vij-Aurora, Bhavana and Aman Sharma. 2015. 'Modi Sarkar Raises Heat on Foreign Funding for NGOs'. *The Economic Times*, 3 June.

Walker, Darren. 2015. 'Why Giving Back Isn't Enough'. *The New York Times*, New York, 17 December.

Wylie, Irving. 1958. 'The Reputation of the American Philanthropist: A Historian's View', *The Social Service Review* 32 (September): 215–22.

Zachariah, Reeba and John Sarkar. 2015. 'Housing Sacks CEO Yadav for Misconduct'. *The Times of India*, 2 July.

Online Access

Azim Premji. 2013. Speech at The Economic Times Lifetime Achievement Awards function, 7 December, azimpremjiuniversity.edu.in/.../mr-azim-premji's-speech-et-awards-dece.

Bill Gates. 2012. 'The Power of Catalytic Philanthropy', http://forbesindia. com/article/philanthropy-awards-2012/the-power-of-catalytic philanthr opy/34209/1?utm=slidebox#ixzz2dSEtDrMx.

Cariappa, Nanda. 2015. 'Subject: Fwd: Grand Salute to this Man', 31 January.

CNBC TV 18, Money Control. 2010. 'Sunil Mittal: Empowering India Through Education', 28 June, http://www.moneycontrol.com/news/ business/sunil-mittal-empowering-india-through-education_466356-1. html?utm_source=ref_article.

Council on Foundations. 'Defining Philanthropy's Role in Society', Council on Foundations, Philanthropy Roundtable, Forum of Regional Association of Grantmakers, http://www.foundationsonthehill.org/docs/

Defining-Philanthropys-Role-in-Society.pdf (accessed on 6 November 2012).

Daniyal, Shoaib. 2015. 'Azim Premji Aside, Why are India's Ultra Rich So Tight-fisted When It Comes to Philanthropy?', *Scroll.in*, 11 July, http://scroll.in/article/740220/azim-premji-aside-why-are-indias-ultra-rich-so-tight-fisted-when-it-comes-to-philanthropy.

Erica Kohl Arenas. 2015. 'Can Philanthropy Ever Reduce Inequality?' *Transformation*, 8 July, https://www.opendemocracy.net/transformation/erica-kohlarenas/can-philanthropy-ever-reduce-inequality.

Giving USA. *The Annual Report on Philanthropy 2014*, http://npengage.com/nonprofit-news/key-findings-from-giving-usa-2014-report/.

Rick Cohen. 2014. 'Can Philanthropic Oligarchy Nurture Economic Justice?', *Transformation*, 15 April, https://www.opendemocracy.net/transformation/rick-cohen/can-philanthropic-oligarchy-nurture-economic-justice.

'Role for Philanthropists in Shaping the Civil Society of the Future', 25 March 2010, downloaded from philanthropy/UK: inspiring giving, at http://www.philanthropyuk.org/news/2010-03-25/role-philanthropists-shaping-civil-society-future on 6 November 2012.

The Business Standard. 2011. 'One Can Create Jobs and Still Be a Santa Claus: Buffet', 25 March, http://articles.timesofindia.indiatimes.com/2011-03-25/edit-page/29187698_1_philanthropy-capitalism-plant-trees.

'Wealth Insights', *Barclays Wealth Report 2013*. Downloaded on 12 June 2015. https://wealth.barclays.com/en_gb/home/research/research-centre/wealth-insights/volume-17.html.

http://data.worldbank.org/indicator/SE.XPD>TOTL>GD>ZS.

http://economictimes.indiatimes.com/articleshow/46064550.cms?utm_source=contentofinterest&utm_medium=text&utm_campaign=cppst.

https://in.answers.yahoo.com/question/index?qid=20100731054136AAb4vQ.

http://www.brainyquote.com/quotes/topics/topic_education.html#ET7Oe6ybFeSRSV7u.99.

http://www.forbes.com/sites/johnkoppisch/2012/06/20/2012-indian-philanthropists/.

http://www.randdcentre.com/benefits.html.

http://www.shivnadarfoundation.org/news.aspx.

http://www.shivnadarfoundation.org/press-releases/Philanthtropy-on-a-wing-with-Shiv-Nadar.pdf.

http://www.nytimes.com/2010/10/06/business/global/06khosla.html?_r=1&pagewanted=all#h[].

Index

About the Author

Pushpa Sundar is a leading authority on philanthropy and corporate social responsibility. She is the author of six books including *Patrons and Philistines: Arts and the State in British India* (1995), *Foreign Aid for Indian NGOs: Problem or Solution?* (2010), and *Business and Community: The Story of Corporate Social Responsibility in India* (2013), and has also contributed extensively to newspapers and journals.

She was a Senior Fellow under the International Fellows in Philanthropy Programme of the Johns Hopkins University, and the Founder Director of the Sampradaan Indian Centre for Philanthropy, New Delhi.

Pushpa gave up her career in the Indian Administrative Service to pursue her interest in development and civil society, and has worked in a variety of national and international organizations, besides serving on the boards of several non profit organizations. She loves flowers and trees, and in her leisure indulges in her interests of gardening, the performing arts and travel.